THE TYPIST'S TREASURY

OR

SECRETARY'S BOOK OF WORDS

*Over 7000 Helpful Points
for those who Type or Write*

BY

KATE STEVENS

*Sometime Examiner in Typewriting to the Union of
Educational Institutions.*

Royal Society of Arts Medallist in Shorthand.

*Winner of £75 Prize in "Daily Sketch" Shorthand-
Typists' Competition.*

Author of "Typewriting Self-Taught."

THIRD EDITION

LONDON
JORDAN & SONS LIMITED
CHANCERY LANE, W.C.2
1944

FIRST EDITION	.	December 1934
REPRINTED	. .	. October 1935
REPRINTED	. .	. July 1936
SECOND EDITION	.	September 1939
THIRD EDITION	. .	April 1944
REPRINTED	. .	September 1945

Made and Printed in Great Britain by
Hazell, Watson & Viney, Ltd., London and Aylesbury

FOREWORD

THIS dictionary has been compiled primarily for Typists and Secretaries, but it is hoped that it will be found useful to many other people, young and old —in fact, to all those who aim at being accurate in their writing and spelling. The book does not set out to give simple grammatical rules, or the elementary principles of typewriting practice, and only for the more difficult words are definitions supplied. The contents are so varied that it is not possible to give a complete classification, but the following headings will indicate the scope of the work. It contains:

Guidance as to modern English usage and construction.

Hints on letter-writing.

Difficult spellings.

Similar place-names.

Hyphenated, non-hyphenated, and combined words that cause confusion.

Unusual or alternative plurals.

Use of capitals.

New terms not yet included in dictionaries.

Colloquialisms.

Difficult pronunciations.

Prefixes and suffixes.

Foreign words that have been anglicized.

Menu terms.

Useful foreign words, especially French, German, and Italian.

Foreign phrases, especially Latin and French.

Abbreviations (general, commercial, and legal).

Initials of societies, etc.

Units of currency of the principal countries.

Terms used in printing and literary work.

Brief hints on the more difficult points in typewriting practice.

Efficiency hints in connection with office work and
appliances.

Appendixes giving correct form of address and
pronunciation of proper names.

Specimen lay-outs of letters.

The author has had recourse to many dictionaries
and reference books, particularly the *Concise Oxford
Dictionary* and Fowler's *Modern English Usage*.
Present-day usage adopted by the best writers has
also been considered in an endeavour to obtain a
consensus of opinion on doubtful points. The results
here presented are the *recommended* forms, but as
the English language is a living thing, constantly
growing and changing, it is impossible to maintain
that every form shown is fixed and unalterable.
The practice in regard to hyphenation is perhaps the
most variable of all, and it is impossible to evolve a
definite rule stating when the parts of compound
words should be separated, when hyphenated, and
when combined.

How to use the Dictionary

The alphabetical arrangement is based on the
assumption that the group of initials or the phrase
is thought of as a whole, or as forming a complete
word. Thus *bystander* appears before *by the by*, and
en bloc after *enameller*.

The appearance of a word in *Ionic Italic Type*
indicates that it is a foreign word and would normally
be set in italic type. The appearance of a foreign
word in *ordinary* type indicates that it has been
absorbed in the English language and no longer
needs differentiation by italics. All German nouns
will be found to have initial capitals, because in the
German language this is the custom followed. Some
very simple words will be noticed, but what is simple
to one reader may prove a trap to another; it may be

that there is no initial capital, that there is an apostrophe, or that a hyphen is needed.

Definitions and statements are necessarily brief, as the work does not claim to be cyclopaedic. It should be noted that the abbreviations marked " legal " are those used when documents are drafted by hand, and the typist copying the written drafts will usually find with such contractions either a horizontal line placed above or the last few letters written above the level of the others.

The author will be grateful for notification of any errors or omissions that might be made good in future editions.

KATE STEVENS.

KATE STEVENS.

LIST OF ABBREVIATIONS USED

abbr.	abbreviation
adj.	adjective
fem.	feminine
Fr.	French
Ger.	German
Gk.	Greek
It.	Italian
Lat.	Latin
masc.	masculine
pl.	plural
Port.	Portuguese
pron.	pronounced
sing.	singular
Span.	Spanish

A

a. Use *a*, not *an*, before all words beginning with the sound of *w* or *y*, as: " a one-sided affair," " a unit "; also before all consonants and aspirated words (except heir, hour, and honour).

A., anna, Indian coin.

A 1, first-class ship in " Lloyd's Register."

A/A, aerodrome to aerodrome.

A.A., air attaché, Associate of Arts, Automobile Association.

A.A.A., Amateur Athletic Association.

A.A.F., Auxiliary Air Force.

A.A.G., Assistant-Adjutant-General.

A.B., able-bodied seaman.

ab (Lat.), off, from, away.

à bas (Fr.), down with.

abatable.

abbé, Frenchman who has studied divinity but holds no benefice.

Abbot's Leigh, Bristol.

Abbotsley, Hunts

abbreviations. Do not abbreviate short words like March; it is not worth while. Avoid ambiguity : an abbreviation familiar to you may be misleading to others. Usually add full-point after abbreviations. Note 1st, 2nd, 4to, etc., are not strictly abbreviations and do not take point, nor do the French forms Mlle, Mme, etc. Longhand abbreviations are usually indicated by placing a stroke above the word or by writing last letter above the line and smaller. *See also under* " counties."

ABC Railway Guide (no points).

Abend (Ger.). evening.

Abercrombie, Fife. *See* Appendix II for pronunciation.

Abercromby, Lancs

Aberystwyth, Wales.

abettor. The *-or* termination is the legal one, and in general use it is commoner than *-er*.

Abingdon, Berks

Abington, Lanark, Limerick, Northants

ab initio (Lat.), from the beginning.

-able. Words ending in *e*, omit it before *-able*. except where pronunciation necessitates its retention, e.g. manageable (*g* would become hard before *a*). The *-able* termination in English is more common than *-ible*.

abolitionist.

à bon compte (Fr.), cheaply.

à bon droit (Fr.), with justice.

ab origine (Lat.), from the beginning.

above-mentioned. Use hyphen when a noun immediately follows, or almost immediately.

Abp., archbishop.

abridgment.

abscess.

absenteeism, the practice of absenting oneself from duty ; formerly used of landlords not residing on their estates.

absente reo (Lat.), the accused being absent ; abbr. *abs. re.*

absinth. (Fr.) : *absinthe.*

absit invidia (Lat.), no offence intended.

absit omen (Lat.), may this bring no evil omen.

abs. re., absente reo (Lat.), the accused being absent.

abst. (legal), abstract.

abstemious.

abstruse.

absurdum (Lat.), absurd.

abutting, adjoining.

a/c, account.

A/C, account current.

A.C., Alpine Club, alternating current.

A.C.A., Associate of the Institute of Chartered Accountants in England and Wales.

accede *to.*

accelerando (It.), increasing speed.

accents. If the nature of the work justifies the change, accents can be fitted to the typewriter in place of fractions. They can be fitted on "dead" keys, that is, when accent is struck the carriage does not move. Otherwise, insert with sharp pencil *through* ribbon. In poetry the accent (grave or acute) is used to show that the termination *èd* is to be sounded as a separate syllable. Stressed and unstressed syllables may be indicated thus : ‾ ˘

accents and diacritical marks. The chief are :

    acute (´)
    cedilla (ç)
    circumflex (ˆ)
    Danish ø is being superseded by ö or ò
    diæresis (¨)

grave (`)
long vowel, or stressed syllable in poetry (‑)
Norwegian, Swedish å
Portuguese ã, õ
short vowel (˘)
Spanish ñ (tilde)
Umlaut (¨)

accessary (*adj.* and *noun*), used of persons or their actions when complicity is implied.

accessible.

accessit (Lat.), he, she, or it, came near—applied to one second in merit.

accessory (*adj.* and *noun*), although it means contributing to a result, emphasizes the subordinate nature of the contribution.

acclimatize.

accommodation.

accompanist.

accordion, a reed instrument.

account, abbr. a/c or acct.

account current, abbr. A/C.

account sales, abbr. A/S.

A.C.C.S., Associate of the Corporation of Certified Secretaries.

accumulator, a group of secondary cells, which store the energy of a current during charging and give it out during discharge.

A.C.F., Automobile Club of France.

A.C.G.B.I., Automobile Club of Great Britain and Ireland.

A.C.G.I., Associate of City and Guilds of London Institute.

achievement. Note that *i* precedes *e*, except after *c* and in a few other words, such as counterfeit, plebeian, seize, weird, and inveigle.

A.C.I.B., Associate of the Corporation of Insurance Brokers.

A.C.I.I., Associate of the Chartered Insurance Institute.

A.C.I.S., Associate of the Chartered Institute of Secretaries.

ackne (legal), acknowledge.

acknowledgment.

A.C.M., Air Chief-Marshal.

à compte (Fr.), on account.

A.C.P., Associate of the College of Preceptors.

A.C.P.A., Associate of the Institution of Certified Public Accountants.

acquittal.

acre, abbr. a.

actionnaire (Fr.), a shareholder.

actors' parts, *see* note under "plays."

Acts of Parliament. These are referred to under the name of the Act. Example: The Companies Act, 1929; or under the progressive title, i.e. the session of Parliament in a given reign, the title of the monarch, and the chapter which the Act occupies on the Statute Book. Example: 19 & 20 Geo. V. c. 23.

acute accent ('). This accent has two uses in English: (1) in dictionaries, after the accented syllable, to show pronunciation (e.g. dis-tor'shun); (2) in poetry, to show that a syllable must be separately pronounced (e.g. "The wingéd hours"). The grave accent may equally well be used for this purpose.

A.C.W.A., Associate of the Institute of Cost and Works Accountants.

A.D., *anno Domini* (Lat.). Place this before the figures.

a.d., *ante diem* (Lat.), before the day.

ad., advt., advert., advertisement.

ad (Lat.), to, toward, with regard to.

ad absurdum (Lat.), to show the absurdity.

adapter, one who adapts; fitting that allows for additional connection (electricity or wireless).

ad arbitrium (Lat.), at pleasure, at will.

ad astra (Lat.), to the stars, to an exalted state.

a dato (Lat.), from date.

A.D.C., aide-de-camp; *pl.* aides-de-camp.

addendum, a thing to be added; *pl.* addenda.

addio (It.), good-bye.

adducible, able to be brought forward or cited.

à demi (Fr.), by halves.

à deux (Fr.), for two; between two.

ad finem (Lat.), near the end; abbr. *ad fin.*

ad hoc (Lat.), for this (purpose).

ad idem (Lat.), to the same point.

a die (Lat.), from that day.

adieu, *pl.* adieux.

ad infinitum (Lat.), for ever.

ad interim (Lat.), meanwhile.

adiós (Span.), adieu.

adj., adjective.

Adj., Adjutant.

adjective, abbr. adj.

Adj.-Gen., Adjutant-General.

adjudicator.

adjustable.

Adjutant, abbr. Adj.

Adjutant-General, abbr. Adj.-Gen. or A.-G.

ad libitum (Lat.), at pleasure; abbr. *ad lib.*

ad litem (Lat.), during the proceedings.

ad literam (Lat.), to the letter, minutely exact.

ad locum (Lat.), at the place; abbr. *ad loc.*

administrator (*masc.*), abbr. admor.

administratrix (*fem.*), abbr. admix.

admissible.

ad modum (Lat.), after the manner of.

admor. (legal), administrator.

ad nauseam (Lat.), to a sickening extent.

adresse (Fr.), address.

à droit (Fr.), to the right.

adsorption, condensation of gases; distinguish from ab-
sorption of gases.

ad valorem (Lat.), according to the value; abbr. *ad val.*

advertise.

advertisement, abbr. ad., advt., advert.

advg. (legal), advising.

adviser.

advising, abbr. advg. (legal).

Advocates, Faculty of, the Bar of Scotland.

æ (diphthong or ligature), used in Danish, French,
Icelandic, and Old English words. Less used in English.

A.E.A., Air Efficiency Award.

Aegean Sea.

aegis, the protecting shield of Zeus; anything which
protects.

aeon, an age; great length of time.

A.E.R.A., Associate Engraver of the Royal Academy.

aerate. Pronounce as three syllables, ā-er-āte.

aerie, also eyrie, nest of bird of prey.

aerodrome.

aerograph, instrument for spraying colour.

aerostat, an air balloon.

Æsculapius, the Roman god of healing.

Æsop.

aestheticism, keen appreciation of the beautiful.

Aet., of age, aged.

A.E.U., Amalgamated Engineering Union.

A.-F., Anglo-French.

A.F., Air Force.

A.F.A., Amateur Football Association; Associate of the
Faculty of Actuaries.

A.F.A.M., Ancient Free and Accepted Masons.

A.F.C., Air Force Cross.

affaire d'amour (Fr.), love affair.

affaire de cœur (Fr.), affair of the heart.

affect, to concern or influence. Do not confuse with effect, to accomplish. Example: "The new secretary desired to effect a change in organization which would not adversely affect the employees."

affiche (Fr.), poster, placard; *affichée*, posted up.

affidavit, a written declaration on oath; abbr. afft. (legal). Type on foolscap paper, with double-line spacing.

affirmatim (Lat.), in the affirmative.

afflatus (Lat.), inspiration.

afft. (legal), affidavit.

Afghanistan.

à fond (Fr.), thoroughly.

aforesaid, abbr. afsd. (legal).

a fortiori (Lat.), with stronger reason.

A.F.R.Ae.S., Associate Fellow of the Royal Aeronautical Society.

A.F.S., Associate of the Faculty of Secretaries; Auxiliary Fire Service.

afsd. (legal), aforesaid.

after-damp, choke-damp (in a mine).

afterthought.

A.-G., Adjutant-General, Agent-General, Attorney-General.

A.-G. (Ger.), *Aktiengesellschaft*, joint-stock company.

Agassiz. *See* Appendix II for pronunciation.

à gauche (Fr.), to the left.

age. Do not use figures in such a sentence as "She was in her twenty-sixth year." *See also* note under "figures."

ageing.

agenda, a list of items to be discussed at a meeting. Sometimes typed on the left of the sheet, so that notes may be written on the right. The word is plural. Sing, agendum.

à genoux (Fr.), on the knees, kneeling.

aggravate. This means to make worse. Do not use it in the loose sense of annoy.

aggrieved.

agneau (Fr.), lamb.

agnosticism, the doctrine of disbelief in the unknowable.

agoraphobia, morbid fear of being in open spaces.

agrarianize, to divide the land equally.

agréable (Fr.), agreeable.

agreement, abbr. agrt. (legal).

agriculturist.

agrt. (legal), **agreement.**

Ah! When standing alone, it takes an exclamation mark. Otherwise it is usually followed by comma, and exclamation mark placed at end of sentence.

à haute voix (Fr.), **aloud.**

A.H.C., Army Hospital Corps.

A.I.A., Associate of the Institute of Actuaries.

A.I.A.C., Associate of the Institute of Company Accountants.

A.I.Arb., Associate of the Institute of Arbitrators.

A.I.C., Associate of the Institute of Chemistry.

A.I.C.S., Associate of the Institute of Chartered Shipbrokers.

aide-de-camp, abbr. A.D.C.; *pl.* **aides-de-camp.**

A.I.G., Assistant-Inspector-General.

aigrette, a spray of feathers or jewels. *See also* note under " egret."

A.I.L., Associate of the Institute of Linguists.

aileron, small plane fixed to main plane of an aeroplane, and used for balancing.

aimable (Fr.), amiable, kind.

A.I.Mech.E., Associate of the Institution of Mechanical Engineers.

A.I.Min.E., Associate of the Institution of Mining Engineers.

A.I.M.T.A., Associate of the Institute of Municipal Treasurers and Accountants.

aîné (Fr.), elder; *fem.* **aînée.**

A.I.P.A., Associate of the Institute of Incorporated Practitioners in Advertising.

Airgraph, postal service using miniature film for transmission.

Air Mail. For particulars of this service *see* leaflet obtainable (free) at any post office.

airplane, officially adopted by U.S. Army and Navy. English equivalent, **aeroplane.**

air-tight.

airworthiness.

à jamais (Fr.), for ever.

A.K.C., Associate of King's College (London).

Aktiengesellschaft (Ger.), joint-stock company; abbr. A.-G.

Al, aluminium (no point).

Ala., Alabama.

A.L.A.A., Associate of the London Association of Certified Accountants.

à la belle étoile (Fr.), in the open air.

à la bonne heure! (Fr.), Well done!

à la carte (Fr.), according to the bill of fare.

à la française (Fr.), in the French style.

à la main (Fr.), at hand.

à la mode (Fr.), in the fashion.

à la napolitaine (Fr.), in the Neapolitan style.

à l'anglaise (Fr.), in the English style.

à la parisienne (Fr.), in the Parisian style.

à la russe (Fr.), in the Russian style.

alas! When standing alone, it takes exclamation mark. Otherwise it is followed by comma, the exclamation mark being placed at end of sentence.

à la suédoise (Fr.), in the Swedish style.

à la viennoise (Fr.), in the Viennese style.

Albania. Unit of currency 1 Albanian franc = 5 lek = 100 centimes.

A.L.B.E., Air League of the British Empire.

Albrighton, Salop

Albury, Herts, Surrey.

Alcester. *See* Appendix II for pronunciation.

Aldborough, Norfolk, Yorks

Aldbrough, Yorks

Aldbury, Herts

Aldeburgh, Suffolk.

Aldebury, Wilts

Alderman. *See* Appendix I for correct form of address.

Aldsworth, Glos

Aldworth, Berks

à l'espagnole (Fr.), in the Spanish style.

alfresco, in the fresh air.

alia (Lat.), other things.

alias (Lat.), otherwise; *pl. aliases.* Generally used in connexion with persons who assume various names.

alibi, the plea that one was elsewhere when an act took place.

" A " Licence, private air pilot's licence.

alignment, alinement, the evenness or otherwise of the typed letters. Capital letters out of register may be due to insufficient depression of shift key. Other irregularities generally indicate wear. Consult a mechanic.

à l'irlandaise (Fr.), in the Irish style.

alkalis, chemical substances that neutralize acids.

all-British (*adj.*).

allée (Fr.), alley, avenue.

allergy, sensitiveness of an individual to certain foods, pollens, etc. *Adj.* allergic.

allez-vous-en! (Fr.), go away!

Allhallows, Kent.

All-Hallows, All Saints' Day, 1st November.

all-in (*adj.*).

allons! (Fr.), Come on! Come along!

allotment.

allotting.

all-over (*adj.*).

all right. Don't confuse this with *although* and *altogether*. Some day *alright* may be sanctioned by usage, but at present the best writers avoid it.

all risks, abbr. A/R.

all-round (*adj.*).

All Saints' Day, 1st November.

All Souls College, Oxford.

All Souls' Day, 2nd November.

allspice, the pepper-plant berry of Jamaica, so called because it combines many different flavours.

alma mater (Lat.), foster-mother—one's University.

Almondbury, Yorks

Almondsbury, Glos

Alnwick, Northumb

Alpes-Maritimes, department of France; abbr. A.-M.

alpine. Use initial capital only when referring to *the* Alps, i.e. Swiss.

alpinist.

A.L.S., Associate of the Linnean Society.

alteration, abbr. alteron. (legal)

alter ego (Lat.), one's second self, a bosom friend.

alteron. (legal), alteration.

Althorp Park, Northants

Althorpe, Lincs

altimeter, an instrument for measuring vertical angular elevation.

alto, *pl.* altos.

altogether, entirely. **All together** means in a body.

aluminium, abbr. Al (no point).

alumnus, pupil of school or university; *pl.* alumni; *fem.* alumna; *fem. pl.* alumnae.

a.m., *ante meridiem* (Lat), before noon.

A.M., Air Ministry; (*Artium Magister*) Master of Arts; Albert medal; (*Ave Maria*) Hail Mary!

amanuensis, *pl.* amanuenses.

ambassador. *See* Appendix I for correct form of address.

A.M.D., Army Medical Department.

amende honorable (Fr.), honourable reparation.

amendt. (legal), amendment.

amenities.

Americanize.

American terms, abbr. A/T (grain trade).

à merveille (Fr.), wonderfully.

amiable.

A.M.I.E.E, Associate Member of the Institution of Electrical Engineers.

A.M.I.Mech.E., Associate Member of the Institution of Mechanical Engineers.

A.M.Inst.C.E., Associate Member of the Institution of Civil Engineers.

A.M.I.R.E., Associate Member of the Institution of Radio Engineers.

A.M.I.Struct.E., Associate Member of the Institution of Structural Engineers.

amoeba, a class of animals of the simplest form; *pl.* amoebae.

amor vincit omnia (Lat.), love surmounts, or overcomes, all things.

amount, abbr. amt.

amour-propre (Fr.), self-esteem.

ampere, unit of measurement of electricity (named after French physicist André M. Ampère) ; abbr. amp.

ampersand, &. Do not use this in a sentence. Used only in the name of a Company (e.g. Jones & Co.) or in quoting numbers (e.g. Seats 36 & 37). Avoid &c. as abbreviation for *et cetera* (etc.). Never say " and cetera."

amphi-, about, around.

amphibian, class of animals, between reptiles and fishes, that can live both on land and in water ; *pl.* **amphibians,** amphibia. Also the name given to an aeroplane that is capable of alighting on both land and water.

amplifier, an apparatus used to reinforce or amplify.

A.M.S., Army Medical Staff.

amt., amount.

amuck.

A.-N., Anglo-Norman.

anaemia.

anaesthetize, to administer an anaesthetic.

analogous, bearing a likeness to.

analyse.

analysis, *pl.* **analyses.**

analyst, one who analyses. *See also* note under "annalist."

ananas (Fr.), pineapple.

anathematize, to pronounce a curse upon.

ancestress.

ancien régime (Fr.), the old régime or order of things.

ancillary, serving, aiding, auxiliary.

, and. Most writers favour the comma before *and* in giving a number of items, e.g. "men, women, and children." *See also* note under "ampersand."

anglais (Fr.) means English (*fem. anglaise*); *anglais* and *anglaise* mean respectively Englishman and Englishwoman.

anglice (Lat.), according to English custom.

anglicize, to convert into English.

Anglo-French, abbr. A.-F.

Anglo-Norman, abbr. A.-N.

animalcule, microscopic animal; *pl.* animalcules. (Lat. *animalculum*; *pl. animalcula*).

anna, Indian coin, 16 to the rupee.

annalist, one who writes or compiles annals. *See also* note under "analyst."

anno Domini (Lat.), abb. A.D.

anno mundi (Lat.), in the year of the world.

anno regni (Lat.), in the year of the reign.

annotator, one who makes notes or comments.

annuity, abbr. anny. (legal).

annus (Lat.), year; *pl.* anni.

annus mirabilis (Lat.), wonderful year.

anny. (legal), annuity.

anon., anonymous.

A.N.S., Army Nursing Service.

Antarctic.

ante (Lat.), before. Used as a prefix in many words. Do not confuse with Greek *anti-*, which changes a word into its opposite.

ante bellum (Lat.), before the war.

antechamber.

antedate, to affix or assign to document or event a date earlier than the true one.

ante diem (Lat.), before the day; abbr. *a.d.*

antediluvian, one who lived before the Flood.

ante meridiem (Lat.), before noon; abbr. *a.m.* English form: antemeridian.

antenna, a feeler of crustacean or insect; *pl.* antennæ.

ante-room.

anthropologist, one who studies humanity as a branch of natural science.

anti- (Greek). When this prefix is used it changes a word into its opposite. Do not confuse with Latin *ante*, before.

anticlimax.

antimony, symbol Sb (no point).

antisabbatarian, one who is opposed to the observance of the Sabbath.

antithesis, contrast; *pl.* antitheses.

antitoxin, a substance that counteracts poison.

antonym, a word of opposite meaning.

Antwerp. Fr.: *Anvers*.

Anwick, Lincs

anyone, but any one if single member of a group.

anything.

anywhere.

Anzac, Australian and New Zealand Army Corps (Dardanelles, 1915).

A.O., Army Order.

a/o, account of.

A.O.C., Army Ordnance Corps; Air Officer Commanding.

A.O.D., Ancient Order of Druids; Army Ordnance Department.

A.O.F., Ancient Order of Foresters.

A.O.H., Ancient Order of Hibernians.

A.O.S., Ancient Order of Shepherds.

août (Fr.), August. It is optional whether the months, in French, take initial caps.

à outrance (Fr.), to the death.

A.P., to be protested (Bills of Exchange); additional premium (Insurance).

A.P.D., Army Pay Department.

à peu près (Fr.), nearly.

apex, *pl.* apexes or apices. Tendency in these words to keep the *x* plural for popular use and the other for scientific.

à pied (Fr.), on foot.

à plaisir (Fr.), at pleasure.

Apollinaris.

apologize.

apostasy, a falling away from, revolt against, one's religion, principles, or party.

apostrophe. This has many uses.

  Possessive: *sing.* the typist's table; *pl.* the typists' tables. Be careful of proper names. Write the name completely first, then add sign of possessive. " Professor Jeans's book." If you omit the final *s* it may *look* all right, but will *sound* as if the name were Jean. Euphony demands that no *s* should be added in such a case as " Moses' law." Avoid two possessives in succession (" My brother's wife's hat "). Avoid making lifeless things possessive (" The curtain's edge ").

Indicating omission, as in poetry and conversation (o'er, we're) ; in proper names, as O'Connor. Note that in M'Clintock and similar names, the sign to be represented by apostrophe is the printer's turned comma.

Plurals of letters and figures: " Distinguish between your u's and n's, and make your 6's clear." Do not add an apostrophe to plurals of abbreviations where the possessive case is not indicated, e.g. M.P.s, J.P.s, etc.

Single quotation mark is made on the typewriter by this same sign ; also the indication of *feet* and *minutes.*

apostrophize, to make an exclamatory address, in the course of a speech, to a particular person.

appal.

appalling.

apparatus.

apparelled.

appartement (Fr.), apartment.

appellant.

appendix, *pl.* **appendixes** or **appendices.** *See* note under " apex."

appetizer.

application, abbr. applon. (legal).

appliqué, appliquéd.

applon. (legal), application.

appointed, abbr. apptd. (legal).

apposite, appropriate.

apprise, to inform.

apprize, to value.

approx., approximately.

appt. (legal), appoint.

appurts., appurtenances.

après-midi (Fr.), afternoon.

apropos, to the purpose. (Fr.: *à propos.*) Examples of English usage: (1) The speaker gave an illustration that was very apropos. (2) Apropos of the decision arrived at last week . . .

A.P.S., Associate of the Pharmaceutical Society.

aq., aqua (Lat.), water.

A.Q.C., Associate of Queen's College (London).

A.Q.M.G., Assistant-Quartermaster-General.

aquarium, *pl.* aquariums.

à quatre mains (Fr.), for two performers (four hands).

aqua vitœ (Lat.), water of life—brandy.

A/R, all risks (marine insurance).

A.R.A., Associate of the Royal Academy (London).

arabic numerals, 1, 2, 3, etc.

A.R.Ae.S., Associate of the Royal Aeronautical Society.

A.R.A.M., Associate of the Royal Academy of Music.

arbitrator.

A.R.C.A., Associate of the Royal Cambrian Academy; Associate of the Royal College of Arts.

arc-en-ciel (Fr.), rainbow; *pl. arcs-en-ciel.*

arch-, archi-, chief, head, ruling.

archaeologist, one engaged in the study of antiquities.

Archbishop, abbr. Abp. *See* Appendix I for correct form of address.

Archbishop of Canterbury is " Primate of all England."

Archbishop of York is " Primate of England."

Archd., Archdeacon.

Archdeacon, abbr. Archd. *See* Appendix I for correct form of address.

archipelago, *pl.* archipelagos.

A.R.C.M., Associate of the Royal College of Music.

A.R.C.O., Associate of the Royal College of Organists.

A.R.C.S., Associate of the Royal College of Science.

Arctic.

Ardleigh, Essex.

Ardley, Oxon

Ardsley, Yorks

A.R.E., Associate of the Royal Society of Painter-Etchers.

aren't, are not. The colloquialism, " Aren't I ? " should be replaced by " Am I not ? "

argent comptant (Fr.), ready money.

argumenti causa (Lat.), for the sake of argument.

argumentum ad absurdum (Lat.), an argument carried to the point of absurdity.

argumentum ad populum (Lat.), an appeal to the people.

A.R.H.A., Associate of the Royal Hibernian Academy.

A.R.I.B.A., Associate of the Royal Institute of British Architects.

Ariz., Arizona.

armadillo, *pl.* armadillos.

Armageddon, the last great battle between good and evil (according to the Revelation of St. John).

arm-chair.

armful, *pl.* armfuls.

armhole.

Arnaud. *See* Appendix II for pronunciation.

A.R.P., Air Raid Precautions.

arrangt. (legal) arrangement.

arrière-pensée (Fr.), ulterior motive; mental reservation.

A.R.S.A., Associate of the Royal Scottish Academy; Associate of the Royal Society of Arts.

arsenic, symbol As (no point).

ars est celare artem (Lat.), true art is to conceal art.

A.R.S.L., Associate of the Royal Society of Literature.

ars longa, vita brevis (Lat.), art is long; life is short.

A.R.S.M., Associate of the Royal School of Mines.

artichaut (Fr.), artichoke.

article de fond (Fr.), newspaper leading article.

artisan, one who practises a trade.

artist, one who is skilled in any art. **Artiste** is sometimes used to designate a professional singer or public performer, but **artist** is becoming more common in this sense.

artium baccalaureus (Lat.), Bachelor of Arts; abbr. B.A.

artium magister (Lat.), Master of Arts; abbr. M.A.

A.R.W.S., Associate of the Royal Society of Painters in Water Colours.

A/S, account sales.

As, arsenic (no point).

A.S.A.A., Associate of the Society of Incorporated Accountants and Auditors.

ascendancy.

asceticism, practising severe self-denial.

A.S.E., Amalgamated Society of Engineers.

as follows. This is idiomatic. Do not use " as follow." Use colon if the enumeration runs on, and colon and dash (:—) if it starts on a fresh line.

Ash-Wednesday.

asperge (Fr.), asparagus.

asphalt.

assagai, a Kaffir spear.

assassin.

assessable.

assessment.

assessor.

assez bien (Fr.), fairly well.

Assheton. *See* Appendix II for pronunciation.

assiettes (Fr.), plates.

assignor.

assigns, abbr. assns. (legal).

assizer, assizor, one who assizes; one of a grand jury.

assn. (legal), association.

assns. (legal), assigns.

association, abbr. assn. (legal).

Assoc.Inst.C.E., Associate of the Institution of Civil Engineers.

Assoc.Inst.T., Associate of the Institute of Transport.

Assoc.M.I.Gas E., Associate Member of the Institution of Gas Engineers.

Assoc.M.I.Min.E., Associate Member of the Institution of Mining Engineers.

Assoc.M.Inst.C.E., Associate Member of the Institution of Civil Engineers.

assurance, usually applied to life, and *insurance* to fire and marine.

asterisk. Form this by typing the small *x* and hyphen.

asthma.

Astrakhan.

astrology, study of supposed influence of stars on human affairs.

astronomy, science of the heavenly bodies.

A/T, American terms (grain trade).

athenaeum, literary or scientific club, etc.

à tout prix (Fr.), at any price.

at par, *see* note under " par."

à travers (Fr.), across.

ats. (law), at the suit of.

attaché, one attached to a legation.

attar of roses.

attending, abbr. attg.

attestn. (legal), attestation.

attg., attending.

Att.-Gen., Attorney-General.

auberge (Fr.), inn.

au contraire (Fr.), on the contrary.

au courant de (Fr.), conversant with.

au désespoir (Fr.), in despair.

au fait (Fr.), conversant, instructed.

au fond (Fr.), at the bottom.

auf Wiedersehen! (Ger.), See you again soon! *Au revoir!*

Aug., August. Avoid abbreviations in letter-writing.

Augereau. *See* Appendix II for pronunciation.

aught, anything.

au gratin (Fr.), with grated cheese or breadcrumbs.

August, abbr. Aug.

Auld lang syne.

au naturel (Fr.), food served uncooked.

au pair (Fr.), board and lodging, without remuneration, usually applied to teachers or governesses.

au pied de la lettre (Fr.), literally.

au prix coûtant (Fr.), at cost price.

Au revoir! (Fr.), Till we meet again!

au rez-de-chaussée (Fr.), on the ground-floor.

Ausgang (Ger.), exit.

Australasian, pertaining to Australia and adjoining islands.

authoritative.

authorized.

authy. (legal), authority.

auto-, self.

autobiography, the story of one's own life.

autogiro, a plane that can land almost vertically.

automaton, *pl.* automata.

autonomy, the right of self-government.

autres temps, autres mœurs (Fr.), manners change with the times.

autumn.

a/v, ad valorem (Lat.), according to value.

A.V., Authorized Version (of the Bible).

avant-propos (Fr.), preface. Same in plural.

A.V.D., Army Veterinary Department.

Avebury. *See* Appendix II for pronunciation.

aviator. The feminine *aviatrix* is not likely to become popular.

A.V.-M., Air Vice-Marshal.

avoirdupois, abbr. avdp.

à volonté (Fr.), at pleasure, at will.

à votre santé! (Fr.), To your health!

A.W.C.S., Association of Women Clerks and Secretaries.

axis, *pl.* axes.

ay, yes; *pl.* ayes (*pron.* i). aye, always (*pron.* ā). This distinction seems likely to prevail, but practice is unsettled.

Ayr, Scotland.

Ayre (Point of), Isle of Man.

Ayscough. *See* Appendix II for pronunciation.

Aytoun. See Appendix II for pronunciation.

B

B/-, bag, bags of.

B.A., Bachelor of Arts.

Ba, barium (no point).

baboon, *fem*. babuina.

bacillus, a microscopic organism, a source of disease; *pl*. bacilli.

backing sheet, a sheet of stout paper to be inserted behind the typing paper, especially if the platen is worn.

back spacer. Its primary use is *not* to make corrections. It is useful in tabular work, when large and small numbers have to be typed in a list. Set the tabulator at a point (say) for the tens, and back-space for the hundreds. Useful for making " combination characters " or for half-space correcting (*q.v.*).

backwoodsman.

bad-tempered.

bagage (Fr.), baggage.

Bagehot. *See* Appendix II for pronunciation.

Baghdad, correct, but present tendency is to use *Bagdad*.

B.Agr.Sc., Bachelor of Agricultural Science.

bakelite, a synthetic insulating material.

baksheesh, Eastern term for a gratuity of money.

balance sheet, to be typed on brief or double foolscap paper. It can be typed on two foolscap sheets, to be neatly pasted together. Type the longer side first; totals must be on the same level.

Balcarres. *See* Appendix II for pronunciation.

balk, **baulk** (noun and verb).

ballad, a simple, sentimental song; simple narrative poem.

ballade, an old French poem, the form of which was revived in France and England in the nineteenth century.

balloon.

balloted.

ball-room.

bandanna, an Indian silk handkerchief.

bandoleer, **bandolier**, a shoulder-belt for cartridges.

Bangkok.

banjo, *pl*. banjos.

bank draft, abbr. B/d.

Bank holidays and public holidays in England and Ireland are: Good Friday, Easter Monday, Whit-Monday, first Monday in August, December 25th and 26th. Ireland has, in addition, March 17th. In Scotland they are: New Year's Day, Good Friday, first Monday in May, first Monday in August, Christmas Day. Edinburgh has an additional day in spring and one in autumn and Glasgow has a Fair Day in July.

bank post bill, abbr. B.P.B.

bankruptcy, abbr. bkcy.

B.A.O., Bachelor of Obstetrics (Ireland).

Barbados.

B.Arch., Bachelor of Architecture (Ireland).

Baring. *See* Appendix II for pronunciation.

barium, abbr. Ba (no point).

Barkston, Lincs and Yorks

Barocci. *See* Appendix II for pronunciation.

barograph, a recording barometer.

barometer.

Baron. *See* Appendix I for correct form of address.

Baroness. *See* Appendix I for correct form of address.

Baronet, abbr. Bart. *See* Appendix I for correct form of address

Baronet's wife. *See* Appendix I for correct form of address.

Baron's daughter. *See* Appendix I for correct form of address.

Baron's son. *See* Appendix I for correct form of address.

baroque, irregularly shaped; denoting style of architecture common in first half of eighteenth century.

barouche, a four-wheeled carriage with a falling top.

barrel, abbr. bl.; **barrels,** abbr. bls.

barrelled.

Barrister-at-Law. Note that this title follows the surname immediately, e.g. W. A. Hirst, Barrister-at-Law, Esq.

Bart., Baronet. Do not use Bt.

Bart's, St. Bartholomew's Hospital, London.

Basle, Switzerland. Fr. *Bâle;* Ger. *Basel.*

bas-relief, a sculpture in low relief (pronounce the s).

bassinette, the more popular spelling. Sometimes *bassinet* is seen. (From Fr. *bassin* = basin.)

basso profondo (It.), lowest male voice.

bateau (Fr.), a boat; *pl. bateaux.*

Bath chair.

baton, music conductor's stick. Fr. *bâton.*

battalion.

battleship.

battre la campagne (Fr.), to beat about the bush.

Baumeister. *See* Appendix II for pronunciation.

Bavaria. Ger. *Bayern.*

bawbee, a halfpenny (Scot.).

Bayard. *See* Appendix II for pronunciation.

bay-window, a window that is advanced from the wall-line. When it is curved in shape it is called a bow-window.

bazar (Fr.), bazaar.

B.B., Bill Book.

B.B.C., British Broadcasting Corporation; Bromo-benzyl-cyanide (tear-gas).

B.C., before Christ. The year precedes the letters; the reverse for A.D. Also British Columbia.

B.C.E., Bachelor of Civil Engineering.

B.Ch., Bachelor of Surgery (Ireland).

B.Ch.D. or B.D.S., Bachelor of Dental Surgery.

B.C.L., Bachelor of Civil Law.

B.Com., Bachelor of Commerce.

B.Comm., Bachelor of Commerce (Ireland).

B.Com.Sc., Bachelor of Commercial Science.

B/d., brought down.

B/D, bank draft.

B.D., Bachelor of Divinity.

bdellium, an Arabian aromatic gum-resin.

bdl., bundle; **bdls.,** bundles.

B.D.S., Bachelor of Dental Surgery.

B/E, Bill of Exchange.

B.E. or B.Eng., Bachelor of Engineering.

Beaconsfield. *See* Appendix II for pronunciation.

Beauchamp. See Appendix II for pronunciation.

Beauclerc. *See* Appendix II for pronunciation.

beau-fils (Fr.), **son-in-law.** Without hyphen, handsome son.

Beaufort. *See* Appendix II for pronunciation.

beau-ideal, highest type of excellence.

Beaulieu. *See* Appendix II for pronunciation.

Beaumarchais. *See* Appendix II for pronunciation.

beau-monde, the fashionable world.

Beaumont. *See* Appendix II for pronunciation.

Beaux-arts (Fr.), fine arts.

béchamel (Fr.), white sauce.

B.Ed., Bachelor of Education.

Bedfordshire, abbr. Beds (no point needed).

bedouin.

bedroom.

Beds, Bedfordshire.

bed-spread.

beehive.

befall.

befe. (legal), before.

beignets (Fr.), fritters.

bel air (Fr.), good bearing.

beldam, an ugly old woman.

bel esprit (Fr.), wit; *pl. beaux esprits.*

bel étage (Fr.), first-floor.

belga, unit of currency in Belgium.

belge (Fr.), Belgian. Initial cap. if used as a noun.

Belgique (Fr.), Belgium

Belgium. Unit of currency 1 Belga = 5 francs = 500 centimes.

believable.

bell. Its purpose is to warn you that the end of the line is approaching, but it will not function unless you have fixed your right-hand margin stop.

belladonna, a poisonous medicinal British plant.

belle-fille (Fr.), daughter-in-law. Without hyphen this means beautiful girl.

belle-mère (Fr.) mother-in-law, stepmother. Without hyphen this means beautiful mother.

belles-lettres, the accepted English form meaning elegant literature (including poetry) regarded as cultured. It is plural.

Bellew. *See* Appendix II for pronunciation.

Bellini. *See* Appendix II for pronunciation.

Bellot. *See* Appendix II for pronunciation.

Belshazzar.

Belvoir. *See* Appendix II for pronunciation.

B.E.M., British Empire Medal.

benedicite (Lat.), bless you.

Benedick, a character in Shakespeare's *Much Ado About Nothing.* Used also to signify a newly married man, especially a "captured bachelor," and sometimes spelt *benedict.*

benefactor.

benefited.

bene vale (Lat.), farewell; abbr. *b.v.*

Benoît. *See* Appendix II for pronunciation.

benzene, aromatic hydrocarbon, obtained from coal-gas. *Benzol* is another name for this.

benzine, obtained from petroleum, and used for removing grease stains. *Benzoline* is another name for this.

beqd. (legal), bequeathed.

bereavement.

beriberi, a disease of the East, caused by a deficiency of vitamin B in the diet.

Berkeley. *See* Appendix II for pronunciation.

Berkshire, abbr. Berks (no point). *See* Appendix II for pronunciation.

Berlioz. *See* Appendix II for pronunciation.

Bertie. *See* Appendix II for pronunciation.

B. ès L., Bachelier ès Lettres (Fr.), Bachelor of Letters.

B. ès S., Bachelier ès Sciences (Fr.), Bachelor of Science.

bête (Fr.), stupid.

bête noire (Fr.), one's pet aversion.

Bethune. *See* Appendix II for pronunciation.

bevelled.

Bewick. *See* Appendix II for pronunciation.

Bexleyheath, Kent.

B/f, brought forward.

bf. (legal), brief.

B.G., Birmingham gauge.

B'ham, Birmingham.

b.h.p., brake horse-power.

bi-, bis-, twice, two ways, double.

Bi, bismuth (no point).

biannual, half-yearly.

biased, the more usual spelling.

Bible, Books of the Bible do not need quotes.

bi-chrome ribbons. These are not generally economical, as the same amount of work does not fall upon both colours. Black record and copying ribbons are used in solicitors' offices. Black and red are used in accountancy work (red for credits, etc.), and for dramatic work (red for all but the spoken part).

Bickleigh, Devon.

Bickley, Cheshire, Kent.

biennial, two-yearly.

biennium, a two-year period.

bientôt (Fr.), soon; *à bientôt,* Good-bye for the present.

bière (Fr.), beer.

bifteck (Fr.), beef-steak.

bigoted.

billet-doux (Fr.), love-letter; *pl. billets-doux.*

billing figures, special characters used on billing machines to avoid possible misreadings. They are open and clear, and 9, for example, has a long tail.

billion, a million millions. In France and U.S.A. it signifies a thousand millions.

book-plate.

Boord. *See* Appendix II for pronunciation.

Borghese. *See* Appendix II for pronunciation.

bos'n, boatswain.

B.O.T., Board of Trade.

bottom of page, approaching. Rule a heavy line on the backing sheet, to warn you that you are nearing foot of page. If using a carbon, gum on to it a small label, cut a small notch at the edge, etc.

boudoir.

bouillon (Fr.), broth.

Bourchier. *See* Appendix II for pronunciation.

bourgeois (Fr.), a middle-class person; *fem. bourgeoise.*

bourgeoisie (Fr.), the middle classes.

Bourke. *See* Appendix II for pronunciation.

Bourn, Cambs

bourn, a stream.

bourne, a limit; a goal.

Bourne, Lincs. *See* Appendix II for pronunciation.

Bourne End, Bucks, Herts.

boutique (Fr.), shop.

bouts-rimés, rhymed endings.

bowdlerize, to expurgate. (T. Bowdler was an expurgator of Shakespeare in 1818.)

bow-window, a curved bay-window.

boxful, *pl.* boxfuls.

boycott, to ostracize (from Captain Boycott, Irish landlord).

Bp., Bishop.

B/P, bill payable.

B.P., British Pharmacopoeia.

b.p., below proof.

B.P.B., bank post bill.

B.Pharm., Bachelor of Pharmacy (Ireland).

B/R, bill receivable; Bordeaux or Rouen (grain trade).

Br, bromide (no point).

Br., brother.

brace, printing term meaning a large, rounded bracket. Make it on the typewriter by typing a succession of brackets.

brackets. The right bracket, repeated, is used for the attestation clause in legal documents, to link a succession of items, or to "hold together," as it were, the items of an Agenda when typed on the left of the sheet, ready for notes to be made on the right. *See also* "parentheses."

brackets [square]. Type the "shilling sign" (/) ; back-space and type the underscore; turn the platen forward one line-space and type the underscore again. This makes a satisfactory square bracket, which will be needed when brackets occur within brackets. Square brackets are used by the printer to enclose a phrase within a quotation; they signify that the writer, and not the author of the quotation, has interpolated the remark.

Brahmin; *fem.* **Brahminee.**

braise, to bake or stew with herbs in covered pan.

braze, to solder.

Brazil. Unit of currency 1 milreis = 100 reis.

Breadalbane. *See* Appendix II for pronunciation.

breakfast-cupful (sometimes one word) ; *pl.* **breakfast-cupfuls.**

break-line, the last line of a paragraph. It should not begin a new page.

brevet d'invention (Fr.), a patent.

bric-à-brac, curios.

brief. Type on brief paper (13 × 16 in.). It is a short account of a client's case, for use of counsel, prepared by the solicitor. Abbr. bf. (legal).

brier-rose.

Brig., Brigadier.

brioche (Fr.), a kind of light, sweet roll.

Britannia, abbr. Brit.

Bro., brother.

broach (verb).

broadcast; past tense and past participle *broadcast* (not broadcasted).

Broad Oak, Carmarthen, Dorset, Hereford, Sussex.

Broadoak, Salop.

brochure, booklet—stitched, not bound.

Broke. *See* Appendix II for pronunciation.

bromine, abbr. Br (no point).

brooch (noun).

Brot (Ger.), bread.

Brougham. *See* Appendix II for pronunciation.

brought down, abbr. B/d.

brought forward, abbr. B/f.

browse.

brussels sprouts.

B/S, Bill of Sale

B.S., B.C., or **B.Ch.,** Bachelor of Surgery.

B/s, bags.

B.Sc., Bachelor of Science.

B.Sc. (Econ.), Bachelor of Science in faculty of Economics.

B.Sc. (Eng.), Bachelor of Science in faculty of Engineering.

B.S.I., British Standards Institution.

B.S.O., British School of Osteopathy.

B.S.S., British Standard Specification.

B.S.T., British Summer-time.

B.Th., Bachelor of Theology.

B.Th.U., British Thermal Unit.

B.T.U., Board of Trade Unit.

bu., bushel.

Bucaresti, national name for Bucharest.

buccaneer.

Buch (Ger.), book; *pl. Bücher.*

Buchanan. *See* Appendix II for pronunciation.

Buchhändler (Ger.), bookseller.

Buckinghamshire, abbr. Bucks (no point).

Bucknall, Lincs, Staffs

Bucknell, Oxon, Salop

Buddhism.

budgeting.

buffalo, *pl.* **buffaloes.**

buffeting.

building, abbr. bldg.

Bulgaria. Unit of currency 1 Lev = 100 stotinki.

bundle, abbr. bdl.; *pl.* **bundles**, abbr. bdls.

bunkum. Original spelling was *buncombe.* Member for Buncombe, in N. Carolina, spoke needlessly in Congress to impress his constituents.

Bunsen. *See* Appendix II for pronunciation.

Burdett. *See* Appendix II for pronunciation.

bureaucracy, undue power of Government officials.

Burghley. *See* Appendix II for pronunciation.

burgomaster, the mayor of a Dutch or Flemish town.

bus, so widely accepted for omnibus that apostrophe is no longer needed; *pl.* buses. Do not use bus as a verb.

bushel, abbr. bu.

Bushey, Herts

Bushy Park, Middlesex.

businesslike.

busybodies.

buttermilk.

button-hole.

B.W.G., Birmingham Wire Gauge.

B.W.I., British West Indies.

by and by.
bye-bye, good-bye.
bygone.
by-law.
bypath.
byplay.
by-product, thing produced incidentally in manufacturing
   something else.
bystander.
by the by.
byway.
byword.

C/-, case, coupon, currency.

C, 100 (roman numerals); carbon, chapter, Lord Chancellor.

C., centigrade, Central.

c., cent, centime, centigram, cents, chapter.

c., *circa* (Lat.), about.

C/A, Capital Account.

C.A., Chartered Accountant (Scottish); Chief Accountant; Court of Appeal; County Alderman.

ca., cases, cathode.

Ca, calcium (no point).

ca'canny, term used for policy of restricting output. (Sc. go cautiously!)

cache, a place for concealing anything; Fr. *cacher*, to hide.

cachet, seal, distinguishing mark.

Cadogan. *See* Appendix II for pronunciation.

café. This has been anglicized as meaning a restaurant. When used to mean coffee, it is a French word.

café au lait (Fr.), coffee with milk.

café noir (Fr.), black coffee.

cafeteria.

caffè (It.), café.

Caiaphas.

Caister, Norfolk.

Caistor, Lincs

Caius College, Camb.; abbr. C.C. *See* Appendix II for pronunciation.

Cal., California.

calceolaria.

calcium, abbr. Ca (no point).

calculator.

calendar, an almanac.

calender, to press in a roller-machine.

calix, cup-like cavity; *pl.* calices. *See also* "Calyx."

calligraphy, good penmanship.

calliper, an instrument for measuring diameters (sometimes caliper).

callisthenics, easy gymnastic exercises, promoting gracefulness of body.

calorie, unit of heat.

calorimeter.

Calveley, Ches.

Calverleigh, Devon.

Calverley, Yorks.

calyx, whorl of sepals forming case of bud; *pl.* **calyces** or **calyxes.**

camaraderie.

Cambridge, abbr. Camb (no point).

Cambridgeshire, abbr. Cambs (no point).

camel-hair brush.

camellia, flower named after G. J. Kamel.

camomile.

camouflage, verb and noun.

campo santo (It., Span.), a cemetery.

Canada. Unit of currency 1 Canadian dollar = 100 cents.

C. & D., collected and delivered.

candelabrum. The plural is **candelabra,** but this is often used as the singular form, with **candelabras** as plural.

C. & F., cost and freight.

candle-power, abbr. c.p.

canonize.

canst.

can't, cannot.

cantate Domino (Lat.), sing to the Lord.

canto, a division of a long poem (in It., a song); *pl.* **cantos.**

canvass, verb.

canyon, deep gorge; Mexican *cañón.*

cap., chapter.

cap-à-pie, from head to foot (armed).

capital account, abbr. C/A.

capitalize.

capitals. Be sparing with these, except in displayed matter, advertisements, etc. They are not needed for small connecting words in titles (e.g. " Songs of the Sea "). They are not generally used for compass points (north-east), nor for the names of the seasons. No hard-and-fast rule can be laid down, however. Use " the North " as representing the north of a country. Note the significance of the capital in " Head " and " Company " in the following sentence: " A distinguished *company* gathered at the dinner, and Lord X sat at the *head* of the table, having on his right the *Head* of an important *Company*." In letter-writing use initial caps for both words of salutation, but only first word of complimentary close. Note how well-established proper names lose their capitals, e.g. indian ink. It is usual for every line of poetry to begin with a capital, the exception being in some instances of ultra-modern verse. Strike the capitals more heavily than the lower-case letters when cutting stencils.

caption, heading of chapter, section, or page, title of illustration, descriptive line on film, picture, etc.

caput (Lat.), section, chapter, head; abbr. *cap.*

car., carat.

caracal, a kind of lynx.

caracul, a sheep.

carafe, water-bottle.

carat, abbr. car. or K.

caraway.

carbon, abbr. C **(no point).**

carbon paper. The three varieties are: single (coated on one side only), double (with pigment both sides), copying. It may be had in colours, and by means of small slips coloured headings may be typed. Economize in the use of carbon paper by shifting its position so that finally the sheet becomes worn evenly all over. Buy good quality. Cut off a little triangle at the corners, to facilitate extracting the carbons from the typed sheets. Grip the typed sheets firmly and pull or shake out the carbon papers.

carburettor, an apparatus for impregnating with carbon; a device for vaporizing petrol.

carcass.

Card., Cardinal.

cardboard, standard sizes: 20×25 in. and $22\frac{1}{2} \times 26$ in.

Cardinal, abbr. Card. *See* Appendix I for correct form of address.

cardinal numbers, 1, 2, 3, 4, etc. In writing, use words (one, two, etc.), up to ten, and generally in isolated cases. Note use of hyphen in thirty-four, etc.

card index. The secretary will find a small boxed card index an excellent way of storing odd items of information in alphabetical order.

cards, typing on. Most modern typewriters take cards easily, but a special attachment can be obtained if necessary.

carême (Fr.), Lent.

care of, abbr. c/o.

caret sign (∧). This well-known sign indicates the omission of a word. It is best made in ink, but " shilling stroke, back-space, underscore " makes a fair substitute, and for a very neat job the paper can be inserted upside down and the small *v* inserted at the appropriate point.

carnaval (Fr.), carnival; Ger. *Carneval.*

Carnegie. *See* Appendix II for pronunciation. ·

caroller, but less popularly caroler.

carotte (Fr.), carrot.

carriage paid, abbr. C.P.

carried down, abbr c/d.

carried forward, abbr. c/f.

carte blanche (Fr.), full discretion.

cartel, combination of business firms with the object of eliminating competition.

carte postale avec réponse payée (Fr.), reply-paid postcard.

case, abbr. C/-.

casein, milk curd.

cases, abbr. ca. or C/s.

cash book, abbr. C.B.

cash on delivery, abbr. C.O.D.

cask, abbr. ck.

Cassilis. *See* Appendix II for pronunciation.

caster, one who casts. *See also* "castor."

Castile, Spanish town.

Castile soap.

cast-iron, use hyphen only when an adjective.

Castleton, Argyll, Derby, Lancs, Yorks

Castletown, Dorset, Isle of Man. A dozen or more places in Ireland have this name, so be careful to indicate the county.

cast-on.

castor. The word meaning pepper-box or chair-wheel should be spelt *caster,* but the *-or* spelling is now common for all meanings, except, of course, *caster,* one who casts.

casus belli (Lat.), the cause of war.

catarrh.

catastrophe.

catch-line, a head-line placed temporarily on proofs.

catchword, the word that attracts attention, as the heading of dictionary paragraph, or the cue word in actor's part.

catechize.

catgut.

catholicism.

cat-o'-nine-tails.

cat's-paw.

cauldron.

cause célèbre (Fr.), law case that attracts much attention.

causerie, informal newspaper article.

cautionary.

caveat actor (Lat.), let the doer beware.

caveat emptor (Lat.), let the buyer beware.

cave canem (Lat.), beware of the dog.

caviare, sturgeon roe.

cayenne.

C.B., cash book; Cavalry Brigade; Common Bench; Companion of the Bath; confined to barracks.

C.B.E., Commander of the Order of the British Empire.

C.C., Caius College; City Council; Civil Court; County Councillor; Common Councillor.

c.c., continuous current; contra credit; cubic centimetre.

cc., chapters.

C.C.A., Controller of Civil Aviation.

C.C.P., Court of Common Pleas.

CD, 400.

c/d, carried down.

c.d. or *cum div.*, with dividend.

C.E., Church of England; Civil Engineer; Christian Endeavour Society.

Ce, cerium (no point).

Cecil. *See* Appendix II for pronunciation.

cedilla (ç), a mark used in French words under letter *c* to indicate that it has the sound of *s*. Type *c* and comma in same position to obtain the effect.

-ceed. There are only three words that end in this syllable, viz. proceed, exceed, and succeed. All others having this sound are spelt with -cede (as precede, intercede), with the single exception of supersede.

cela va sans dire (Fr.), that goes without saying.

céleri (Fr.), celery.

celerity.

'cello, short for violoncello. The performer is a 'cellist.

"Cellophane" (trade name).

cellular.

C.E.M.A., Council for the Encouragement of Music and the Arts.

ce n'est que le premier pas qui coûte (Fr.), it is only the beginning that is difficult.

censer, incense vessel.

censor, an official who licenses or suppresses books, plays, etc.; Roman magistrate.

cent, American coin (no point) ; abbr. c., ct., or *℀*. Form this by typing small c and the solidus through it.

centavo, South American coin, one-hundredth of a peso.

centenarian, a person 100 years old.

centesimo, Italian coin, one-hundredth of a lire.

centi-, one-hundredth.

centigrade, abbr. C. or Cent.

centigram, abbr. c. or cg.

centilitre, abbr. cl. (·07 gill).

centime, French coin ; abbr. c. (one-hundredth of a franc).

centimes, abbr. cts.

centimetre, abbr. cm. (·394 in.). No change for plural.

centring headings. Place headings in centre of work, not paper. Assuming paper is central on platen and that the work is to be centralized on the paper, count letters in heading, divide by two, and subtract result from 40, i.e. centre of scale. This gives point at which to commence. If machine has centring scale, bring pointer to zero, tap out number of characters, and the figure on scale will be the commencing point. For short headings, bring printing point to middle of work and back-space half as many times as there are letters in heading.

centum (Lat.), 100 ; abbr. C or cent (no point).

ceramic.

cerise, a light-red colour ; Fr. *cerise,* cherry.

cerium, abbr. Ce (no point).

Cert.A.I.B., Certificated Associate of the Institute of Bankers.

c'est-à-dire (Fr.), that is to say.

c'est la guerre (Fr.), it is according to the customs of war.

c'est tout dire (Fr.), that is saying everything.

c'est une autre chose (Fr.), that is quite another thing.

ceteris paribus (Lat.), other things being equal.

Ceylon. To describe the natives use Sinhalese, rather than Singhalese, Cingalese, etc.

c/f, carried forward.

cf. (Lat.), *confer,* compare.

c.f.i., cost, freight, and insurance.

C.F., Chaplain to the Forces.

C.G., Captain-General ; Captain of the Guard ; Commissary-General ; Consul-General.

C.G.M., Conspicuous Gallantry Medal.

C.H., Companion of Honour ; Custom House.

C.H.A., Co-operative Holidays Association.

chacun à son goût (Fr.), everyone to his taste.

chairman. This word is generally used also when there is a lady in the chair. A speaker, on rising to address a meeting, would say, " Madam Chairman, Ladies and Gentlemen."

chalet.

Chalmers. *See* Appendix II for pronunciation.

chambre à coucher (Fr.), bedroom; *pl. chambres à coucher.*

chameleon.

chamois-leather.

champignon (Fr.), mushroom.

'Change, Exchange.

changeable.

channelled.

chapeaux bas! (Fr.), hats off !

Chapelton, Devon, Lanark.

Chapeltown, Antrim, Banff, Down, Kerry, Yorks

chaperon.

chapter, abbr. c.; *pl.* cc.

charabanc, the popular spelling, with **charabancs** as plural. The real French word is *char-à-bancs*; *pl. chars-à-bancs.*

characterization.

charge, abbr. chge. (legal).

chargeable.

charges for typewriting work. *See* " typewriting charges."

charlotte, pudding of apple (or other fruit) and bread-crumbs. **Charlotte russe,** custard and sponge cake.

Charteris. *See* Appendix II for pronunciation.

chasse (Fr.), the hunt, the huntsmen, etc.

chassé (Fr.), gliding step in dancing.

châsse (Fr.), a shrine.

chassis, framework of motor-car, etc. No change for plural.

chastisement.

chateau, a castle; *pl.* **chateaux.**

châteaux en Espagne (Fr.), " castles in the air."

chatelain, lord of the manor; *fem.* **chatelaine.**

chauffeur. The feminine *chauffeuse* is not very popular.

Ch.B., *Baccalaureus Chirurgiae,* Bachelor of Surgery.

Ch.Div., Chancery Division.

Cheddar.

chef (Fr.), a cook.

chef-d'œuvre (Fr.), one's masterpiece.

chef d'orchestre (Fr.), the leader of the orchestra; *pl. chefs.*

Chekhov (Anton).

chemin de fer (Fr.), railway; *pl. chemins.*

cheque-perforating type. Typewriters can be fitted with this type. It perforates the paper and prevents fraudulent alteration.

cherchez la femme (Fr.), look for the woman.

cherub, *pl.* cherubs, cherubim.

chervonetz, unit of currency of Russia, equal to 10 old Russian gold roubles.

Cheshire, abbr. Ches (no point).

chestnut.

cheval de bataille (Fr.), a fad, hobby-horse (*cheval*, horse).

chge. (legal), charge.

chic, style, stylish.

chicken-pox. This is singular.

Chief Justice, abbr. C.J.

chiffonier, a sideboard.

childlike.

chilli, dried pod of capsicum.

China. Unit of currency 1 Tael.

chiropodist, *pron.* ki.

chiropractic, the science of palpating and adjusting the movable articulations of the human spinal column by hand. (The operator is called a chiropractor.)

chirruping.

Chisholm. *See* Appendix II for pronunciation.

chlorine, abbr. Cl (no point).

chlorophyll, the green colouring matter in plants.

Cholmeley, Cholmondeley, Chomley. *See* Appendix II for pronunciation.

choreography, the designing of ballet. The person responsible is called a *choreographer* or *choreographist*.

chores, American word for errands or odd jobs.

chorused.

chou (Fr.), cabbage; *pl. choux.*

chou-fleur (Fr.), cauliflower; *pl. choux-fleurs.*

chou marin (Fr.), seakale.

choux de Bruxelles (Fr.), brussels sprouts.

Christ Church College, Oxford, abbr. Ch. Ch.

Christianize.

Christie's, a famous auction-room in London.

Christmas-time.

Christ's Hospital, Horsham, Bluecoat School.

Christ's College, Cambridge, abbr. Chr. Coll. Cam.

chromolithography, the art of making colour-printed lithographs.

chronologize, to make a record of dates and events.

chrysalis, *pl.* chrysalises, chrysalides.

church. Use small *c* when referring to the building, and capital for body of followers, such as the Baptist Church.

churchwarden.

chute, slide, etc. (*pron.* shoot).

C.I., Channel Islands.

cicerone, a guide; *pl.* ciceroni.

C.I.D., Criminal Investigation Department.

C.I.E., Companion of (the Order of) the Indian Empire.

Cie (Fr.), *compagnie*, company (no point).

C.I.E.E., Civil Institute of Electrical Engineers.

c.i.f., cost, insurance, freight.

c.i.f.c., cost, insurance, freight, and commission.

c.i.f.e., cost, insurance, freight, and exchange.

ci-gît (Fr.), here lies.

cilium, a hair-like appendage; *pl.* cilia.

cipher.

C.I.R., Commissioners of Inland Revenue.

circa (Lat.), about; abbr. *c.*

circuitus verborum (Lat.), roundabout expression, circumlocution.

circularizing, the sending out of circulars.

circumcise.

circumflex accent (^) can be formed by combination of acute and grave, if these are on the machine. Otherwise, write in by hand.

circumstances. " In the circumstances " more accurately conveys the meaning of being in the midst of one's surroundings than does " under the . . ."

Cirencester. *See* Appendix II for pronunciation.

citron (Fr.), lemon.

C.I.V., City (of London) Imperial Volunteers.

Civil Court, abbr. C.C.

Civil Service, abbr. C.S.

C.J., Chief Justice.

ck., cask, casks.

Cl, chlorine.

cl., centilitre, class, clause.

clairvoyant, *fem.* clairvoyante.

claptrap.

clarinet, clarinettist, the spellings favoured by musicians, though clarionet is in more general use.

claustrophobia, morbid fear of being in closed spaces.

clean proof, one with few errors, or one pulled after correction.

cleaning typewriter. See "typewriter, care of."

clearness' sake (for).

Clergyman. See Appendix I for correct form of address.

Clerk. See Appendix II for pronunciation.

Clerk of the Peace, abbr. C.P.

Clerk of the Privy Council, abbr. C.P.C.

Clerke. See Appendix II for pronunciation.

cliché, a hackneyed literary phrase; a stereo or electro block.

clientele, a body of clients, followers, etc.

clique, cliquy.

clockwise.

cloisonné (Fr.), enamel with inlaid wire pattern.

close-up (noun or adj.). Examples: "The too frequent use of close-ups sometimes spoils the continuity of a film story"; "He craned his neck in order to obtain a close-up view of the proceedings."

Clowes. See Appendix II for pronunciation.

C.L.R., Central London Railway.

C.M., Chirurgiae Magister, Master of Surgery; Corresponding Member.

cm., centimetre. No change for plural.

C.M.G., Companion of (the Order of) St. Michael and St. George.

c/o, care of.

C.O., Commanding Officer, Conscientious Objector.

Co, cobalt.

Co., company, county.

co-, col-, com-, con-, cor-, with, together, altogether.

coal-field.

coal-mine.

coast-line.

coastwise.

cobalt, abbr. Co (no point).

Cockburn. See Appendix II for pronunciation.

co. claim (legal), counterclaim.

coco-nut.

C.O.D., Cash on delivery.

codl. (legal), codicil.

co-education, educating boys and girls together.

coefficient, a number placed before and multiplying another quantity, known or unknown (Algebra).

coexist.

cognizant.

coheir, coheiress.

coiffeur (Fr.), hairdresser.

coiffure, style of hairdressing; head-dress.

Coke. *See* Appendix II for pronunciation.

Col., Colonel, Colossians.

col., counsel.

colander, a strainer.

colcannon, Irish dish of cabbage and potatoes.

Coliseum, London.

collaborator.

collapsible.

collator, one who compares copies of documents one with another.

collectable.

colloq., colloquial, colloquially, colloquialism.

Cologne; in Ger. **Köln.**

Colombia, S. American republic.

colon. Came into use before the full-stop, but not frequently employed nowadays. Precedes a remark that explains or amplifies statement made in first part of sentence. The most common use is to introduce a list of items; when this begins on a new line, type the colon and dash together, thus :—

Colonel, abbr. Col.

Colonial Bishops. *See* Appendix I for correct form of address.

colonization.

coloration.

Colosseum, Rome.

Colossians, abbr. Col.

colour-scheme.

Colquhoun. *See* Appendix II for pronunciation.

Columbia, U.S.A.

column selector, device on typewriter that is of great use in billing work. It allows the carriage to jump to any point previously set, whereas the tabulator key sends it from column to column in rotation.

Com., Commander.

combated.

Combe. *See* Appendix II for pronunciation.

combination characters. One character may be typed over another, by holding down the space bar whilst the two keys are struck in succession, or by using the back-spacer. This method is useful for making signs not on the typewriter, e.g. dollar, cap. S and shilling mark ($); asterisk, small *x* and hyphen.

comdg., commanding.

Comdt., Commandant.

Comédie Française (Fr.), the home of the French classical drama.

Comines. *See* Appendix II for pronunciation.

comma. Beware of this important stop. Its misplacement or omission may make a world of difference. It is used to indicate a short pause, to separate a parenthetical clause from the rest of the sentence, etc. Note that it need not be used after the number of the house in a street. It should not precede or follow a dash.

Commandant, abbr. Comdt.

commanding, abbr. comdg.

Commanding Officer, abbr. C.O.

commanditaire (Fr.), a sleeping partner.

commando, *pl.* **commandos.**

comme ci, comme ça (Fr.), indifferently, so-so.

comme il faut (Fr.), in good form.

commensurate.

commenter.

Commissary-General, abbr. C.G.

commissionaire; Fr. form *commissionnaire.*

commissioner, abbr. commr. or com.

committed.

committee.

Common Bench, abbr. C.B.

commonplace (*adj.*).

common sense. Note that the hyphen is necessary only when these words are combined to form an adjective, as in " a common-sense proposition." The words should never be written as one word. The other use is shown in, " The typist has plenty of common sense."

Common Serjeant, abbr. C.S. or Com.-Serj.

commr. or com. (legal), commissioner.

communiqué (Fr.), an official report.

compagnia (It.), company; abbr. *Comp^a.*

compagnie (Fr.), company; abbr. *Cie* (no point).

comparative.

compare, abbr. cf. (Latin *confer*), or cp.

compared *with* (to note agreement or difference); *to* (to suggest similarity).

compass points. No caps are necessary; e.g. north-north-west. When abbreviating use caps, but place full stop after last letter only, e.g. NNE. When the word forms part of a name, the initial cap. is needed, e.g. South Australia, the Middle West.

compenson. (legal), compensation.

complainant.

complement, a completion.

compliment, an act or expression of courtesy.

complimentary close. *Respectful:* Yours obediently, Your obedient servant. *Formal:* Yours faithfully, Yours truly. *Less formal:* Yours very truly. *Friendly:* Yours sincerely, Yours very sincerely. Make the salutation correspond; do not combine "Dear Sir" and "Yours sincerely" or "My dear Johnson" and "Yours obediently."

compos mentis (Lat.), in possession of one's faculties, sane.

compote, fruit stewed in syrup.

comprised.

Compton. *See* Appendix II for pronunciation.

Comptroller General. Accountant and Comptroller General, H.M. Customs; of Patent Office; but Controller of Insurance Department, Ministry of Health; Controller of Stamps, Inland Revenue, etc. Consult Whitaker's Almanack.

Com.-Serj., Common Serjeant.

comte (Fr.), Count; *fem. comtesse.*

con., *contra* (against).

concede.

concerng. (legal), concerning.

concurring.

condenser.

conferrable.

confidant, *fem.* **confidante.** Put the stress on the last syllable. The French equivalents are *confident, confidente.*

confiserie (Fr.), sweetmeats.

Coniston, Lancs, Yorks

Conistone, Yorks

Conn., Connecticut.

connexion should be used when referring to a sect or denomination, e.g. the Methodist connexion. In other senses *connection* is the more usual form.

connoisseur.

conscience' sake. Note that enphony demands this exceptional use of apostrophe.

consensus, agreement (of opinion).

Consols, Consolidated Funds.

consommé, clear soup.

conson. (legal), consideration.

conspectus, a general view.

Constable. *See* Appendix II for pronunciation.

consulate, office of a consul.

consultn. (legal), consultation.

consumable.

consummatum est (Lat.), it is finished.

contained (legal), abbr. contd.

contce. (legal), continuance.

contd. (legal), continued, contained.

continent. When reference is made to " *the* Continent," the capital is needed, but not otherwise.

continually, happening frequently ; **continuously** means uninterruptedly.

continuation sheet. Head this with the name, number of sheet, and the date, and begin to type near the top of the sheet, not half-way down.

continued, abbr. contd. (legal).

continuous current, abbr. c.c.

continuous stationery. Commercial forms are fed into the typewriter without interruption, the typist merely having to detach the sets at the perforations.

contra (Lat.), against ; abbr. *con.*

contra credit, abbr. c.c.

contract, abbr. contt. (legal).

contralto, *pl.* contraltos.

contrariwise.

contrary *to*.

contrast *with*.

contretemps, a mishap, a hitch.

contributory.

contt. (legal), contract.

convce. (legal), conveyance.

convener.

conversationist, preferred to *conversationalist.*

conversazione, *pron.* äts.

conveyance, abbr. convce. (legal).

convolvulus, *pl.* convolvuluses.

coomb, a hollow in a hill.

co-operate. In this and similar words, use hyphen.

Copenhagen, in Dan. *Köbenhavn.*

copper, abbr. Cu (no point).

co. pt. or **copart.** (legal), counterpart.

copy (*noun*). To the printer this means matter to be set up in type. To the typist a fair or clean copy is one that is transcribed from a rough copy.

copy-holder. Notebook covers which hold the book and (by means of a cord contrivance) stand beside the machine, will prevent eye-strain. Other copy-holders are obtainable which raise the notebook higher.

copying, charges for, *see* under "typewriting charges."

copy of a letter. Always type COPY at top left-hand corner, and type the signature, placing before it the word (in parentheses) *signed*.

coram judice (Lat.), before the court or a judge.

coram nobis (Lat.), before us, in our presence.

Corbould. *See* Appendix II for pronunciation.

co-respondent (in divorce cases).

cornfield.

cornucopia, the horn of plenty; *pl.* **cornucopias.**

Cornwall, abbr. Corn (no point).

corps, sing. and pl.

corpus Christi (Lat.), body of Christ.

Corpus Christi College, abbr. C.C.C.

correction marks. These are the chief marks used in proof-correcting:

℧	Take out.
#	Insert space.
⊙	Adjust a type that has been inverted.
⊂	Close up.
⊙	Insert full stop.
⁄	Insert comma.
⅋⅋	Insert quotation marks.
H	Insert hyphen.
□	Indent the first word.

cap. Change into capitals words underlined—three lines.

s. caps. Change into small capitals the words underlined—two lines.

l.c. Change into lower case words underlined—one line.

ital. Change into italics words underlined—one line.

rom. Change into roman type words underlined—one line.

N.P. Begin new paragraph at point indicated by square bracket.

run on. No new paragraph to be made. (Link the two pars. by a line.)

stet. Cancelled word to remain. Place dots beneath it.

tr/ Transpose.

w.f. Wrong fount.

correlate.

corroborator.

cost, insurance, and freight, abbr. c.i.f.

cosy. Use this spelling for adjective and noun.

coterie.

Couch. *See* Appendix II for pronunciation.

couldn't.

couldst.

councillor, member of a council.

counsel, abbr. col. (legal).

counsellor, one who gives advice.

counterclaim, abbr. co. claim (legal).

counter-clockwise.

counterfeit. Note—this is one of the exceptions to the rule " *i* before *e* except after *c*."

counterpart, term used in legal offices to mean a duplicate, or one of two corresponding copies of a deed, abbr. co. pt. *or* copart (legal).

Countess. *See* Appendix I for correct form of address.

counties. No full stop is needed after abbreviations for counties, e.g. Bucks, Herts, Lancs, etc.

countrified.

County Court Judges. *See* Appendix I for correct form of address.

coup d'éclat (Fr.), a brilliant exploit.

coup d'état (Fr.), sudden or illegal change in government.

Couper. *See* Appendix II for pronunciation.

coupon, abbr. C/-.

court martial, *pl.* courts martial.

Coutts. *See* Appendix II for pronunciation.

couturière (Fr.), dressmaker.

Covent Garden.

Coventry. *See* Appendix II for pronunciation.

Cowling, Yorks

Cowlinge, Suffolk.

Cowper. *See* Appendix II for pronunciation.

coxswain, *pron.* koxn; abbr. cox (no point).

Cozens. *See* Appendix II for pronunciation.

cp., compare.

C.P., carriage paid; Charter Party; Common Pleas.

c.p., candle-power.

C.P.R., Canadian Pacific Railway.

C.P.R.E., Council for the Preservation of Rural England.

C.P.S., *Custos Privati Sigilli*, Keeper of the Privy Seal.

cr., credit, creditor.

C.P.A., Certified Public Accountant.

C.R., *Custos Rotulorum*, Keeper of the Rolls; Company's Risk.

crape, gauze-like black fabric used for mourning.

crèche.

Creighton. *See* Appendix II for pronunciation.

crêpe de Chine (Fr.).

cretonne.

crevette (Fr.), prawn.

Crichton. *See* Appendix II for pronunciation.

cringeing.

crisis, *pl.* crises.

criterion, *pl.* criteria.

criticize.

critique, a review of literary or artistic work.

crochet, crocheting (*pron.* krōshǐing).

croquet, game.

croquette (Fr.), rissole.

Cross Gates, Yorks

Crossgates, Fife.

crosswise, *-wise* is a more common ending than *-ways* in this and similar words.

crystallize.

C/s, cases.

C.S., Civil Service; Court of Session; close shot (film scenario term); Common Serjeant; *Custos Sigilli*, Keeper of the Seal.

C.S.I., Companion of the (Order of the) Star of India.

C.S.M., Company Sergeant-Major.

C.T.C., Cyclists' Touring Club.

C.T.L., Constructive total loss.

C.U., Close-up (film scenario term).

Cu, cuprum (copper).

cubic centimetre, abbr. c.c.

Cui bono? (Lat.), Who gains by it?

cul-de-sac, *pl.* culs-de-sac.

cum (Lat.), with.

Cumberland, abbr. Cumb or Cumbd (no point).

cum bona venia (Lat.), with your kind indulgence.

cum dividend, with dividend; abbr. c.d. *or* cum div.

cum grano salis (Lat.), with a grain of salt; with reserve.

cum privilegio (Lat.), with privilege.

cumulus, a cloud form; *pl.* **cumuli.** Also *adj.*, but when used more broadly, spelt *cumulous.*

cuneiform, the ancient wedge-shaped Assyrian and Persian script.

curb (*verb*). But *kerbstone.*

curé (Fr.), a rector or vicar.

currency, abbr. C/-. For units of currency, *see* under names of the various countries.

curriculum, *pl.* **curricula.**

Currie, Midlothian.

Curry, Sligo, Somerset.

curt., current.

Curties. *See* Appendix II for pronunciation.

curtsy (*noun*), a bow made by a woman. Also *verb.*

Custos Privati Sigilli, Keeper of the Privy Seal; abbr. C.P.S.

Custos Rotulorum, Keeper of the Rolls; abbr. C.R.

Custos Sigilli, Keeper of the Seal; abbr. C.S.

cut-and-dried (*adj*).

cut-in letter, one at the beginning of a chapter.

cutis (Lat.), skin. Term used in anatomy to mean the true skin, under the epidermis.

C.V.O., Commander (of the Royal) Victorian Order.

c.w.o., cash with order.

C.W.S., Co-operative Wholesale Society.

cwt., hundredweight. Do not add *s* for plural.

cyclopaedia. The more common form is encyclopaedia, but cyclopaedic is more usual as the adjective.

Cymric, Welsh; *pron.* kum-rik.

cynosure.

cyst.

Czecho-Slovakia. Adjective Czecho-Slovak.

D

D, 500 (roman numerals), Deputy, Duke, *Deus* (Lat. = God), *Dominus* (Lat. = Lord).

d., date, daughter, day, deceased or died, dollar, *denarius* (penny), dime.

d', **da**, **de**, **du**. Before persons' names these may have caps or lower-case letters. Follow the signature of your correspondent.

D/A, days after acceptance, deposit account, discharge afloat, documents against acceptance.

D.A.A., Diploma of the Advertising Association.

da capo or *capo al fine* (It.), repeat to the word *fine*; abbr. D.C.

dagger (†), a reference mark, used next in order after the asterisk. Sometimes used before a person's name to signify that he has died. It can be formed by typing capital I and hyphen.

dahlia, a Mexican plant, named after Dahl, a Swedish botanist.

Dáil Eireann. Chamber of Deputies in Eire parliament.

Dalhousie. *See* Appendix II for pronunciation.

Dalton. *See* Appendix II for pronunciation.

Dalziel. *See* Appendix II for pronunciation.

damageable.

dame de compagnie (Fr.), lady's companion.

Danke! (Ger.), Thanks! Thank you!

danse macabre (Fr.), dance of death.

danseuse, a female dancer.

Danzig. Unit of currency 1 Gulden = 100 pfennig.

D.A.Q.M.G., Deputy-Assistant Quartermaster-General.

daren't.

dare say.

dash. Type a hyphen with a space before and after. The printer has a special sign, longer than the hyphen. The dash is increasingly popular in the place of parentheses in a sentence. It is placed after the full stop that ends a quotation and before the name of the author.

data, plural of datum (*q.v.*).

datable.

date. Type this in full on letters, and in the logical order: day, month, year Avoid full stop after 16th, 23rd, etc., as these are not abbreviations. In quoting a number of years, use the shortest form, e.g. 1933-6, not 1933-36.

"Date as postmark," sometimes seen printed on postcards, but to be avoided.

datum, a thing known or assumed; generally used in the plural (data) to mean a collection of facts or materials upon which to work.

d'aujourd'hui en huit (Fr.), this day week.

daurs. (legal), daughters.

Davy lamp, miner's wire-gauze safety lamp.

day. Holidays, festivals, etc., to have initial caps. Note that days of the week, in French, may have small initials or caps.

Day Book, abbr. D.B.

daylight.

days after acceptance, abbr. D/A.

days after date, abbr. D/d.

day's date, abbr. D/d.

days' sight, abbr. D/s.

day-time.

D.B., Day Book.

D.B.E., Dame Commander of (the Order of) the British Empire.

D.C., District of Columbia; *da capo*; direct current.

D.C.A., Director of Civil Aviation.

D.C.L., Doctor of Civil Law.

D.C.M., Distinguished Conduct Medal.

D.C.S., Deputy Clerk of Session.

D/d, days after date; day's date.

D/D, domicile to domicile; demand draft.

D.D., Doctor of Divinity.

dd., delivered.

D.D.S., Doctor of Dental Surgery.

"dead" key, one fitted with an accent. On depression of this key the typewriter carriage does not move.

Dean. *See* Appendix I for correct form of address.

Dean of Faculty, abbr. D.F.

Dear Sir. Note initial S, but lower-case f in "Yours faithfully." (*See* note on "complimentary close.")

death-rate.

debacle, in figurative language means a collapse or stampede. Fr. *débâcle*.

debatable.

debonair, accomplished, affable.

de bonne grâce (Fr.), willingly.

déboutonné (Fr.), unbuttoned; careless.

debris, *pron.* dĕ-brē.

debtor, abbr. Dr.

début (Fr.), first appearance in society or on the stage. *Débutante* is nowadays restricted to the meaning of a lady presented at Court.

déc. (Fr.), *décédé* (*fem. décédée*), deceased; *décembre*, December.

decade, a group of ten (usually years).

decasualization, scheme to avoid the necessity for the unemployed to seek poor relief.

deced. or decd. (legal), deceased.

décédé (Fr.), deceased; *fem. décédée*; abbr. *déc.*

December, abbr. Dec.

décembre (Fr.), December. Upper or lower-case initial may be used for the month in French; abbr. *déc.* or *X*bre.

decennial, recurring every ten years.

decentralize, to distribute what has been centralized.

dcciduous, shed periodically or normally (leaves, etc.).

decigram, 1·54 grain; abbr. dg.

decimal point. Use the full stop. In typing there is no need to raise it above the line.

décime (Fr.), ten centimes.

deckle edge, the rough, untrimmed edge of paper.

declaration, *abbr.* declon. (legal).

déclassé (Fr.), one who has sunk in the social scale; *fem. déclassée.*

declon. (legal), declaration.

décolleté (Fr.), wearing low-necked dress; *fem. décolletée.*

decolorize.

D.Econ.Sc., Doctor of Economic Science (Ireland).

décor (Fr.), all that contributes to the general appearance of a room; arrangement of stage scenery.

decree *nisi*, order for divorce, unless cause to the contrary is shown within a period.

de die in diem (Lat.), from day to day.

deducible.

deductible.

de facto (Lat.), in fact; actual.

defce. (legal), defence.

defendant.

défense d'afficher (Fr.), stick no bills.

défense de fumer (Fr.), no smoking.

défense d'entrer (Fr.), no admittance.

defensible.

defensor fidei (Lat.), defender of the faith; abbr. D.F. —on coins usually F.D.

deference.

deferred.

dégoût (Fr.), disgust.

de gratia (Lat.), by favour.

degree. This can be represented on the typewriter by the small *o* raised.

degrees (University). A full stop, but no space, should appear between the letters, and a comma after each group. Note the exceptions, LL.B., LL.D. *See* note under " initials."

dehors (Fr.), outside, foreign to.

Dei gratia (Lat.), by the grace of God.

Deity. All pronouns and synonyms representing the Deity should have initial caps.

déjeuner (Fr.), breakfast.

de jure (Lat.), by right of law.

Del., Delaware.

deld. or dd., delivered.

délicatesses (Fr.), delicacies. In Ger. *Delicatessen.*

delirium, *pl.* deliriums.

delirium tremens, state brought about by heavy drinking; abbr. d.t.

delivered, abbr. deld., dd.

demarcation.

demobilize.

démodé (Fr.), out of fashion; *fem. démodée.*

demonetize, to deprive of standard value as money, to withdraw from circulation.

demoralize.

denarius (Lat.), penny; *pl. denarii.*

D.Eng., Doctor of Engineering.

Denmark. Unit of currency, 1 Danish crown (krone) = 100 öre.

denouement, the unravelling of a plot. Fr. *dénouement.*

de nouveau (Fr.), afresh.

de novo (Lat.), afresh.

deodorize, to deprive of smell.

Deo gratias (Lat.), God be thanked.

Deo volente, God willing; abbr. D.V.

dép., département (Fr.), shire.

departmentalize.

dependant (*noun*).

dependence.

dependent (*adj.*).

déplacé (Fr.), out of place; *fem. déplacée.*

depopularize, to make unpopular.

depopulate, to deprive of inhabitants.

deposit account, abbr. D/A.

depositary, person to whom something is entrusted.

deposition (legal), abbr. deposn.

depositor, one who deposits.

depository, place where something is deposited.

deposn., deposition.

depot.

deprecate, to express disapproval of.

depreciate, to disparage or belittle; to diminish in value.

de profundis (Lat.), out of the depths.

deputy-consul, abbr. D.C.

Deputy-Lieutenant, abbr. D.L.

dérangé (Fr.), disturbed, disconcerted.

de-rating, Government measure for assisting industry by reducing the rates on factories, etc.

Derbyshire, abbr. Derby

de règle (Fr.), in order.

de rigueur (Fr.), required by etiquette.

dernier cri (Fr.), the very latest.

dernier ressort (Fr.), a desperate expedient.

derogatory *to.*

des (Fr.), of the (plural).

dès (Fr.), since.

désagrément (Fr.), disagreeableness, annoyance.

descdt., descendant.

descron. (legal), description.

déshabillé (Fr.), wearing a négligé garment or being negligently dressed. English equivalent *dishabille.*

desiccated, dried up.

desideratum (Lat.), something desired or wanted; *pl. desiderata.*

dessertspoonfuls.

dessin (Fr.), drawing.

desuetude, discontinuance of practice or custom.

detector, a rough form of galvanometer for detecting the presence of a current in a circuit as a test for its continuity.

deterrent.

detonator, a capsule filled with some fulminating substance to fire a high explosive.

detour, a roundabout way. Fr. *détour.*

detractor, one who takes away the reputation of another.

de trop (Fr.), superfluous.

Deus avertat! (Lat.), God forbid!

deus ex machina (Lat.), something providential that happens just in time to solve a difficulty. (Literally a god from the machinery, referring to gods shown in ancient theatre.)

Deus misereatur! (Lat.), God be merciful!

Deus vobiscum! (Lat.), God be with you!

development.

devitalize, to deprive of vitality.

Devon, Devonshire.

dexterous, skilful.

D.F., *defensor fidei* (Lat.) (defender of the Faith), Dean of Faculty.

D.F.C., Distinguished Flying Cross.

D.F.M., Distinguished Flying Medal.

dft., draft.

dg., decigram.

D.G., *Deo gratias* (Lat.), By the grace of God, or God be thanked.

dhurrie, Indian carpet.

di-, dif-, dis-, apart, asunder, not.

diacritical marks, those used to indicate different sounds of a letter (e.g. accent, cedilla, diaeresis).

diaeresis, formerly used (in English words) over the second of two vowels to show that they were to be pronounced separately (e.g. reëstablish). Present practice is to omit the sign or to use a hyphen, and to restrict the use of the diaeresis to foreign and technical words. If the sign is not on the keyboard it may be represented by the double quote.

diagnose, to determine the nature of a disease from its symptoms.

diagnosis, *pl.* diagnoses.

dialectic, argument.

dialling.

diaphragm, muscular wall separating the abdomen from the thorax.

diarrhoea.

dice, cubes used in games.

dictum, a saying; *pl.* dicta. *Obiter dicta* (Lat.), things said by the way.

dictum de dicto (Lat.), hearsay report.

didn't.

Didot. *See* Appendix II for pronunciation.

didst.

die, *pl.* dies (stamps); dice (cubes used in games).

dies irae (Lat.), the day of wrath.

dies non juridicus (Lat.), a day on which the judges do not sit; abbr. *dies non.*

dietetic.

dietitian, one who studies diets in relation to health.

different *from,* not *to.*

digestible.

dilettante, *pron.* diletantē. An amateur, one who cultivates an art for amusement; *pl.* dilettanti.

dime (U.S.A.), ten cents; abbr. d.

diminuendo (It.), less loudly; abbr. *dim.*

dinar, unit of currency of Yugo-Slavia.

dinghy, small boat.

dining-room.

diphtheria, *pron.* diftheria.

diphthongs, *pron.* difthongs. Æ used less than formerly; either the simple *e* is written, as in medieval, or the æ œ are written separately as in Caesar, homoeopathy. If it is desired to type two vowel characters close together it can be done on most machines by partially depressing the back-spacer key, or by holding the carriage in position. (*See* note on " ligature.")

diplomatist, preferable to diplomat.

direct current, abbr. D.C.

direction, abbr. diron. (legal).

dirigo (Lat), I direct or guide.

diron. (legal), direction.

disappoint.

discharge, abbr. dischge. (legal)

discharge afloat, abbr. D/A.

dischge. (legal), discharge.

disciplinary.

discoloration.

discron. (legal), discretion.

disfranchise, to deprive of rights of citizenship, especially of the vote.

dishabille (*pron.* dĭsabēl), partly dressed, or negligently dressed. Fr. *déshabillé.*

dishevelled, with untidy hair.

disillusionize, to free from illusion or enchantment.

disinterested means free from bias or from selfish motives. It is often used for uninterested, which simply means lacking in interest.

disorganize.

dispatch.

Dissenter.

dissipé (Fr.), dissipated; *fem. dissipée*.

dissociate.

dissoluble. This is the common word for all meanings, but dissolvable is sometimes used in the sense of dissolving something in a liquid or dissolving Parliament, etc.

distil.

distillation.

disyllable, a word of two syllables.

ditto, abbr. do. or ,, . When typing, use the double quote for this sign.

divide et impera (Lat), divide and govern.

division (÷). This sign can be formed on the typewriter with the colon and hyphen.

division at line-ends. *See* note under "line-end division."

divorcee. Tendency to use this for a divorced person of either sex. Strictly *divorcé (masc.)* and *divorcée (fem.)*

D.Lit., Doctor of Literature (London or Belfast).

D.Litt., Doctor of Letters (Birmingham, Bristol, Durham, Oxford, Reading, Wales, Aberdeen, Edinburgh, Glasgow, St. Andrews). Doctor of Literature (National University of Ireland). *See* also Litt.D.

D.M., Deputy Master; Doctor of Medicine (Oxford).

D.Mus., Doctor of Music. Use this form if the degree was taken at London or Oxford University, and Mus.D. if it was taken at Cambridge.

do., ditto or ,, —the same.

D.O., Diploma in Osteopathy.

doct. (legal), document.

documents against acceptance, abbr. D/A.

documents against payment, abbr. D/P.

Doddington, Cambs, Kent, Northants, Northumb

Dodington, Somerset.

dogmatize, to assert authoritatively.

dolce far niente (It.), pleasant idleness.

dollar. Form this on the typewriter by using capital S and solidus, $. It should precede the figures, and be typed close up.

Domesday Book. *Note*—in other senses *doomsday*.

domicile to domicile, abbr. D/D.

Domine dirige nos! (Lat.), O Lord direct us! (motto of the City of London).

Dominion Day in Canada, 1st July.

Dominus noster (Lat.), our Lord.

Dominus vobiscum (Lat.), the Lord be with you.

don't.

doomsday.

D.O.R.A., Defence of the Realm Act.

dormeuse (Fr.), sleeping-carriage.

Dorset. Note that this is the name of the English county, not Dorsetshire.

dossier, set of documents.

dots. *See* note under " leader dots."

douane (Fr.), customs.

double-bass (music).

double entendre (Fr.), phrase with two meanings.

double line. You can type an effective double line by turning forward the platen slightly (using the variable line space mechanism) before typing the second line.

double-shift machine. This has three characters on a key, and three, instead of four, rows of keys. It means that a double-shift key mechanism must be used, and the method is going out of favour, even for portable machines.

Dougal. *See* Appendix II for pronunciation.

douzaine (Fr.), dozen.

downstairs.

doyen, the senior member of a body.

d'oyley. This seems to be the most popular spelling, but there are various others. Named after Mr. Doily, its inventor.

dozen or dozens, abbr. doz.

D/P, documents against payment.

D.P.A., Diploma in Public Administration.

D.P.H., Diploma in Public Health.

D.Ph., D.Phil., Doctor of Philosophy.

Dr., debtor, doctor.

dr., drachma, dram, drams.

drachma, unit of currency of Greece.

draft. In typing the draft of a document, use stout paper, leave wide margins, and type in treble spacing. It may have to undergo considerable revision; abbr. dft. Draft paper (for legal work) measures $16 \times 10\frac{1}{2}$ ins.

dramatis personae (Lat.), list of characters in a play.

draughtsman.

drawing (legal), abbr. drg.

drg. (legal), drawing.

D.R.G.M., *Deutsches-Reichsgebrauchsmuster* (Ger.), German registered design. (Points between the initials are not necessary in German.)

droit (Fr.), right (legal or moral).

droite (Fr.), right hand.

dropped head, a printer's term for a chapter heading, which begins lower than the matter on the other pages.

Drucker (Ger.), printer.

drunkenness.

D/s, days' (after) sight.

D.S.C., Distinguished Service Cross (Naval).

D.Sc., Doctor of Science (London, Oxford, etc.). Sc.D. is used if degree was taken at Cambridge or Dublin University.

D.S.M., Distinguished Service Medal.

D.S.O., Distinguished Service Order.

d.t., delirium tremens.

D.Th., Doctor of Theology

du. *See* note under "d'."

duc (Fr.), Duke.

duce (It.), leader.

Duchesne. *See* Appendix II for pronunciation.

Duchess. *See* Appendix I for correct form of address.

Duchess, Royal. *See* Appendix I for correct form of address.

Duguid. *See* Appendix II for pronunciation.

Duke, abbr. sometimes used, D. Fr. *duc. See* Appendix I for correct form of address.

Dukeries, a district, mainly in Nottinghamshire, that comprises several ducal estates.

Duke, Royal. *See* Appendix I for correct form of address.

Duke's daughter. *See* Appendix I for correct form of address.

Duke's son. *See* Appendix I for correct form of address.

dulce domum (Lat.), sweet home.

dullness.

dumb-bell.

dumbfound.

dum spiro, spero (Lat.), while I live, I hope.

Dundreary.

Durchgangszug (Ger.), a through train; abbr. *D-Zug*.

Durham. Use Co. Durham when requiring to distinguish county from town.

dux (Lat.), leader; *pl. duces.*

D.V., *Deo Volente* (Lat.), God willing.

D.V.S., Doctor of Veterinary Science.

D.W., deadweight, dividend warrant.

dwg.-ho. (legal), dwelling-house.

dwt., pennyweight (no change for plural).

Dysart. *See* Appendix II for pronunciation.

D-Zug. (Ger.), *Durchgangszug*, a through train.

E., Earl, east.

e (It., Port.), and.

è (It.), is.

e. In poetry the letter *e* has an accent (acute or grave) when it is intended that the syllable *-ed* is to be sounded separately, e.g. "Nods, and becks, and wreathéd smiles." Alternatively, some writers use an apostrophe in place of the *e* when the syllable is *not* to be sounded separately, leaving the reader to assume that when *-ed* appears it *is* to be sounded separately.

each. This is singular. Example : "Each of the books has twenty illustrations." "Between each" is wrong, although widely accepted. "Insert a space between each line" should read ". . . between each line and the next" or "Insert spaces between the lines."

E. & O.E., errors and omissions excepted.

Eardley. *See* Appendix II for pronunciation.

Earl, abbr. E. *See* Appendix I for correct form of address.

Earle. *See* Appendix II for pronunciation.

Earl's daughter. *See* Appendix I for correct form of address.

Earl's son. *See* Appendix I for correct form of address.

Earl's wife. *See* Appendix I for correct form of address.

earmark.

easemt. (legal), easement.

east, abbr. E. *See* note under "north."

Easter Sunday is next after the full moon that follows, or falls on, 21st March.

easygoing.

eau-de-Cologne.

eau-de-Nil, pale-green shade (literally water of Nile).

Ebor, York.

Ecce Homo (Lat.), Behold the Man.

échalote (Fr.), shallot.

échantillon (Fr.), sample.

éclat, conspicuous success.

economic, having relation to the science of economics.

economical, thrifty.

economize.

écossais (Fr.), Scottish; *fem. écossaise.*

écrevisse (Fr.), crayfish, lobster.

ecstasy.

Ed., editor, edition.

edelweiss, Alpine flower; *pron.* ā-dl-vīs.

Edin., Edinburgh.

éditeur (Fr.), publisher.

editor, in French, *directeur, rédacteur en chef.*

educationist.

-ee. This termination is common in law, to indicate the recipient as contrasted with the giver, e.g. lessor, lessee; transferor, transferee. Tendency to use loosely in words like evacuee and billetee.

E.E., errors excepted.

effect. Do not confuse with affect, q.v.

effluvium, noxious odour; *pl.* effluvia.

e.g., *exempli gratia* (Lat.), for example. The abbreviation is always preceded by a comma.

E.G.M., Medal of the Order of the British Empire (for gallantry). Displaced in 1940 by the George Medal.

egoism, the theory that regards the self as the centre of all interest. Egotism is self-conceit and the practice of talking about oneself. Note egoist and egotist.

egret, a variety of heron. *See* note under " Aigrette."

Egypt. Unit of currency 1 Egyptian pound=100 piastres.

Ei (Ger.), egg; *pl. Eier.*

E.I.C., East India Company.

eighties. *See* note under " thirties."

Eingang (Ger.), walk in; entrance.

Eintreten (Ger.), come in.

Eire, formerly Irish Free State. *See* Appendix II for pronunciation.

Eisteddfod, *pl.* eisteddfodau.

either. Use this when speaking of two things, not more, and follow it by singular verb and " or " (not " nor ").

electronic music, that played by means of an electrical instrument invented in 1926 by Professor Leo Theremin.

electroplating.

elf, *pl.* elves.

Elgin. *See* Appendix II for pronunciation.

eligibility.

eliminate, to cancel; to take out as not being necessary.

elision, the omission of a vowel or syllable, as in poetry. Indicate by apostrophe.

élite (Fr.), the select few.

elite type, the size of typewriter type that gives twelve letters to the inch. Very popular for private and semi-private correspondence.

ellipsis, the omission of words in a sentence. Use three points to mark omission, and four when it is the end of a sentence.

Ely. *See* Appendix II for pronunciation.

Elysium, *pl.* Elysiums; *adj.* Elysian.

E.M., Edward medal; Earl Marshal.

em, the unit for measuring printed matter. Also abbreviation for electromotive.

embalmment, preserving from decay.

embargo, prohibition; *pl.* embargoes.

embarkation.

embarrassed.

embassy, residence of ambassador; deputation to a sovereign.

embezzlement, fraudulently appropriating money.

embryo, *pl.* embryos.

emeritus (Lat.), one who has retired after having honourably performed some duty.

E.M.F., electromotive force.

emigrant, a person who leaves a country to reside in another. *See also* note under " immigrant."

Emp., Emperor, Empress.

empanelled, name entered on a panel.

emphasize.

Empire Day, 24th May, birthday of Queen Victoria.

employee. This has been accepted as the English form, for both masculine and feminine.

empressement (Fr.), earnestness, alacrity.

enameller.

en bloc (Fr.), in the mass.

en clair (Fr.), term used in cabling to denote plain language as distinct from code.

enclose. Do not use herewith with enclose; it is redundant.

enclosures. Always indicate these; the practice saves error at both ends. There are various methods, e.g. small coloured seal gummed to the letter; Enc. typed at foot of letter; diagonal ink line in margin at point where enclosure is mentioned.

encumbrance. Legal abbr. encumb.

encyclopaedia. Note that the adjective is usually cyclopaedic.

endorsement, typed on outside of folded document.

Contains date, names of parties, brief description of contents, name of solicitor carrying through the transaction.

endwise, *-wise* is more common than *-ways* in this and similar words.

ENE., east-north-east.

en famille (Fr.), at home, with the family.

enfant gâté (Fr.), spoilt child.

en fête (Fr.), making holiday.

enforceable.

enfranchise, to grant civic privileges to.

en garçon (Fr.), as a bachelor.

engrossment, a legal term for the copy of a document that is ready for signature.

enhance. This means heighten, intensify, exaggerate, raise (price), etc. It is often wrongly used.

en passant (Fr.), in passing.

en règle (Fr.), in order.

enrol, but enrolled, enrolling.

ensemble, the general effect. Fr. *tout ensemble*.

ensure. Use this in ordinary meanings, but *insure* in connection with insurance matters. (*See* note under " assurance.")

entente cordiale (Fr.), cordial understanding between States.

enthrall, preferable to enthral.

entomology, study of insects. etymology, the study of the formation of words.

entr'acte (Fr.), the interval between acts of a play.

en train (Fr.), in progress.

entrecôte (Fr.), the undercut of sirloin.

entrée, a made dish, served between fish and meat courses.

entre nous (Fr.), between ourselves.

envelop (*verb*).

envelope addressing. Start a little more than half-way down, or the Post Office stamp may obliterate the addressee's name. Display the address artistically, making left and right margins fairly even. It is a Post Office regulation that addresses on envelopes should be typed (or written) parallel to the length, and not across.

envelopes. The commercial size is $6 \times 3\frac{1}{2}$ in., small commercial is $5\frac{1}{2} \times 3\frac{1}{4}$ in., but a square envelope is sometimes used for business letters. The paper must be folded to correspond. *See* note under " folding."

en vérité (Fr.), in truth.

Envoy Extraordinary and Minister Plenipotentiary.
See Appendix I for correct form of address.

enwrapped.

epaulet, shoulder ornament, strictly that worn by military and naval officers.

epi-, upon, over.

épice (Fr.), spice.

epidiascope, a lantern for projecting, by means of mirrors, non-transparent pictures.

epigram, a pithy phrase.

épigramme (Fr.), **a meat dish.**

épinards (Fr.), spinach.

Epsom-salt.

E.P.T., Excess Profits Tax.

equalization.

equation (=). Type two hyphens to make this sign (if it is not on the machine.) They can be placed one slightly below the other by use of variable line-space mechanism.

equilibrium.

-er. Many words indicating agents or doers terminate either in *-er* (English) or *-or* (Latin). The *-er* class is by far the larger. *See also* -or.

eraser. The thin, circular eraser is recommended. A soft rubber is useful for a preliminary application, or a combined (hard and soft) eraser may be preferred.

ergo (Lat.), therefore.

errare est humanum (Lat.), to err is human.

erratum, an error in writing or printing; *pl.* **errata.** An erratum slip is a small printed leaflet inserted in a book, drawing attention to a mistake or mistakes on certain pages.

errors and omissions excepted, abbr. E. & O.E.

Erskine. *See* Appendix II for pronunciation.

erysipelas, inflammation of the skin.

escalator.

escudo, unit of currency of Portugal.

ESE., east-south-east.

Eskimo, *pl.* Eskimos.

espagnol (Fr.), Spanish; *fem. espagnole.*

Esperantist, one who speaks Esperanto, an invented universal language.

estaminet (Fr.), café, inn.

este. (legal), estate.

estimating words. This can be done by taking the average number of words to a line and multiplying by the number of lines. The typist can make for herself a table, showing the words to a page of quarto, foolscap, etc., and with varying margins and line-spacing.

estimator.

Estonia. Unit of currency 1 kroon = 100 cents.

E.S.U., electrostatic units.

étage (Fr.), floor, storey.

et al. (Lat.), *et alii,* and others; *et alibi,* and elsewhere.

etc., abbreviation for et cetera. Do not use &c. Avoid etc., etc. Once is enough.

etceteras.

ethnology, the science that treats of the varieties of the human race.

et sequens, and the following, abbr. *et seq.; pl. et sequentes,* abbr. *et sqq.*

Et tu, Brute! (Lat.), You, too, Brutus!

etymologically, according to etymology, i.e. the study of the formation of words.

eugenics, science of the physical welfare and development of the race.

Euler. *See* Appendix II for pronunciation.

euphemism, a mild expression used in place of a harsh one. Say a euphemism, not an.

euphony, agreeable sound.

euphuism, a high-flown style of writing (originally in imitation of Lyly's *Euphues,* 1580).

eurhythmics, study of rhythmic movement, with music. Introduced by Monsieur J. Dalcroze.

evangelize.

evaporize.

evce. (legal), evidence.

evenness.

even pages, the left-hand pages of a book, which are those bearing the even numbers.

evermore.

every. This is singular, and must be followed by singular verb and pronoun.

everybody.

everyday (*adj.*).

everyone, but every one for members of a group individually.

evidence, abbr. evce. (legal).

Ewart. *See* Appendix II for pronunciation.

Ewing. *See* Appendix II for pronunciation.

ex., examined, exchange, executed, out of, without, example, exception.

exacerbate, to irritate (person); to aggravate (disease, anger, etc.).

exaggeration.

examined, abbr. exd.

ex cathedra (Lat.), with authority (literally, from the chair).

exceptionable means "open to exception" and *unexceptionable* means "giving no opening for criticism." Do not confuse with the more common word *exceptional.*

excerpt, an extract; *pl.* excerpta.

exchange, abbr. ex.

exclamation mark (!), used frequently in poetry and conversational matter. May be placed in brackets to indicate dissent from views of the author quoted. The sign can be included in keyboard in place of a fraction. Otherwise, make it by combining the apostrophe and full stop. (*See* note under "combination characters.")

ex contractu (Lat.), according to or arising out of contract.

ex curia (Lat.), out of court.

exd. (legal), examined.

ex dividend, without dividend; abbr. ex div.

executed, abbr. ex.

exempli gratia (Lat.), for example; abbr. e.g.

exeunt omnes (Lat.), they all leave the stage.

ex gratia (Lat.), by favour.

exhibitor.

exhilaration, animation.

ex hypothesi (Lat.), from the hypothesis.

ex libris, from the library of. Used commonly on, and sometimes to mean, a book-plate; abbr. ex lib.

ex officio (Lat.), *adj.* and *adv.* In virtue of one's office. Use hyphen when it comes before a noun, e.g. "an *ex-officio* member."

exor(s). (legal), executor(s). **Extrix.** or exrx., executrix.

exorbitant, excessive.

exorcize, to drive out evil spirits.

ex parte (Lat.), on one side only; biased.

expenses, abbr. exs.

experimenter.

experto crede (Lat.), believe one who has experience to justify his opinion.

ex post facto (Lat.), after the deed is done.

Ex-President.

expressis verbis (Lat.), in express terms.

ex pte. (legal), *ex parte,* on one side only; biased.

exs., expenses.
ex-Service men.
ex tacito (Lat.), tacitly.
extemporize, to speak, compose, etc. off-hand.
extolled.
extra judicium (Lat.), outside the court.
extraneous, not belonging to the subject.
extravaganza, burlesque.
extrix. or exrx. (legal), executrix.
exuberance.
Exzellenz (Ger.), Excellency; abbr. *Exz.*
eyeball, also similar words—no hyphen.
eyewitness.

F

F., Fahrenheit.

f., following, fathom.

f., forte, loud.

F.A.A., Fellow of the Central Association of Accountants.

f.a.a., free of all average.

Fabre. *See* Appendix II for pronunciation.

façade, front of building.

facia.

facile princeps (Lat.), easily the first.

facetiae (Lat.), humorous writings or sayings.

façon de parler (Fr.), way of speaking.

facsimile, an exact copy; *pl.* facsimiles.

jacta non verba (Lat.), deeds, not words.

factotum, a man of all work.

jactum est (Lat.), it is done.

fade-out, term used in cinematography.

Fahrenheit, abbr. F. or Fahr.

F.A.I., Fellow of the Auctioneers' Institute.

fair copy, a term used, mostly in legal offices, to mean a neat, clear copy made from a corrected draft; abbr. f.co.

faire suivre (Fr.), "letters to be forwarded"; abbr. F.S.

fairway, golfing term meaning the stretch of trimmed turf between tee and green, free from hazards.

fait accompli (Fr.), accomplished fact.

Falconer. *See* Appendix II for pronunciation.

fall, American word for autumn.

fal-lal, piece of finery.

familiarize.

fanfold, a method of billing in which the forms are printed in continuous strips.

fantasia, musical composition of fantastic nature.

fantasy, a fanciful artistic production.

fantoccini (It.), marionettes.

f.a.q., fair average quality.

farce (Fr.), stuffing, force-meat.

farci (Fr.), stuffed.

farewell.

farinaceous, mealy.

farm-house.

Farquhar. *See* Appendix II for pronunciation.

Farquharson. *See* Appendix II for pronunciation.

farther, tendency to restrict this to the literal sense, and to use further when the notion of space or distance is absent.

F.A.S., Fellow of the Antiquarian Society.

f.a.s., free alongside ship.

Fascism, a system of government inaugurated by Signor Mussolini in Italy. The word is derived from the Latin *fasces*, a bundle of rods with an axe bound with them, borne before the Roman magistrates and signifying justice. **Fascist** = a believer in the system.

fata Morgana (It.), a kind of mirage.

Father (R.C.); abbr. Fr.

faubourg (Fr.), a suburb. Capital F when used with name.

faun, a woodland creature; *pl.* **fauns.**

fauna, singular noun used as collective; *pl.* (rarely needed) **faunas or faunae.** The word means the animals of a country or period.

faute de mieux (Fr.), for want of something better.

fauteuil, arm-chair; *pl.* **fauteuils.**

faux pas (Fr.), a slip (literally, false step).

favour. Avoid this word in letter-writing, and particularly "esteemed favour."

F.B.A.A., Fellow of the British Association of Accountants and Auditors.

F.B.I., Federation of British Industries.

F.B.S., Fellow of the Botanical Society.

F.C.A., Fellow of the Institute of Chartered Accountants in England and Wales.

F.C.C.S., Fellow of the Corporation of Certified Secretaries.

F.C.G.I., Fellow of the City and Guilds of London Institute.

F.C.I., Fellow of the Institute of Commerce.

F.C.I.B., Fellow of the Corporation of Insurance Brokers.

F.C.I.I., Fellow of the Chartered Insurance Institute.

F.C.I.S., Fellow of the Chartered Institute of Secretaries.

fcp., foolscap.

F.C.P., Fellow of the College of Preceptors.

F.C.P.A., Fellow of the Institution of Certified Public Accountants.

F.C.W.A., Fellow of the Institute of Cost and Works Accountants.

F.D., *fidei defensor* (Lat.), Defender of the Faith.

Fe, ferrum (iron).

feasible.

Featherstonehaugh. *See* Appendix II for pronunciation.

February, abbr. Feb. Avoid abbreviations in letter-writing.

fecit (Lat.), he or she made it.

feeding paper backwards. If papers have been stapled together, a sheet can be fed in from the bottom. First feed in a loose sheet. Then insert your document between that sheet and the front of the platen. Pull out loose sheet.

feet, abbr. ft. or '.

feldspar, a mineral, a principal constituent of granite.

felo de se (Lat.), suicide; *pl. felos de se.*

Fels-naptha.

femme de chambre (Fr.). chambermaid; *pl. femmes de chambre.*

femme de charge (Fr.), housekeeper.

Fenwick. *See* Appendix II for pronunciation.

ferreted.

ferrule, metal ring on the end of a stick.

ferrum, iron; abbr. Fe (no point).

fertilizer.

F.E.S., Fellow of the Entomological Society; Fellow of the Ethnological Society.

festa (It.), festival.

festina lente (Lat.), hasten slowly.

fête.

fête-champêtre (Fr.), outdoor fête.

fetish.

feu (Scot.), ground rent; *pl. feus.*

feu (Fr.), deceased; *fem. feue*; also fire, *pl. feux.*

feuille (Fr.), a sheet.

feuilleton, ruled-off portion at foot of newspaper (especially French) devoted to story or light literature. Term is less used than formerly.

feux d'artifice (Fr.), fireworks.

février (Fr.), February.

ff, fortissimo, very loud.

ff. Proper names beginning with ff may or may not have an initial capital. *Examples:* ffitch, ffolliott, fforde, ffoulkes, ffrench.

F.F.A., Fellow of the Faculty of Actuaries.

fff, fortississimo (It.), as loud as possible.

F.F.P.S., Fellow of the Faculty of Physicians and Surgeons.

F.F.S., Fellow of the Faculty of Secretaries.

f.g.a., free of general average.

F.G.S., Fellow of the Geological Society.

F.I.A., Fellow of the Institute of Actuaries.

F.I.A.C., Fellow of the Institute of Company Accountants.

fiancé, *fem.* fiancée.

F.I.Arb., Fellow of the Institute of Arbitrators.

fiasco, *pl.* fiascos.

fiat (Lat.), let it be done.

F.I.B., Fellow of the Institute of Bankers.

F.I.B.D., Fellow of the Institute of British Decorators.

F.I.C., Fellow of the Institute of Chemistry.

fichu, light ornamental collar worn by women.

F.I.C.S., Fellow of the Institute of Chartered Shipbrokers.

F.I.D., Fellow of the Chartered Institute of Directors.

fiddlededee!

fidei defensor (Lat.), Defender of the Faith.

fidgeted.

Field-Marshal, abbr. F.M.

Field Officer, abbr. F.O.

fieri facias (Lat.), abbr. *fi. fa.*, cause it to be done; a writ empowering the sheriff to levy execution on a debtor.

fifties. *See* note under "thirties."

fig., figure, figuratively.

figures, generally expressed as words in literary work. Use words always for numbers one to nine; for indefinite statements (e.g. "It was fourteen or fifteen feet high"); for the opening of a sentence; on cheques, estimates, and legal documents. Do not mix words and figures; say 7 p.m., nine o'clock, 5000, six thousand. Note that *one* in typing is represented by small letter l and not by capital I. Occasionally a special key for the figure *one* is provided on the typewriter.

F.I.Inst., Fellow of the Imperial Institute.

F.I.L., Fellow of the Institute of Linguists.

Fildes. *See* Appendix II for pronunciation.

filet (Fr.), fillet.

filigree, ornamental work in gold or silver threads.

filleted.

film scenario abbreviations:

C.U., close-up.

C.S., close shot.

L.S., long shot.

M.S., medium shot.

Pan, panoramic. Sometimes *pam* to avoid confusion with abbreviation for panchromatic.

F.I.M.T.A., Fellow of the Institute of Municipal Treasurers and Accountants.

finable, liable to a fine.

finale, last item of a performance.

finesse, artifice.

finger-end, *pl.* **finger-ends.**

finger-nail.

finis, the end. Used on last page of book, etc., but less than formerly.

Finland. Unit of currency 1 mark (Finnish " markka ") = 100 penniä.

finnan-haddock.

fiord, more correctly fjord (Norwegian).

F.I.R.E., Fellow of the Institute of Radio Engineers.

fire-arms.

fire-proof.

fire-screen.

fireside.

first-born.

first-class (*adj.*), but " in the first class."

first-fruits.

f.i.t., free of income tax.

fivefold.

F.J.I., Fellow of the Institute of Journalists.

F.K.C., Fellow of King's College (London).

fl., florin.

fl., *floruit* (Lat.), flourished, i.e. period (failing exact dates) at which a person was alive.

F.L.A., Fellow of the Library Association.

F.L.A.A., Fellow of the London Association of Certified Accountants.

flaccid.

flageolet, small wind instrument.

flageolet (Fr.), a kidney-bean.

flagship.

flagstaff.

flamboyant, showy (literally flame-like).

flan, open pastry tart containing fruit, savoury, or custard filling.

flannelette.

flavorous.

fledgeling, a bird that has just begun to fly.

Fleisch (Ger.), meat.

fleur-de-lis, heraldic lily ; *pl.* **fleurs-de-lis.**

flexible.

flier. Present tendency is to use flier for " one who flees " and flyer for " one who flies."

flora, the flowers of a country or period ; *pl.* **floras or florae.** *See* note under " fauna."

florin, abbr. fl.

floruit (Lat.), flourished. *See* note under "*fl.*"

flotation, act of floating.

flotsam and jetsam. Flotsam = lost goods afloat; jetsam = goods thrown into sea to lighten vessel in danger of wreck, and (in modern use) washed ashore.

flowerpot.

F.L.S., Fellow of the Linnean Society.

flutist, preferable to flautist.

fly-leaf, blank leaf of circular or at beginning of book, etc.

F.M., Field-Marshal.

F.M.S., Federated Malay States.

F.O., firm offer; Foreign Office.

fo., folio.

F.O.A., Fellow of Advertising.

f.o.b., free of board.

F.O.C., from own correspondent; father of chapel (printers' term).

fo'c'sle, forecastle.

focus, *pl.* **focuses.** Scientific: *foci.*

focused.

fogy, *pl.* **fogies.**

foie gras (Fr.), specially prepared liver of the goose.

folding. The correct folds for letter-paper are:

   (*a*) *Octavo:* once for square envelope, twice for commercial.

   (*b*) *Quarto:* once, and once again, for square envelope; across and then in three for commercial.

   (*c*) *Foolscap:* bottom to top, then again. Always use foolscap envelope.

folio. Typing of technical, legal, and other matter is charged by the folio, i.e. 72 words, but lengthy literary matter by the thousand. In America a folio is 100 words. Folio is also a printer's term meaning a sheet of paper folded in two leaves only. Abbr. fo.

folk-song.

follower, the name given to second page of a letter. On it should be typed the name of addressee, number of page, and date.

following, abbr. f.

follow-up, the name given to a reminder-letter sent to a prospective purchaser.

fonda (Sp.), an inn.

fondue (Fr.), savoury dish in which melted cheese is used.

food-stuff.

fool-proof.

foolscap, typewriting paper, measures 13 × 8 in.

foot, feet, abbr. ft. Sign '. Say one-and-a-quarter-foot, two feet.

foot-and-mouth disease, abbr. F.M.D.

foot-hold.

footlights.

footnotes. If a typescript is being prepared for the printer, the footnote should be typed immediately after the passage to which it refers. A line should be typed above and below it.

footpath.

foot-wear.

f.o.r., free on rail.

forasmuch.

forbear, to abstain; ancestor.

force majeure (Fr.), irresistible compulsion; diplomatic coercion; strike, war, etc., that excuses fulfilment of a contract.

forceps (*sing.* and *pl.*), surgical pincers.

forearm.

forecastle, abbr. fo'c'sle.

foreclose, to end a mortgage by seizure of the estate.

forego, to go before.

foreign words. These tend (*a*) to lose their accents, and (*b*) to be printed in roman and not italic type, when they are fully established in the English language (e.g. clientele, vice versa).

foreshorten.

forestall.

for ever.

forgather, to meet.

forget-me-not.

forgettable.

forgivable.

forgo, to abstain from.

formally, in a formal manner.

format, the size and shape of a book or journal.

former. Use this in referring to the first of two only. "Former" and "latter" are usually avoided by careful writers.

formerly, belonging to a past time.

form letters, duplicated or printed letters used in publicity work. The typist is often called upon to match in the names and addresses.

formula, *pl.* **formulas** (popular), **formulae** (scientific).

Forsyth. *See* Appendix II for pronunciation.

forte (It.), loud; abbr. *f.*

Fortescue. *See* Appendix II for pronunciation.

fortes fortuna adjuvat (Lat.), fortune favours the brave.

forties. *See* note under "thirties."

fortissimo (It.), very loud; abbr. *ff.*

fortississimo (It.), as loud as possible; abbr. *fff.*

fortuitous, accidental.

Foulis. *See* Appendix II for pronunciation.

Foulkes. *See* Appendix II for pronunciation.

fount, set of type of one particular face and size. (*See* "w.f.")

four-bank keyboard, the most usual form of typewriter keyboard, "bank" being the technical term for "row."

fourfold.

f.p.a., free of particular average.

F.P.L.A., Fellow of the Institute of Poor Law Accountants.

F.P.S., Fellow of the Philological Society.

Fr., Father, Frau, French.

fr., franc, from.

fr. (Ger.), *frei.*

fractions. If many fractions are to be used, it is possible to have the keyboard fitted with combination characters, that is, separate type for the numerators and denominators, so that many varieties can be made up. Express fractions in words when they are isolated. Note use of hyphen, e.g. two-thirds, thirty-five sixty-seconds.

frais (Fr.), outlay, expenses; (*adj.*) fresh, new, lively.

F.R.A.M., Fellow of the Royal Academy of Music.

framboise (F.), raspberry.

framework.

franc, abbr. fr.

française (*à la*) (Fr.), in the French style.

France. Unit of currency 1 French franc = 100 centimes.

franchise, right of voting.

franking machines. These are supplied by the Post Office. They obviate the need for sticking stamps on envelopes.

frappé (Fr.), iced.

F.R.A.S., Fellow of the Royal Astronomical Society.

Frau (Ger.), Mrs., wife; *pron.* frow; abbr. *Fr.*; *pl. Frauen.*

Fräulein (Ger.), Miss, unmarried lady; *pron.* froilīn; abbr. *Frl.*; *pl.* same.

F.R.B.S., Fellow of the Royal Botanic Society.

F.R.C.O., Fellow of the Royal College of Organists.

F.R.C.P., Fellow of the Royal College of Physicians.

F.R.C.S., Fellow of the Royal College of Surgeons.

F.R.C.V.S., Fellow of the Royal College of Veterinary Surgeons.

F.R.Econ.S., Fellow of the Royal Economic Society.

free alongside ship, abbr. **f.a.s.**

freehd. (legal), freehold.

free-lance.

free of particular average, abbr. **f.p.a.**

frei (Ger.), free; abbr. *fr.*

freight prepaid, abbr. **frt. ppd.**

French, abbr. Fr.

french chalk.

french polish.

frequency of letters. *E, t, a, i, o, s, r,* are generally stated as being the most frequently occurring letters in the English language.

frère (Fr.), brother, friar; *pl. frères*; abbr. *Fres.*

Fres, abbr. for *frères* (Fr.), brothers.

fresco, a painting upon plaster; *pl.* frescoes.

freshwater, one word when used as adjective, e.g. " freshwater fishing."

F.R.G.S., Fellow of the Royal Geographical Society.

F.R.Hist.Soc., Fellow of the Royal Historical Society.

F.R.H.S., Fellow of the Royal Horticultural Society.

friar's balsam.

F.R.I.B.A., Fellow of the Royal Institute of British Architects.

fricandeau (Fr.), braised veal; *pl. fricandeaux.*

fricassee, a stew.

frier, one who fries; frier or fryer in other senses.

Fries. *See* Appendix II for pronunciation.

frieze, coarse cloth; term used in architecture.

frit (Fr.), fried; *fem. frite.*

Frl., Fräulein (Ger.).

F.R.Met.Soc., Fellow of the Royal Meteorological Society.

F.R.M.S., Fellow of the Royal Microscopical Society.

frolicked.

from, abbr. fr.

fromage (Fr.), cheese.

frowzy.

F.R.P.S., Fellow of the Royal Photographic Society.

F.R.S., Fellow of the Royal Society.

F.R.S.A., Fellow of the Royal Society of Arts.

F.R.S.E., Fellow of the Royal Society (Edinburgh).

F.R.S.L., Fellow of the Royal Society of Literature.

F.R.S.S., Fellow of the Royal Statistical Society.

frt. ppd., freight prepaid.

Frühstück (Ger.), breakfast.

fryer. *See* frier.

F.S.A., Fellow of the Society of Antiquaries.

F.S.A.A., Fellow of the Society of Incorporated Accountants and Auditors.

F.S.I., Fellow of the Chartered Surveyors' Institution.

F.S.S., Fellow of the Royal Statistical Society.

ft., feet, faint.

fth., fathom.

fuchsia.

fuelling.

Führer (Ger.), leader.

fulfil.

fuller's earth.

fullness.

full stop. Used in abbreviations, with no spaces, e.g. L.R.A.M. Omitted from certain abbreviations, e.g. IOU, MS., LL.D., pp. Used to indicate omission in quoted sentences; type three points at beginning or in middle of sentence, and four at the end. Use it between the figures of pounds, shillings and pence, for easier reading. Note printers' tendency to omit it in printed headings, etc. Do not use it after 1st, 2nd, 8vo, per cent, Mlle, Yorks, etc.

fulsome.

function. This, as a noun, may pass when meaning a formal meeting, but should not be used for any and every kind of gathering.

fungus, *pl.* funguses (popular); fungi (scientific): *adjs.* fungous, fungoid.

für (Ger.), for; abbr. *f.*

furbelow, a flounce.

furore, frenzied admiration. (Lat. *furor* = rage.)

furor poeticus (Lat.), poetic fire.

furor scribendi (Lat.), mania for writing.

further, *see* note under " farther."

fuselage, the framework of the body of an aeroplane.

fusillade, simultaneous discharge of firearms.

F.Z.S., Fellow of the Zoological Society.

G

G., gauge, gramme.

Ga, gallium.

G.A., general average.

gage, a pledge.

gainsay.

galantine, a dish of veal or chicken without bones.

Galen. *See* Appendix II for pronunciation.

Gallagher. *See* Appendix II for pronunciation.

galley proofs. These are supplied before the matter is made up into pages. Alterations are more easily made and with less cost. They are strips containing about 20 in. of type.

Galli-Curci.

gallium, abbr. Ga (no point).

gallon of water (fresh) weighs 10 lb.; (salt) 10·272 lb.

gallop, a horse's movement; galop, a dance.

Gallup, George, originator of Gallup Poll, a method of ascertaining public opinion.

Gallwey. *See* Appendix II for pronunciation.

galosh, an overshoe. In boot trade golosh, meaning the vamp, or front part of the shoe.

galvanize.

gambolling.

gamin, a street arab.

gammon, a cured ham.

gamut, range, scope.

gaol, the " g " spelling is used officially; but jail is in common use.

garage, originally a noun, now also used as a verb.

garçon (Fr.), waiter, boy, bachelor.

Garde nationale (Fr.), national guard.

gare (Fr.), railway station.

gargantuan, enormous.

Garioch. *See* Appendix II for pronunciation.

garni (Fr.), furnished; garnished. *Fem. garnie.*

garrulous, talkative.

Gasthaus (Ger.), inn; *pl. Gasthäuser.*

Gasthof (Ger.), hotel; *pl. Gasthöfe.*

gastritis.

gastronome, one who appreciates good food.

gâté (Fr.), spoiled; *fem. gâtée.*

gâteau (Fr.), cake.

gateway.

gauche, awkward; gaucherie, awkwardness.

gauche (Fr.), left; awkward.

gauge, a measure.

gazetteer.

G.B., Great Britain.

G.B.E., Knight Grand Cross of (the Order of) the British Empire.

G.C., George Cross, instituted 1940.

G.C.B., Knight Grand Cross of the Bath.

G.C.I.E., Knight Grand Commander of the Indian Empire.

G.C.M.G., Knight Grand Cross of (the Order of) St. Michael and St. George.

G.C.S.I., Knight Grand Commander of the Star of India.

G.C.V.O., Knight Grand Cross of the (Royal) Victorian Order.

Geb. (Ger.), *Gebrüder,* brothers.

Geddes. *See* Appendix II for pronunciation.

Gee. *See* Appendix II for pronunciation.

geisha, Japanese dancing girl. Plural same.

gelatinize.

gelée (Fr.), frost, jelly. (*geler* = to freeze.)

Gen., General.

gendarme (Fr.), policeman.

gendarmerie (Fr.), force of gendarmes.

Generalissimo (It.), supreme commander.

generalize.

generator, apparatus for producing electricity, gases, steam, etc.

genesis, origin; *pl.* geneses.

genius, *pl.* geniuses (men), genii (spirits). Singular form genie, for spirit, is sometimes used.

Genlis. *See* Appendix II for pronunciation.

genus, a group; *pl.* genera.

Geoffrey. *See* Appendix II for pronunciation.

Geoghegan. *See* Appendix II for pronunciation.

Gepäck (Ger.), luggage.

gérant (Fr.), manager, principal, editor.

Gerard. *See* Appendix II for pronunciation.

Germany. Unit of currency 1 Reichsmark=100 Reichspfennigs.

Ges., Gesellschaft (Ger.), Company.

Gesellschaft (Ger.), a Company or Society; abbr. *Ges.*

gestorben (Ger.), deceased; abbr. *gest.*

geyser, hot spring throwing up mud or water. (In Iceland called geysir.) Also apparatus for heating water.

G.H.Q., General Headquarters.

gibe, preferred to *jibe*.

gibier (Fr.), game.

gigot (Fr.), leg of mutton. *Des manches à gigot* = leg-of-mutton sleeves.

gilt-edged.

gipsy, *pl.* gipsies.

gist.

give-and-take. Hyphens are needed when the phrase becomes an adjective, as in " a give-and-take arrangement."

glace (Fr.), an ice-cream.

glacé (Fr.), iced.

gladiolus, *pl.* gladioli.

Glamorganshire, abbr. Glam (no point).

glamorous.

glamour.

glassful, *pl.* glassfuls.

Glauber's salt.

glengarry, a Scottish cap.

glockenspiel, musical instrument, consisting of bells or bars.

gloria in excelsis (Lat.), glory to God in the highest.

gloria Patri (Lat.), glory be to the Father.

Gloucester. *See* Appendix II for pronunciation.

Gloucestershire, abbr. Glos (no point).

glow-worm.

glutinous, resembling glue.

gluttonous, greedy.

glycerin, spelt thus by chemists, but glycerine in everyday usage.

G.M., George Medal (for gallantry). Instituted in 1940.

G.m.b.H., Gesellschaft mit beschränkter Haftung (Ger.), limited liability company.

G.M.I.E., Grand Master of the Indian Empire.

G.M.K.P., Grand Master of the Knights of St. Patrick.

G.M.M.G., Grand Master of (the Order of) St. Michael and St. George.

G.M.S.I., Grand Master of the Star of India.

G.M.T., Greenwich Mean Time.

godmother.

godsend.

God-speed.

Goethe. *See* Appendix II for pronunciation.

gofer, thin cake made of batter.

goffer, to crimp with heated irons.

good-bye (corruption of " God be with you ").

goodness' sake (for), euphony demands that the possessive s should be omitted.

good night, two words except when adjective, as "a good-night kiss."

goodselves, avoid this as commercial jargon.

goodwill, one word when used as the noun meaning kindly feeling, and also in the sense of "the goodwill of a business."

Gorgonzola.

gossiping.

got. Avoid this: say "I have a book," not "I have got ..."

Gough. *See* Appendix II for pronunciation.

Gould. *See* Appendix II for pronunciation.

gourmand, a glutton. Spell with *u*, but gormandize has *u* omitted.

goût (Fr.), taste.

gouverneur (Fr.), governor; *fem. gouvernante.*

Governors of Colonies. *See* Appendix I for correct form of address.

Gower. *See* Appendix II for pronunciation.

G.P., general practitioner; Graduate in Pharmacy.

G.P.O., General Post Office.

gr., grain, grains.

Graf (Ger.), a count; *fem. Gräfin.*

grain, abbr. gr.

gramme, 15·432 grains; abbr. grm.

gramophone.

granddaughter.

grande vitesse (Fr.), fast passenger train or fast goods train; abbr. G.V.

grandfather.

grand'mère (Fr.), grandmother.

grand'messe (Fr.), high mass.

grandmother.

grand-nephew.

grand-père (Fr.), grandfather.

grand seigneur (Fr.), a great lord.

grangerize, to illustrate a book by pictures cut from other works. (From J. Granger, who published in 1769 a History of England with blank leaves for illustrations.)

graphology, reading character from handwriting.

gras (Fr.), fat, greasy. *Gros* = big.

grass-lands.

gratia Dei (Lat.), by the grace of God.

gratin. *See* "au gratin."

gratis.

grave accent (`). *See* under "*e.*"

gravelled.

gravestone.

gravure, abbreviation for photogravure.

Greece. Unit of currency 1 drachm = 100 lepta.

greengage.

Greenhalgh. *See* Appendix II for pronunciation.

Greig. *See* Appendix II for pronunciation.

grenadine, dress fabric; dish of meat or poultry fillets braised.

grey.

greyhound.

grievance.

grillé (Fr.), grilled.

grimy.

grippe (Fr.), influenza.

grm., gramme, grammes.

groseille (Fr.), currant.

gross weight, abbr. gr. wt.

Grosvenor. *See* Appendix II for pronunciation.

grotto, *pl.* grottoes.

grovelled.

Grüss Gott! (Ger.), Good-day! (literally "God's greeting!")

Gruyère, Swiss town; also name of a cheese, in which use it needs no capital.

gr. wt., gross weight.

guarantor.

guerre (Fr.), war.

guerrilla warfare, irregular warfare.

guilder, unit of currency of the Netherlands.

Guildford, Surrey.

guild-hall, but Guildhall, London, with the article "the."

Guilford Street, London, W.C.1.

guillotine, machine for beheading, paper-cutting machine, parliamentary term.

gulden, unit of currency of Danzig.

gullible, easily deceived.

gun-metal.

Gurkhas, Indian soldiers.

Guten Morgen (Ger.), Good morning.

Guten Tag (Ger.), Good day.

gutta-percha.

G.V., *grande vitesse* (Fr.), fast passenger train, or fast goods train.

G.W.R., Great Western Railway.

gymkhana, sports display.

gymnasium, *pl.* gymnasiums.

H

H, hard lead pencil. *B* is soft, and *HB* (the most popular) between the two. Also the symbol for hydrogen.

habeas corpus (Lat.), writ by which the physical presence, or *body*, of person named in it can be compelled to be brought before the Court.

habitat, natural abode.

habitué, habitual visitor.

hachis (Fr.), mincemeat.

hackneyed.

Hadleigh, Essex, Suffolk.

Hadley, Herts, Salop, Worcester.

hadst.

haemorrhage.

haggis, a Scottish dish.

hailstone.

hairbreadth (*adj.*), otherwise hair's breadth. Examples: "A hairbreadth escape." "He succeeded by a hair's breadth."

hairdresser.

hair-space, the thinnest space used in printing.

Hakluyt. *See* Appendix II for pronunciation.

halb (Ger.), half, semi-.

half a dozen. This and similar forms need no hyphens. Note "a half-dozen."

half-bound, used to describe a book that has leather back and corners, and cloth sides.

half-caste.

half-crown.

half-hour.

half-past.

halfpenny.

halfpennyworth; abbr. ha'p'orth.

half-plate (photography), $6\frac{1}{2} \times 4\frac{3}{4}$ in.

half-price.

half-space correcting. This is the name given to the process by which four letters are compressed into the space of three, and so on. It is done by partially depressing the back-spacer key, or by holding the carriage in position. On some makes of typewriter, however, the construction does not permit of this operation.

half-title, the title of a book, with no descriptive matter, that appears on the leaf preceding that containing the full title.

half-tone block, one in which the various tones are made by dots.

halle (Fr.), market.

Hallelujah.

hall-mark:

Hambleden, Bucks

Hambledon, Hants, Surrey.

Hambleton, Lancs, Rutland, Yorks

Hampshire, abbr. Hants (no point).

Handbuch (Ger.), handbook, manual.

handfuls.

Händler (Ger.), dealer.

hangar, shed for housing aeroplane.

hanging paragraph, one in which the first line projects beyond the rest.

haphazard.

harassed.

hard-and-fast rule.

Hardinge. *See* Appendix II for pronunciation.

Hardwick, Bucks, Norfolk, Notts

Hardwicke, Gloucester.

harebell.

hare-brain.

hare-lip.

harem.

hareng (Fr.), herring.

haricot (Fr.), thick stew.

haricots verts (Fr.), French beans.

Harlesden, Middlesex.

Harleston, Norfolk.

Harlestone, Northamptonshire.

harmonize.

harum-scarum.

hasard (Fr.), hazard.

hâte (Fr.), haste.

Haus (Ger.), house.

haute bourgeoisie (Fr.), upper middle-class.

hauteur, arrogance (same in French).

haute volée (Fr.), the upper ten.

haut-goût (Fr.), taint, high flavour.

haut ton (Fr.), high fashion.

have. Avoid doubling, as in " I should have liked to have gone." Write " I should like to have gone," or " I should have liked to go."

Hawarden. *See* Appendix II for pronunciation.

haystack.

HB, lead pencils that are hard and black—in popular use. *B* are softer, *H* harder.

H.B.M., His (or Her) Britannic Majesty.

H.C., House of Commons.

H.C.F. or h.c.f., highest common factor.

H.C.J., High Court of Justice.

hdqrs., headquarters.

H.E., His Eminence, His Excellency.

He, helium.

headache.

head-dress.

headings, centring, *see* note under "centring headings."

head-lines, running, lines at head of page containing, generally, on the left the book title and on the right the chapter title.

Head Master. Practice is very unsettled as between this form and Headmaster. Both are used by official bodies in their publications, but the *Head Master* form is probably more popular for ordinary use.

headquarters, abbr. H.Q. or hdqrs.

head space, the space left at the top of a page of typescript. Typists more often err in leaving insufficient space than too much.

headway.

healthful.

heartburn.

hearthstone.

Heathcote. *See* Appendix II for pronunciation.

Hebridean.

hedgerow.

Heer (Ger.), Army Captain.

heer (Dutch), Mr., Sir.

Heil! (Ger.), Hail!

heilig (Ger.), holy.

heirloom.

heirs, abbr. hrs. (legal).

hektograph copying process. This involves typing the original with hektograph ribbon and placing it on a preparation of gelatine, glue, or clay.

helium, abbr. He (no point).

hell (Ger.), bright. The German word for hell is *Hölle*.

hello, hallo. These appear to be the most popular forms; other variants are *hullo, halloo, hollo, hulloa, holla.*

helpmate, helpmeet.

Hepburn. *See* Appendix II for pronunciation.

hepta-, seven.

Herausgeber (Ger.), editor, publisher.

Herculean, of extraordinary strength; exceptionally strong.

hereafter, abbr. hrar. (legal).

hereby, hereunder. These and similar words do not take hyphen.

hereinafter, abbr. hrnar. (legal).

heretofore, abbr. htofore.

herewith. Do not use with enclose. It is redundant.

Herr (Ger.), Mr., Sir. Envelopes are usually directed An Herrn Schiller; note the *n* to make the Herr dative after To (*An*); *pl. Herren; fem. Herrin, pl. Herrinnen.*

Herr (der), (Ger.), the Lord.

Hertford. *See* Appendix II for pronunciation.

Hertfordshire, abbr. Herts (no point).

Hervey. *See* Appendix II for pronunciation.

Herzog (Ger.), duke.

Herzogin (Ger.), duchess.

hetero-, other, different.

heterogeneous, of another kind (opposite of homogeneous).

hexa-, six.

H.F., Holiday Fellowship.

H.F., high frequency.

Hg, mercury.

H.H., His (or Her) Highness, His Holiness.

hhd., hogshead.

hiccup.

Hic jacet (Lat.), Here lies.

hieroglyphics.

Hier spricht man Deutsch (Ger.), German spoken here.

higgledy-piggledy.

high frequency, abbr. H.F. (use hyphen when as adjective).

Highlander.

high resistance, abbr. H.R. (use hyphen when as adjective).

high-water mark, abbr. H.W.M.

highwayman.

H.I.H., His (or Her) Imperial Highness.

Hillingdon, Middlesex.

Hillington, Norfolk.

hill-top.

hindmost.

Hindu, Hinduism.

hingeing.

hire-purchase.

H.L., House of Lords.

H.M., His (or Her) Majesty.

H.M.A., His (or Her) Majesty's Airship.

H.M.C., His (or Her) Majesty's Customs.

H.M.I., His (or Her) Majesty's Inspector.

H.M.I.S., His (or Her) Majesty's Inspector of Schools.

H.M.O.W., His (or Her) Majesty's Office of Works.

H.M.S., His (or Her) Majesty's Ship, or Service.

H.M.S.O., His (or Her) Majesty's Stationery Office.

hobbledehoy.

Hof (Ger.), yard, hotel.

hogshead, abbr. hhd.

holland, a kind of linen.

hollandais (Fr.), Dutch; *fem. hollandaise.*

hollyhock.

Holmes. *See* Appendix II for pronunciation.

Holmeswood, Lancs

Holmewood, Derby

Holmwood, Surrey.

Holy Week, the week before Easter Day.

homard (Fr.), lobster.

Home Counties. These are Essex, Hertfordshire, Kent, Middlesex, and Surrey.

home-made.

homespun.

Homfray. *See* Appendix II for pronunciation.

homing.

homme à tout faire (Fr.), jack of all trades.

homme d'affaires (Fr.), business man, agent.

homme d'église (Fr.), churchman.

homme de lettres (Fr.), literary man.

homme de robe (Fr.), lawyer.

homo-, same, similar, together.

homo (Lat.), human being.

homoeopathy, medical system based on the principle that like cures like.

homonym, a word with same spelling but different meaning.

Hon., Honourable, honorary.

Hon. C.F., Honorary Chaplain to the Forces.

Honi soit qui mal y pense (Fr.), Evil be to him who evil thinks.

honoraires (Fr.), fee, honorarium.

Honorar (Ger.), honorarium.

honorarium, a voluntary fee for professional services; *pl.* **honorariums.**

honoris causa (Lat.), for the sake of honour.

honourable.

Hon. Sec., Honorary Secretary.

hoof, *pl.* hoofs, hooves.

hook-in, the term used when a line of poetry is too long, and the extra words are typed just above or below.

Horace. *See* Appendix II for pronunciation.

hora fugit (Lat.), time flies.

hors (Fr.), beyond.

hors concours (Fr.), not competing for prize.

hors de combat (Fr.), disabled.

hors d'œuvre, appetisers served at beginning of a meal.

horse-chestnut.

horsehair.

horseshoe.

Hosanna.

hostelry.

hôte (Fr.), innkeeper, guest.

Hôtel de ville (Fr.), town hall.

Hôtels-Dieu (Fr.), hospitals.

Hotham. *See* Appendix II for pronunciation.

Houghton. *See* Appendix II for pronunciation.

house-agent.

householder.

housekeeper.

housemaid.

house-surgeon.

How-do-you-do?

howr. (legal), however.

H.P., half pay, high pressure, horse-power (sometimes h.p.).

H.P.N. or h.p.n., horse-power nominal.

H.Q., headquarters.

h.r., high resistance.

hrar. (legal), hereafter.

H.R.H., His (or Her) Royal Highness.

hrnar. (legal), hereinafter.

hrs. (legal), heirs.

H.S.A., Hospital Savings Association.

H.S.H., His (or Her) Serene Highness.

H.S.M., His (or Her) Serene Majesty.

H.T. or h.t., high tension.

htofore. (legal), heretofore.

huckaback, a rough towelling.

Hudson Bay, North America. Note Hudson's Bay Company.

Huguenot, a French Protestant.

huîtres (Fr.), oysters.

hullabaloo.

Humanum est errare (Lat.), To err is human.

humerus, the arm bone, above the elbow.

humorist. This has become the more generally accepted spelling, but the older spelling humourist is still used.

humorous.

humpback.

hunchback.

hundred, abbr. C (no point).

hundredweight, abbr. cwt. for singular and plural. (A combination of *C* for hundred and *wt.* for weight.)

Hungary. Unit of currency 1 pengö = 100 filler.

Huntingdonshire, abbr. Hunts (no point).

hurly-burly.

hurrah.

H.W.M., high-water mark.

hydrangea.

hydro-. This prefix, in miscellaneous terms, means "having to do with water" (from Greek *hudro*).

hydrocarbon.

hydro-electric, producing electricity by friction of water or steam.

hydrogen, abbr. H (no point).

hydrostatics, the science of equilibrium of liquids.

hygeist, from Hygeia, goddess of health.

hygiene.

hymeneal, from Hymen, god of marriage.

hymnologist, student of hymn literature.

hyper-, above.

hyperbole, exaggerated statement; *pron.* hī-per′bŏ-lē.

hypercritical, over-critical.

hyphen. No space to be typed before or after the hyphen (spaces make it into a dash). This sign causes more mental confusion than all the rest put together. Use it when it helps the sense or the pronunciation. Note changing tendencies. Words formerly hyphenated, when established, may drop the hyphen, as *housekeeper*. Note its value in the following typical illustrations:

Similar *vowels* or awkward groups of consonants: re-establish, Tees-side.

Prefixes: neo-paganism, ex-Chancellor.

Adjectival phrases: a free-and-easy manner, a six-year period, a hard-headed business man, base- and acid-forming substances.

Figures: half-past five, a half-inch (half an inch is preferable), twenty-one thirty-seconds, one-and-twenty.

Note the difference between reproducing a play and re-producing a play.

See also note under "line-end division."

hypnology, study of the phenomena of sleep (from Greek *hupnos*, sleep).

hypnotism, deep sleep produced artificially.

hypnotize.

hypo-, from Greek *hupo*, under, below, slightly.

hypochondriac, one suffering from morbid depression.

hypocrisy.

hypocritical, concealing real motive.

hypothesis, *pl.* hypotheses.

I. On most typewriters there is no special sign for the unit figure. Operators should not use a capital I (a mistake that suggests lack of training), but small *l*. The symbol for iodine is I. *See* note under " figures."

Ian. *See* Appendix II for pronunciation.

I.B.C., International Broadcasting Company.

ibidem (Lat.), in the same place; abbr. *ib.* or *ibid.*

-ible. *See* note under " -able."

ich (Ger.), I.

Ich dien (Ger.), I serve (Prince of Wales's motto).

Ici on parle français (Fr.), French spoken here.

I.C.S., Indian Civil Service, International Correspondence Schools.

idealize.

idem (Lat.), the same; abbr. *id.*

idiosyncrasy, peculiarity of temperament.

idolater.

i.e., *id est* (Lat.), that is. Should be preceded by comma.

Iesus hominum Salvator (Lat.), Jesus, Saviour of men; abbr. I.H.S.

ignis fatuus (Lat.), will-o'-the-wisp.

ignoramus, *pl.* ignoramuses.

Ignorantia legis neminem excusat (Lat.), Ignorance of the law is no excuse.

I.H.P. or **i.h.p.,** indicated horse-power.

IIII, the roman numeral four—sometimes appears thus on the clock-face, but everywhere else as IV.

I'land, Icelandic for Iceland.

île (Fr.), island.

Ill., Illinois.

ill-advisedly.

ill-favoured.

illuminate.

ill will.

I.L.O., International Labour Office of the League of Nations, Geneva.

I.L.P., Independent Labour Party.

I.M., Imperial Measure.

imbuing, inspiring, tingeing deeply.

im Jahre (Ger.), in the year; abbr. *i.J.*

immanent, indwelling.

immeasurably.

immigrant, a person who comes into a country to take up residence. *See also* note under " emigrant."

imminent, about to happen.

immobilize.

immortalize.

immovably.

immunize, to render immune or exempt.

imp., imperial.

imp. (Lat.), *imperator,* emperor.

impasse, position from which there is no escape.

impce. (legal), importance.

impedimentum, commonly used in plural—impedimenta.

imperator (Lat.), emperor; abbr. *I., imp.*

imperilling.

imperturbable.

impingeing.

implicite (Lat.), by implication.

imply, to indicate something in speech or writing. *See* " infer."

importance (legal), abbr. impce.

impostor.

impracticable, not feasible, not able to be done. *See* note under " practical."

impresario, manager of company of actors or singers.

imprimatur (Lat.), a licence to print a book; let it be printed.

imprimeur (Fr.), printer.

imprimis (Lat.), in the first place.

imprint. This is seen on the title-page of a book or periodical. It gives name of publisher, place, and date.

improvize, extemporize.

impugn.

I.M.S., Indian Medical Service.

in., inch, inches.

inamorato, lover; *fem.* inamorata.

inasmuch.

in camera (Lat.), in secret instead of in open Court. Fr. *à huis clos.*

in cathedra (Lat.), in the chair of office.

incendiarism.

inch, abbr. in, or ".

incipit (Lat.), here begins (book, etc.).

incognito (It.), with one's name concealed, under disguised character; *fem. incognita* (rarely used); abbr. incog.

inconnu (Fr.), unknown; *fem. inconnue.*

incorporeal (legal), having no material existence.

incorrigible.

incumbrance (legal), otherwise *en-.*

in curia (Lat.), in open court.

incurring.

in custodia legis (Lat.), in legal custody.

indefensible.

indemy. (legal), indemnity.

indentation. The first line of each paragraph should be indented five or ten spaces, according to taste. *See also* under "poetry."

independent.

index, *pl.* indexes or indices. *See also* note under "apex."

Index Expurgatorius, list of passages to be expunged in books otherwise permitted.

Index Librorum Prohibitorum (Lat.), list of books that the Roman Catholic Church forbids its followers to read.

India. Unit of currency 1 rupee = 16 annas.

indian ink.

indictment, pron. inditement.

indigestible.

indispensable.

individual, avoid using this word for person.

indre. (legal), indenture.

in dubio (Lat.), in doubt.

ineffaceable.

in equilibrio (Lat.), equally balanced.

in excelsis (Lat.), in the highest degree.

in extenso (Lat.), in full, at full length.

in extremis (Lat.), at the point of death.

infer, to gather or deduce from what has been said or written. *See* "imply."

inferior characters, figures placed a little below the line of writing, as in algebraic formulae.

inflexion, preferred to *inflection.* Note also connexion. Reflexion, however, is less common than reflection.

informn. (legal), information.

infra (Lat.), below; abbr. *inf.*

infra dignitatem (Lat.), undignified; abbr. *infra dig.*

infra-red rays, rays of radiant heat of lower frequency than those of the red end of the visible spectrum.

Inge. *See* Appendix II for pronunciation.

Ingelow. *See* Appendix II for pronunciation.

ingénu (Fr.), ingenuous person; *fem. ingénue.*

Ingres. *See* Appendix II for pronunciation.

inhance. (legal), inheritance.

In hoco signo vinces (Lat.), Under this standard thou shalt conquer.

In hoc signo spes mea (Lat.), In this sign is my hope.

Inigo. *See* Appendix II for pronunciation.

in initio (Lat.), in the beginning; abbr. *init.*

initialled.

initials. To facilitate reference, it is usual in some business houses to type the initials of dictator and typist at the head of the letter. No points should be used; e.g. JE/HS. The initials of a person's name are typed with a space after each full stop, but the letters following the name are typed without spaces, the groups being separated by commas, e.g. R. D. Foster, Esq., M.A. LL.B. "Degrees" usually follow this order: first dignities conferred by the Crown, then University degrees, and finally, degrees conferred by non-University bodies. When addressing a letter to someone whose initials or Christian name you do not know, use a dash e.g. — Jones, Esq.

in loco parentis (Lat.), in the place of a parent.

in medias res (Lat.), into the midst of things.

in memoriam (Lat.), in memory of.

innamorato, Italian spelling of *inamorato,* lover; *fem. innamorata.*

Innes. *See* Appendix II for pronunciation.

innings, singular or plural.

innocuous, harmless.

in nuce (Lat.), in a nutshell.

in pace (Lat.), in peace.

in perpetuum (Lat.), for ever.

in persona (Lat.), in person.

inquiry, the generally recommended form and certainly to be used for an official inquiry.

in re (Lat.), in the matter of.

in respect *of.*

I.N.R.I., *Iesus Nazarenus, Rex Iudaeorum* (Jesus of Nazareth, King of the Jews).

in situ (Lat.), in its original situation.

in so far.

insomuch.

inst., instant.

install.

instalment.

instanter (Lat.), at once.

in statu quo (Lat.), in the former state.

in statu quo ante bellum (Lat.), as it was before the war.

instil.

instrons. (legal), instructions.

instructor.

insure, *see* note under " ensure."

int., interest.

intdd. (legal), intended.

Integer vitae (Lat.), Let your life be blameless.

intelligentsia (Russian), spelt less often with *z*, term used in the first place in Russia to mean the intellectual classes.

intended (legal), abbr. intdd.

inter alia (Lat.), among other things.

inter alias (Lat.), among other persons.

inter-departmental.

intérêt (Fr.), interest.

intermarriage.

internationalize.

inter nos (Lat.), between ourselves.

interpretative.

interrogation, note of, *see* note under " question mark."

interrogs. (legal), interrogatories.

interrupter.

inter se (Lat.), among themselves.

inter vivos (Lat.), between living persons.

intestacy, arising from being intestate, i.e. dying without making a will.

in the interim, meanwhile.

in to, separate or combined as the sense demands, e.g. " She went in to dinner"; " The message was sent in to us"; " They will go into the question"; " He stepped into the car."

in totidem verbis (Lat.), in so many words.

in toto (Lat.), entirely, as a whole.

intra muros (Lat.), within the walls.

in transitu (Lat.), in transit; abbr. *in trans.*

invaluable. This means valuable to a high degree. To express the absence of value use valueless, worthless, etc.

inveigle, to entice. Use into with this verb. Note that

inveigle is one of the exceptions to the rule "*i* precedes *e* except after *c*."

inventory.

inverted commas, *see* note under "quotation marks."

invigilator, one who supervises at an examination.

I.O., India Office.

I/O, Inspecting Order.

iodine, symbol I (no point).

I.o.M., Isle of Man.

I.O.O.F., Independent Order of Odd Fellows.

IOU, signed document acknowledging debt (no points between initials).

I.o.W., Isle of Wight. Also I.W.

ipecacuanha, a South American root.

ipse dixit (Lat.), he himself said it; dogmatic statement.

ipsissimis verba (Lat.), the actual words.

ipso facto (Lat.), by that very fact.

ipso jure (Lat.), by unquestioned right.

Ir, iridium.

iridescence, shimmering with rainbow colours.

I.R.O., Inland Revenue Office.

iron, symbol Fe (no point).

iron-mould.

ironwork.

irradiate.

irreconcilable.

irrefragable, indisputable.

irrelevant, not bearing on the matter in hand.

irreparable, *see* note under "reparable."

irresistibly.

Isidore. *See* Appendix II for pronunciation.

I.S.M.A., Incorporated Sales Managers' Association.

I.S.O., Imperial Service Order.

isochromatic, sensitive to yellow and green, as applied to photographic plate or film.

Istanbul, formerly Constantinople.

I.S.W.G., Imperial Standard Wire Gauge.

italicize, to print words in italic type.

italic type. The underscoring of a word in a manuscript is an instruction to the printer to set it in italics. Apart from purposes of emphasis, italics are chiefly used for: (1) foreign words and phrases, (2) titles of books, newspapers, plays, etc., (3) names of botanical species, (4) words that require to be mentioned by name (e.g. "The word *Private* should be written in the bottom left-hand corner of an envelope")). For the typist's purposes—when matter is not intended for printing—the quotation marks will take the place of italics in most cases.

Italy. Unit of currency 1 lira = 100 centisimi.

It is me. This is permissible in speech, but the correct form " It is I " should generally be used in writing.

it's. This is a contraction of *it is,* the apostrophe indicating the omission. *Its* is the possessive pronoun.

Iveagh. *See* Appendix II for pronunciation.

I.W., Isle of Wight. Also I.o.W.

-ize. Most verbs with this sound get their endings from the Greek izo, and the usual practice is to spell them with *z*, not *s*. A small number of verbs, however, have no connection with Greek, and are spelt with *s,* notably advertise, compromise, despise, exercise, supervise, surprise.

J

J., Justice. Placed after the name of a Judge of the High Court, e.g. Talbot, J., means Mr. Justice Talbot.

J/A, joint account.

ja (Ger.), yes; *pron.* yah.

Jacobean, pertaining to the time of the Stuart Kings of England.

Jaeger.

J.A.G., Judge-Advocate-General.

Jahr (Ger.), year; *pl. Jahre.*

jailer, *see* note under "gaol."

jambon (Fr.), ham.

James. Do not abbreviate.

James's. This is preferred to James' as the possessive. *See* note under "apostrophe."

Jan., January. Avoid abbreviations in literary work and correspondence.

Jansen. *See* Appendix II for pronunciation.

januis clausis (Lat.), with closed doors.

janvier (Fr.), January. Initial capital is now sometimes used in French; abbr. *J^er.*

Japan. Unit of currency 1 yen = 100 sen.

japanned, covered with hard varnish and embellished with figures.

jardinière, used in England to mean ornamental pot or stand for display of flowers in a room. *A la jardinière* (a menu term) means with a garnish of vegetables.

Jas., James, an undesirable abbreviation.

jasmine, flower of the genus Jasminum. The spelling jessamine is not recommended.

Javanese.

je (Fr.), I.

Je ne sais pas (Fr.), I do not know.

Je ne sais quoi (Fr.), I do not know what.

jeopardize, to hazard.

jeremiad, a lamentation.

jerry-builder.

jetsam, *see* under "flotsam and jetsam."

jettison, the throwing overboard of cargo.

jeu (Fr.), game; *pl. jeux.*

jewel.

jewelled, jeweller, jewellery. Also **jewelry.**

Jill (Jack and). Gill is the more correct (though less

popular) form, as it is an abbreviation of the French Gillian.

JJ., Judges of the High Court. (Address: Mr. Justice X, etc.)

Jno., an ugly abbreviation for John, and represents no saving of time, as the one letter omitted is replaced by the full stop.

jog-trot.

Johnsonian, stilted. From Samuel Johnson, who compiled the Dictionary in 1755. Also *noun,* Johnsonese.

joie de vivre (Fr.), great happiness.

joint-stock, use hyphen when noun follows.

jour (Fr.), day; *à jour* = open-work; *au jour* = by daylight.

jour de l'an (Fr.), New Year's Day.

journal (Fr.), newspaper; *pl. journaux.*

journalese, colloquial term meaning " newspaper English."

J.P., Justice of the Peace.

Jubilate Deo (Lat.), Rejoice in God.

J.U.D., *Juris utriusque Doctor* (Lat.), Doctor of Civil and Canon Law.

Judges. *See* Appendix I for correct forms of address.

judgment. This is the more usual spelling nowadays, though the *e* is retained in the Revised Version of the Bible, and some modern writers prefer it.

judgt. (legal), judgment.

judicature, abbr. judre. (legal).

judicium capitale (Lat.), capital judgment.

judicium Dei (Lat.), the judgment of God.

judre. (legal), judicature.

Jugendherbergen, the German youth hostel movement, which was the first in the world.

juggernaut, an Indian idol; term used of anything that ruthlessly crushes.

juillet (Fr.), July. Initial capital is now sometimes used in French.

juin (Fr.), June. *See* note above.

ju-jitsu, a Japanese system of wrestling. Variants of this spelling are in use.

julienne (Fr.), a thin soup.

June, do not abbreviate.

Junior. This is used to distinguish son from father, when both bear the same Christian name. It should appear immediately after the name, followed by Esq.; abbr. Jun.

jure divino (Lat.), by divine law.

jure humano (Lat.), by human law.
jure mariti (Lat.), by a husband's right.
jurisdon. (legal), jurisdiction.
jus (Fr.), gravy.
jus ad re (Lat.), right to immediate possession.
jus ad rem (Lat.), right to a thing; a right to a property not yet in possession.
jus civile (Lat.), civil law.
jus civitatis (Lat.), right of the state.
jus divinum (Lat.), divine law.
jus gentium (Lat.), law of nations.
jus mariti (Lat.), right of husband to property of his wife.
jus naturae (Lat.), the law of Nature.
jus possessionis (Lat.), the right of possession.
jus relictae (Lat.), right of the widow.
jus supra vim (Lat.), right before might.
justifying, a term used by the printer for levelling the margins of letterpress. The typist should do her best to justify margins by skilful line-end division; on her letters she can line up the date with the right-hand margin level.
justitia omnibus (Lat.), justice for all.

K

K, carat, potassium (no point).

Kaffee (Ger.), coffee.

kaleidoscope, an optical instrument showing coloured figures.

kari à l'indienne (Fr.), Indian curry.

Karlovy Vary, national name for Carlsbad.

Kartoffeln (Ger.), potatoes.

K.B., King's Bench, Knight Bachelor, Knight of the Bath.

K.B.D., King's Bench Division.

K.B.E., Knight Commander of (the Order of) the British Empire.

kc., kilocycle.

K.C., King's Counsel.

K.C.B., Knight Commander of the Bath.

K.C.I.E., Knight Commander of the Indian Empire.

K.C.M.G., Knight Commander of (the Order of) St. Michael and St. George.

K.C.S.I., Knight Commander of the Star of India.

K.C.V.O., Knight Commander of the (Royal) Victorian Order.

Kearney. *See* Appendix II for pronunciation.

Keble. *See* Appendix II for pronunciation.

kedgeree, a dish of fish, rice, eggs, etc.

keepsake.

Keith. *See* Appendix II for pronunciation.

Kekewich. *See* Appendix II for pronunciation.

Kellner (Ger.), waiter; *fem. Kellnerin.*

Kenmare, Kerry.

Kenmore, Perthshire.

Kennard. *See* Appendix II for pronunciation.

kerb-stone, preferred to curb-.

kerosene.

Kerr. *See* Appendix II for pronunciation.

ketchup, more popular than catchup.

keyboard, universal. The present arrangement of the keys on a typewriter is standardized. It was originated in 1873 by the inventor of the first Remington machine. Three-bank machines (that is, with three rows of keys and double-shift keys) are becoming obsolete. *See* note under " typewriter, the first."

keyhole.

keying. This expression is used to signify the method adopted by most advertisers in order to classify the responses to their advertisements. The reader is asked to write to a particular number or Department, and this is the "key" to the paper in which the advertisement appears.

key-note.

keystone.

kg. or kilo, kilogram.

K.G., Knight of (the Order of) the Garter.

K.G.C.B., Knight Grand Cross of (the Order of) the Bath.

Khayyám, Omar, Persian poet.

Killala, Mayo.

Killaloe, Clare.

Killaloo, Londonderry.

Killea, Londonderry, Tipperary.

Killeagh, Cork.

Killylea, Armagh.

Killyleagh, Belfast.

kilocycle, abbr. kc.

kilogram, abbr. kg. or kilo

kilometre, abbr. km.

kilowatt, 1000 watts; approximately 1·34 British horse-power; abbr. kW.

kilowatt hours, abbr. kW. hr.

kimono.

kindly. "You are kindly requested"—beware of this absurdity.

King, The. *See* Appendix I for correct form of address.

Kingsdon, Somerset.

Kingsdown, Kent, Wilts

Kingston, Cambs, Devon, Dorset, Kent, Som, Surrey.

Kingstown, Cumb, Dublin.

Kington, Herts

Kirkby. *See* Appendix II for pronunciation.

kleptomania, a mania for pilfering.

K.L.H., Knight of the Legion of Honour.

K.M., Knight of Malta.

km., kilometre.

Knight. *See* Appendix I for correct form of address.

Knight's wife. *See* Appendix I for correct form of address.

Knollys. *See* Appendix II for pronunciation.

knowledgeable.

Köln (Ger.), Cologne.

kosher, food prepared according to Jewish law.

K.P., Knight of (the Order of) St. Patrick.

kromeskies, balls of a savoury mixture (meat or fish) dipped in batter and fried.

krona, unit of currency of Sweden.

krone, unit of currency of Norway and Denmark, pl. **kronen.**

kroon, unit of currency of Estonia.

K.R.R., King's Royal Rifles.

K.T., Knight of (the Order of) the Thistle.

Kt. Bach., Knight Bachelor.

Kuchen (Ger.), cake.

Kursaal, building for use of visitors. German word meaning hall.

kW., kilowatt.

kW. hr., kilowatt hours.

Kyrle. *See* Appendix II for pronunciation.

L

L, 50 (roman numerals), Lady, lake, left.

l., line.

£, symbol meaning pounds, to be placed before the figures.

L.A., Legislative Assembly, Literate in Arts.

L.A.A., London Association of Certified Accountants.

labelled.

labels, typing on. If any difficulty is experienced in typing on small labels, they can be slipped into slots made in a sheet of paper, after the method of the postcard albums. The paper can remain in the machine while each successive label is inserted.

Laborare est orare (Lat.), To work is to worship.

labore et honore (Lat.), with labour and honour.

laborious.

Labor ipse voluptas (Lat.), Labour itself is a pleasure.

Labor omnia vincit (Lat.), Labour conquers all things.

laburnum.

labyrinth, a maze.

L.A.C., Licentiate of the Apothecaries' Company.

lac, use comma after the number of lacs, e.g. 12,42,000 means 12 lacs, 42,000 rupees.

lachrymose, tearful.

lackadaisical, affected, languishing.

lacrosse, North-American ball game.

lacuna, a gap; *pl.* lacunae, lacunas.

Lady (wife of Baronet or Knight), abbr. L. *See* Appendix I for correct form of address.

Lady Day, 25th March.

ladylike.

lady's maid, *pl.* ladies' maids.

laisser-aller (Fr.), freedom from restraint.

laisser-faire (Fr.), to let things, or people, alone; Government abstention from interference.

laissez-passer (Fr.), permit; same in plural.

lait (Fr.), milk; *au lait* = with milk.

laitue (Fr.), lettuce.

Lammas, 1st August.

lamp-post.

lampshade.

Lancashire, abbr. Lancs (no point).

Lance-Corporal, abbr. L.-Corp.

landmark.

Land's End, Cornwall.

Landwehr (Ger.), militia.

Lane End, Bucks

Lanes End, Kent.

languorous, drooping, slack.

Langwith, Notts

Langworth, Lincoln.

lanolin, a basis for ointments (extract from sheep's wool; *lana* = wool).

lapel, turned-back part of coat.

lapin (Fr.), rabbit.

lapis philosophorum (Lat.), the philosopher's stone.

Lapp, native of Lapland.

lapsus calami (Lat.), a slip of the pen.

lapsus linguae (Lat.), a slip of the tongue.

lard, fat.

lard (Fr.), bacon.

lares et penates (Lat.), household gods.

large-sized.

largess, gifts bestowed freely.

laryngitis.

larynx, cavity in throat that holds the vocal cords; *pl.* larynges.

lat, unit of currency of Latvia.

lat., latitude.

late-fee letter, one that is accepted after the ordinary evening hour for collection, on payment of an additional fee of ½d. (Gt. Britain and Ireland).

lath, thin piece of wood.

Latham. *See* Appendix II for pronunciation.

lathe, a machine for turning wood, metal, etc.

Latin. *I* and *j* are the same in Latin, and the tendency is to use *j*. Latin plurals in *i* should be pronounced with long *i* and in *es* with long sound *ēz*.

Latine dictum (Lat.), spoken in Latin.

latter. This should be used in referring to the last of two things, not of a number. " Former " and " latter " are usually avoided by good writers, as they often result in awkward constructions that pull up the reader. Never use such a form as: " The document was handed to Mr. Jones, and the latter signed it."

Latvia, *adj.* Latvian or Lettish. Unit of currency of Latvia is 1 lat = 100 santims.

laudanum (*pron.* lodnum).

Laudon. *See* Appendix II for pronunciation.

Laughton, Lincs, Sheffield, Sussex.

Launton, Oxon

Laus Deo (Lat.), Praise be to God.

Laus propria sordet (Lat.), Self-praise is no recommendation.

lawgiver.

lawn-tennis.

law reports. References to these usually take the following form: *Dunster* v. *Brown*, 1924; 1 K.B. 250, meaning that the case of Dunster *versus* Brown, tried in the year 1924, is reported in King's Bench reports, vol. 1, page 250.

lawsuit.

lay and lie. These are often confused. Lay is transitive and must have an object (e.g. to lay a cloth). *Present tense:* I lay, I am laying. *Past:* I laid, I was laying. *Perfect:* I have laid, I have been laying.

Lie is intransitive (lie down, lying in bed). *Present:* I lie, I am lying. *Past:* I lay, I was lying. *Perfect:* I have lain, I have been lying.

Layard. *See* Appendix II for pronunciation.

lay-out, a term used in advertising to mean the rough plan of an advertisement. It is also used to indicate the arrangement of typewritten work. The typist should be an artist in her endeavour to secure a good lay-out.

L.B., *Baccalaureus Literarum*, Bachelor of Letters.

l.b., leg-bye.

lb., *libra, librae*, pound, pounds. Note no *s* to be added.

l.b.w., leg before wicket.

L/C, Letter of Credit.

L.C., Lord Chamberlain, Lord Chancellor.

l.c., lower case, i.e. not capitals.

L.C.C., London County Council.

L.Ch., Licentiate in Surgery.

L.C.J., Lord Chief Justice.

L.C.M. or l.c.m., least common multiple.

L.-Corp., Lance-Corporal.

L.C.P., Licentiate of the College of Preceptors.

l/cr., lettre de crédit.

L.Div., Licentiate in Divinity.

L.D.S., Licentiate of Dental Surgery.

£E, Egyptian pound(s).

le. (legal), lease.

leader dots. As the name indicates, these guide the eye across the page, say, from an index item to its page number. The typist should use them when they are a help, but not otherwise. They should not be typed in continuous lines, as this wears the platen, but in groups of two, separated by three spaces.

leaderette, a short editorial paragraph.

leading (*pron.* ledding), separating lines of type by interposing leads (strips of metal). Matter thus spaced out is said to be leaded.

leading article, one of the longer articles in a newspaper, giving editorial opinion.

leaf, sometimes referred to as a page by the ordinary reader, consists (to the printer) of two pages.

lease, abbr. le. (legal).

leaves, abbr. ll.

Lebewohl! (Ger.), Farewell!

le bon Dieu (Fr.), God Almighty.

Leconfield. *See* Appendix II for pronunciation.

left, abbr. L. In stage directions left should mean when looking towards the audience.

leg before wicket, abbr. l.b.w.

leg-bye, abbr. l.b.

legenda (Lat.), things to be read.

légumes (Fr.), vegetables.

Leicestershire, abbr. Leics

Leigh. *See* Appendix II for pronunciation.

Leighton. *See* Appendix II for pronunciation.

Le jeu ne vaut pas la chandelle (Fr.), The game is not worth the candle.

lengthwise, *-wise* is more common than *-ways* in this and similar words.

lens, *pl.* lenses.

lentille (Fr.), lentil.

Lepidoptera (*pl.*) (Gk.), insects with scale-covered wings, including butterflies and moths.

Le Queux. *See* Appendix II for pronunciation.

lese-majesty, treason. Fr. *lèse-majesté.*

L.èsL., Licentiate of Letters.

letter endings, *see* note under " complimentary close."

letter of credit, abbr. L/C

letters, abbr. lres. (legal).

letters, folding of, *see* note under " folding."

lettre d'avis (Fr.), letter of advice.

lettre de change (Fr.), bill of exchange.

lettre de crédit (Fr.), letter of credit; abbr. l/cr.

leu, unit of currency of Rumania.

lev, unit of currency of Bulgaria.

levee, reception (of men only) held by sovereign.

Lever. *See* Appendix II for pronunciation.

lex loci (Lat.), the law or custom of the place; local custom.

lex scripta (Lat.), the written or statute law.

L.F., low frequency.

L.F.P.S., Licentiate of the Faculty of Physicians and Surgeons.

L.G., large grain, Life Guards.

L.G.B., Local Government Board.

L.H.A., Lord High Admiral.

L.H.C., Lord High Chancellor.

L.H.T., Lord High Treasurer.

Li, lithium.

liaison, joining, illicit intimacy, co-ordination between allies, thickening used in cookery, slurred note in music.

libelled.

libra (Lat.), pound; *pl. librae*; abbr. L., £, l., lb. (no *s* to be added for plural).

libraire (Fr.), bookseller; *librairie* (Fr.), bookshop. Library, in Fr. *bibliothèque*.

libretto (It.), words of a musical work; *pl. libretti*. The writer of such words is a librettist.

libro (It.), a book; *pl. libri*.

L.I.C., *Licencie Institute Comptable.*

licence (*noun*); **license** (*verb*).

licentia vatum (Lat.), poetic licence.

Liddington, Wilts

Lidlington, Beds

lie and lay, *see* note under "lay and lie."

Lied (Ger.), song; *pl. Lieder*. (Tendency in England to use small letter instead of capital.)

lief, gladly. ("I would as lief do . . .")

lieu, in lieu of = in the place of.

lieu (Fr.), place.

lieue (Fr.), league. French league about 2½ miles, English 3.

Lieutenant, abbr. Lieut. or Lt.

lifelong, lasting through life. Livelong = entire, whole.

lifetime.

ligature, the joining of two or more letters in printing. Special signs for the ligatures can be fitted on the typewriter. The ligatures æ and œ are used in foreign words, but in English there is a strong tendency to print the letters separately. Care must be taken when copying from printed matter not to confuse æ (ae) and *œ* (oe), as in some founts of type there is hardly any distinction. *See also* note on "diphthongs."

lighted, lit. Use either for past tense, but lighted is commoner for past participle. Use lighted for the adjective ("a lighted match").

lighthouse.

lightning.

likeable.

likelihood.

lilliputian, tiny (similar to the inhabitants of Lilliput, in *Gulliver's Travels*).

limelight.

limestone.

Limited, abbr. Ltd. or Ld. Some limited companies use a comma before Limited; others do not. The typist should follow the style of the correspondent's letter heading. For addressing of limited companies, *see* under "Messrs."

Lincolnshire, abbr. Lincs (no point).

Lindsay. *See* Appendix II for pronunciation.

Lindsey, political division of Lincolnshire, the others being Holland and Kesteven.

line, abbr. l.; *pl.* ll.

lineaments, features.

line-end division. Pay attention to this; an even right-hand margin adds greatly to the beauty of your work. The chief points are: (*a*) Do not divide a monosyllabic word. (*b*) Divide according to pronunciation. (*c*) Do not divide the last word on a page. (*d*) Do not divide a word that already has a hyphen in it. (*e*) A hyphen should never be placed at the beginning of a line.

linen-draper.

linendrapery.

line-spacing, *see* note under "spacing."

lines, ruling. When the typist is producing a tabular statement with many columns, it will save time (unless a number of carbon copies are being taken) to do the ruling in ink rather than by means of the underscore on the typewriter. A useful tool is a special (adjustable) ruling pen, obtainable at small cost. On some machines, however, a continuous line can be obtained by depressing the underscore and running the carriage backwards and forwards, and a vertical line by depressing the apostrophe and revolving the platen. Do not mix typed and ink rules in one piece of matter.

lingerie (Fr.), underwear.

lingua franca, a mixed jargon serving as a medium between different peoples.

liniment, embrocation.

Linton, Burton-on-Trent, Cambridge, Hereford, Kent, Northumb, Yorks *Lynton* is in Devon.

Lions, Gulf of, in French *golfe du Lion*. *See* also " Lyons."

lipsalve.

lipstick.

liquefy.

liqueur.

liquon. (legal), liquidation, the winding-up of the affairs of a Company.

liquorice.

lira, Italian unit of currency; *pl.* **lire;** abbr. L.

lita., unit of currency of Lithuania.

literally. Think of the real meaning of this word, and do not use it when you mean something quite different, as in " I was literally bowled over by the news."

literals, term used in printing to signify errors made by the compositor and not the author, e.g. defective types, turned letters, etc.

literati (Lat.), men of letters or learning.

literatim (Lat.), letter for letter.

lithium, symbol Li (no point).

Lithuania. Unit of currency 1 lita = 10 cents.

litre, 1·76 pint; abbr. L. or lit.

Litt.D., Doctor of Letters (Cambridge, Leeds, Liverpool, Manchester, Sheffield, Dublin). *See* also D.Lit. and D.Litt.

littérateur (Fr.), author, literary man.

Litteratur (Ger.), literature.

littérature (Fr.), literature.

livre (Fr.), *masc.* book; *fem.* pound.

L.J., Lord Justice.

L.JJ., Lords Justices.

ll., leaves, lines.

-ll, spelling hint: many words ending in double l, when compounded, use only one l, e.g. belfry, spoonful, welfare.

L.L.A., Lady Licentiate of St. Andrews, Lady Literate of Arts.

llama.

LL.B., *Legum Baccalaureus* (Lat.), Bachelor of Laws.

LL.D., *Legum Doctor* (Lat.), Doctor of Laws.

L.L.I., Lord-Lieutenant of Ireland.

LL.M., *Legum Magister* (Lat.), Master of Laws.

Lloyd's marks. For wooden ships, A1, A1 (in red), AE1; for steel, 100A, A. Older marks were 100 A1 and 90 A1.

L.M.S., London, Midland and Scottish Railway, also London Missionary Society.

L.N.E.R., London and North Eastern Railway.

L.N.U., League of Nations Union.

loath, averse. Sometimes spelt *loth.*

loathe, to hate.

local. Do not use this word on envelopes in place of the post town.

locale, commonly used for the French *local,* meaning the place where something happened.

localize.

loch, Scottish word for lake.

lock-out, employers' action in shutting out employees of a factory or mine; *pl.* **lock-outs.**

loco citato (Lat.), in the place cited.

locum tenens (Lat.), one holding another's place. (Colloquially : locum.)

locus standi (Lat.), legal standing in a matter, right to interfere.

lodestar.

lodgment, sometimes spelt lodgement.

loggerheads *(at)*, disagreeing with.

loggia (It.), gallery or arcade; *pl. loggias* or *loggie.*

longe (Fr.), loin.

longhand.

Long Marston, Herts, Warwickshire.

Long Marton, Westmorland.

Longton, Lancs

Longtown, Cumberland, Monmouth.

longwise, *-wise* is more common than *-ways* in this and similar words.

looking-glass.

look-out, *pl.* **look-outs.**

loophole.

loquacious, talkative.

loquitur (Lat.), speaks; abbr. *loq.*

Lord-Advocate. *See* Appendix I for correct form of address.

Lord Chamberlain, abbr. L.C.

Lord Chancellor, abbr. L.C. *See* Appendix I for correct form of address.

Lord Chief Baron, abbr. L.C.B.

Lord Chief Justice, abbr. L.C.J. *See* Appendix I for correct form of address.

Lord High Commissioner. *See* Appendix I for correct form of address.

Lord Justice, abbr. L.J.; *pl.* **Lords Justices.**

Lord Justice-General. *See* Appendix I for correct form of address.

Lord-Lieutenant, abbr. L.L.; *pl.* **Lord-Lieutenants.**

Lord Mayor, *pl.* **Lord Mayors.** *See* Appendix I for correct form of address.

Lord Privy Seal, abbr. L.P.S.

Lords of Session. *See* Appendix I for correct form of address.

lorgnette (Fr.), opera-glasses; pair of eye-glasses having a handle.

Loudon. *See* Appendix II for pronunciation.

louring, frowning.

lovable.

"**Love's Labour's Lost,**" play by Shakespeare.

lower-case, a printer's term for the small letters. In typewriting, the letters that are typed without first depressing the shift key. Abbr. l.c.

low frequency (use hyphen when an adjective), abbr. L.F.

L.P.T.B., London Passenger Transport Board.

L.R.C.P., Licentiate of the Royal College of Physicians. (E. is added to indicate Edinburgh and I. for Ireland.)

L.R.C.S., Licentiate of the Royal College of Surgeons.

lres. (legal), letters.

L.R.I.B.A., Licentiate of the Royal Institute of British Architects.

L.S., *locus sigilli* (Lat.), the place of the seal. In making a copy of a document that has a seal affixed, type L.S. at the place where the seal appears. L.S. also means long shot (film scenario term).

L.S.A., Licentiate of the Society of Apothecaries.

L.S.D., or **£ s. d.**, abbr. for *Librae, solidi, denarii*, pounds, shillings, and pence. (Note, no point after £)

L.T., abbreviated form of L.P.T.B., London Passenger Transport Board; also low tension (sometimes l.t.).

£T, *lira Turca*, Turkish pound.

Lt.-Col., Lieutenant-Colonel.

Lt.-Gen., Lieutenant-General.

L.Th., Licentiate in Theology.

Lucerne, Ger. *Luzern*.

L.U.E., instructions for an actor, meaning left upper entrance, i.e. left when facing audience, and upper, at back of stage.

lukewarm.

lupus in fabula (Lat.), the wolf in the fable.

lusus naturae (Lat.), a freak of nature.

Luton, Beds

Lutton, Cambs, Northants

luxurious. Use this of houses, food, people, etc. *Luxuriant* implies rich growth—vegetation, hair, etc.

L.W.L., load-water-line.

L.W.M., low-water mark.

lycée (Fr.), grammar or secondary school.

lynx, animal of the cat tribe; *pl.* **lynxes.** Lynx-eyed = sharp-sighted.

Lyons. Fr. *Lyon.*

Lyth, Caithness.

Lythe, Yorks

M

M. 1000 (roman numerals).

M., Majesty, Marquess, member; French *Monsieur* (never Mons.); German *mark*; Latin *Magister*, Master.

m., married, masculine, meridian, metre, mile, minute.

M.A., *Magister Artium*, Master of Arts.

ma'am, colloquial for madam.

Mac. Follow strictly the form used by the person to whom you are writing. It may be Macpherson, MacPherson, McPherson, McPherson, or M'Pherson. When making an index, imagine it always to be spelt Macp- and place it accordingly. When typing such names note that no space or full stop follows the Mac or Mc.

macadamizing, system of road-making invented by John McAdam in 1819.

macaroni, *pl.* macaronies.

macaroon.

macassar, oil.

Macbean. *See* Appendix II for pronunciation.

Maccabean, of the Maccabees, Jewish princes. Note " Judas Maccabeus."

macédoine (Fr.), a mixture of fruit or vegetables.

ma chère (Fr.), my dear (*fem.*); *mon cher* (*masc.*).

Machiavellian, cunning in politics.

Mackay. *See* Appendix II for pronunciation.

mackerel, *pl.* mackerel *or* mackerels.

Maclachlan. *See* Appendix II for pronunciation.

Macleod or MacLeod. *See* Appendix II for pronunciation.

macramé, trimming made of knotted thread or cord.

macrocosm, the universe. (Greek *macros*, long, large.)

macron, the mark over a vowel to indicate that it is long, e.g. ē.

Madagascar, note the *adj.* Malagasy.

madam. This is really a combination of *ma* and *dame*, meaning my lady. There is no plural, so it is necessary to borrow from the French and say " Dear Mesdames " when writing to a firm of ladies. Note the colloquial forms of madam, viz. ma'am, marm, m'm, and mum. The only use of Madame is as a title, both in English and French; the abbreviation for it is Mme (no point), not Mdme, and in the plural, Mmes (no point).

Mädchen (Ger.), girl; same for plural.

Madeley, Crewe, Shropshire.

Mademoiselle (Fr.), means Miss; abbr. Mlle, not Mdlle; *pl. Mesdemoiselles,* abbr. Mlles. Use no point after these abbreviations.

Madley, Hereford.

maestoso (It.), majestically.

maestro (It.), master, music teacher, composer.

Ma foi! (Fr.), Really! Upon my word!

magasin (Fr.), shop, store, warehouse, etc.

Magdalen College, Oxford; *pron.* mawdlin. Similarly, Magdalene College, Cambridge.

magi, plural of magus, wise man; *pron.* j.

magister (Lat.), master.

magister ceremoniarum (Lat.), Master of Ceremonies; abbr. M.C.

Magna Charta, *pron.* carta.

Magna est veritas et praevalet (Lat.), Great is truth and it prevails.

magnanimity, generosity.

magnesium, abbr. Mg (no point).

magnetize.

magnum opus (Lat.), the chief work of an author.

M.Agr.Sc., Master of Agricultural Science (Ireland).

Maharaja, Indian title, *fem.* Maharanee.

Mahon. *See* Appendix II for pronunciation.

Maids of Honour. *See* Appendix I for correct form of address.

main (Fr.), hand; *main droite* = right hand; *main gauche* = left hand.

mainspring.

maintce. (legal), maintenance.

Mainwaring. *See* Appendix II for pronunciation.

maison (Fr.), house.

maisonnette. This is a French word, and it seems only right to adopt it with its French spelling, but it is often seen in house agents' notices and elsewhere with one *n* only.

maître (Fr.), master, ruler, Councillor. *Maître d'hôtel* = steward, butler. *A la maître d'hôtel* = method of dressing a cooked dish.

Majesty, abbr. M.; *pl.* MM.

major-domo, house steward.

makeshift.

make-up, actor's disguise, or the materials used for this. Do not hyphenate when it is a verb.

mal-, male-, ill, badly.

malade imaginaire (Fr.), imaginary invalid.

male fide (Lat.), in bad faith.

malapropism, misuse of word, especially in substitution for one resembling it. (From Mrs. Malaprop in Sheridan's *The Rivals*.)

malapropos, unseasonably, inopportunely; Fr. *mal à propos*.

Malay, the language.

Malaya, the country.

Malays, the people.

malcontent, person inclined to rebellion.

mal de mer (Fr.), sea-sickness.

Malden, Surrey.

Maldon, Essex.

mal entendu (Fr.), misunderstood.

malentendu (Fr.), misapprehension.

malgré lui (Fr.), in spite of himself.

malingerer, one who pretends illness in order to escape duty.

malodorous, evil-smelling.

malum in se (Lat.), a thing inherently wrong.

malum prohibitum (Lat.), a thing prohibited by law, although not necessarily wrong.

manacled, fettered.

manageable.

mañana (Sp.), to-morrow.

manche (Fr.), *masc.* a handle; *fem.* a sleeve.

Manche (La) (Fr.), the English Channel.

Manchester, abbr. Manch., M'chester, or M/C, but beware of abbreviations that are significant to you but may not be recognized by others!

Manchukuo, formerly Manchuria.

mandarin, Chinese official.

mandat (Fr.), power of attorney, warrant, etc.

mandatary, a person to whom a mandate is given.

mandatory (*adj.*), conveying a command.

mandat-poste (Fr.), money order.

mandolin.

manganese, abbr. Mn (no point).

manifesto, *pl.* manifestos.

manifolding, process of taking carbon copies. *See* note under " carbon paper."

manikin, dwarf, artist's lay-figure.

manipulator.

mannequin. In French the word may mean manikin, puppet, insignificant person, etc., but in English it is used for the human model on whom clothes are displayed.

manoeuvre(r).

man-of-war, *pl.* men-of-war.

Manston, Dorset.

mantelpiece.

mantilla (Sp.), a veil or short mantle.

Manton, Rutland, Wilts

manufacturer, abbr. mfr.

manus (Lat.), the hand. *Sing.* and *pl.*

manuscript, abbr. MS.; *pl.* MSS. Manuscripts should, if possible, be typed; indeed, some editors will not read handwritten MSS. Type on one side only, and number pages at the top. (*See* notes under "pagination" for useful hints.) Use quarto paper. Never roll a MS.

manuscrit (Fr.). manuscript.

Manuskript (Ger.), manuscript.

Manxman, native of the Isle of Man.

Maori, native of New Zealand; *pron.* mowri; *pl.* Maoris.

maquereau (Fr.), mackerel.

M.Ar., Master of Architecture (U.S.A.).

marabou, feather.

marabout, North African hermit.

marabout (Fr.), a large coffee-pot.

maraschino, a liqueur; *pron.* maraskēno.

M.Arch., Master of Architecture (Ireland).

March, may be abbreviated to Mch., if space is a consideration, but not in correspondence.

marchese (It.), marquess; *fem. marchesa,* marchioness.

Marchioness. *See* Appendix I for correct form of address.

marconigram, wireless telegraph message.

Marden, Hereford, Kent, Wilts

marginalia (Lat.), marginal notes.

marginal stop. If the right-hand marginal stop is not fixed, there will be no ring of the bell to warn the operator that the line-end is approaching.

margin release, a useful device for allowing the typing to extend beyond the margin (left or right) that has been fixed by the margin stop.

margins. Be generous with your margins. In letters the left-hand margin is generally greater than the right. By judicious line-end division of words, secure as straight a right-hand margin as possible.

mariage de convenance (Fr.), marriage of convenience.

Marina (Gk.), Mary, Maria, Marian.

marinade (Fr.), pickle used for enriching the flavour of meat or fish.

marionette, puppet worked by strings. Fr. *marionnette*. "Human marionette" is description often used when operator's own face is seen.

Marjoribanks. *See* Appendix II for pronunciation.

mark, German coin. Abbr. M (no point) ; does not take sign of plural.

markka, Finnish mark, unit of currency.

marks used in proof-correcting. *See* note under "correction marks."

Marloes, Pembrokeshire.

Marlow, Bucks

marque de fabrique (Fr.), trade-mark.

Marquess or Marquis. *See* Appendix I for correct form of address.

Marquess's daughter. *See* Appendix I for correct form of address.

Marquess's son. *See* Appendix I for correct form of address.

marquis (Fr.), marquis or marquess ; *fem. marquise* = marchioness.

marriageable.

married, abbr. m.

marron (Fr.), chestnut.

Marsden, Yorks

marshal, marshalled.

Marston, Cheshire, Oxford, Yorks

Marton, Cheshire, Lincs, Montgomery, Warwickshire, Yorks

marvel, marvellous.

Marylebone, formerly Mary-le-bone ; *pron.* măr-ĭ-bŭn.

M.A.S., Master of Applied Science.

masculine, abbr. m.

mashie, a golf club.

Massachusetts, abbr. Mass.

massacring.

masseur, *fem.* masseuse.

Master of the Rolls, abbr. M.R.

mat, a felt or rubber mat placed under the typewriter reduces the noise and vibration, and will prevent "creeping" on a polished surface.

matador, man who kills bull in Spanish bull-fight.

match-box.

matchwood.

maté, a Brazilian tea.

matelot (Fr.), seaman.

matelote (Fr.), fish-stew.

mater (Lat.), mother.

materfamilias (Lat.), the mother of a family.

materia medica (Lat.), collectively of substances used in the art of healing, science of drugs.

mathematician.

matin (Fr.), morning.

matinée, entertainment by day, almost always in afternoon, e.g. theatrical performance.

matrix, a mould; *pl.* **matrixes** or **matrices**. *See* note under " apex."

Maugham. *See* Appendix II for pronunciation.

mausoleum, magnificent tomb (from that of King Mausolus in Central Asia in fourth century B.C.)

mauvais goût (Fr.), bad taste.

mauvais sujet (Fr.), worthless fellow.

maximum, *pl.* **maxima**; abbr. max.

maybe, perhaps.

May Day, 1st May.

mayonnaise (Fr.), salad dressing.

Mayor of a Borough. *See* Appendix I for correct form of address.

Mayor of a City. *See* Appendix I for correct form of address.

mayst.

mazurka, a Polish dance.

M.B., *Medicinae Baccalaureus* (Lat.), Bachelor of Medicine.

M.B.A.N., Member of the British Association of Naturopaths.

M.B.E., Member of (the Order of) the British Empire.

Mc, *see* note under " Mac."

M.C., Military Cross; Master of Ceremonies.

M/C, Manchester. Use abbreviations with discrimination.

M.C.E., Master of Civil Engineering.

M.Ch., *Magister Chirurgiae* (Lat.), Master of Surgery.

M.Ch.Orth., Master of Orthopaedic Surgery.

M.C.L., Master of Civil Law.

M.Com., Master of Commerce (Birmingham and Manchester).

M.Comm., Master of Commerce (Ireland).

M.C.P., Member of the College of Preceptors.

M.D., *Medicinae Doctor* (Lat.), Doctor of Medicine.

m.d., month's date.

M.D.S., Master of Dental Surgery.

M.E., Mechanical Engineer, Middle English, Mining Engineer, Most Excellent.

mea culpa (Lat.), by my fault.

meadow-land.

mealie, an ear of Indian corn.

mealy-mouthed, soft-tongued.

meantime.

meanwhile.

measurable.

mechanization.

M.Econ.Sc., Master of Economic Science (Ireland).

M.Ed., Master of Education.

medallist.

medical signs. These can be fitted on the typewriter, in place of keys containing fractions, etc.

medieval, the æ form is disappearing.

Mediterranean.

medium, agency, means, etc.; *pl.* **media**. In spiritualism the word means a person through whom communications from the dead are obtained; *pl.* **mediums**.

meeting-place.

me judice (Lat.), according to my judgment.

Melbourn, Herts

Melbourne, Derby, Yorks

mêlé (Fr.), mixed; *fem. mêlée.*

mêlée, used as an English word to mean a mixed fight, skirmish.

Melhuish. *See* Appendix II for pronunciation.

melioribus auspiciis (Lat.), under better auspices.

mem., memo., memorandum.

memento, *pl.* mementos.

memorabilia (Lat.), things to be remembered, noteworthy things.

memorandum, *pl.* memoranda or memorandums. Abbr. mem., memo.

memoriter (Lat.), from memory.

memorize.

Mempes. *See* Appendix II for pronunciation.

mem-sahib (Ang.-Ind.), married European lady.

ménage (Fr.), domestic establishment.

mendacity, falsehood.

Mendelssohn-Bartholdy, Felix, German composer.

mendicity, begging.

men-folk.

M.Eng., Master of Engineering.

Mens agitat molem (Lat.). Mind animates matter.

mens legis (Lat.), the spirit of the law.

mens rea (Lat.), a guilty intent.

mens sana in corpore sano (Lat.), a sound mind in a sound body.

mentd. (legal), mentioned.

mente captus (Lat.), an idiot.

Mentone. Fr. *Menton*. *See* Appendix II for pronunciation.

menu (Fr.), bill of fare; *pl. menus*.

Menzies. *See* Appendix II for pronunciation.

meo periculo (Lat.), at my own risk.

meo voto (Lat.), by my wish.

Mephistopheles, a spirit of evil who figures in Goethe's "Faust."

mercerized, having silky gloss (named after J. Mercer, the patentee).

merchandise.

merci (Fr.), thank you; or, no, thank you.

mercury, symbol Hg (no point).

meridian, circle passing through celestial poles and zenith of any place on the surface of the earth; abbr. m.

merlan (Fr.), whiting.

Mersham, Kent.

Merstham, Surrey.

Merton, Devon, Oxon

mésalliance (Fr.), marriage with one of inferior social position.

Mesdames, prefixed to the names in addressing a firm of ladies, when one or both are married. The salutation of any letter addressed to ladies is " Dear Mesdames." It may be possible to address an individual, such as the Secretary, and then use " Dear Madam." *See* note under " madam."

Mesdemoiselles, *pl.* of Mademoiselle; abbr. Mlles (no point).

messe. (legal), messuage.

Messieurs (Fr.), abbr. MM.

Messrs. This is the plural of Mr., and equivalent of the French Messieurs. It should appear before the title of a firm that contains personal names (e.g. Messrs. Day & Knight), but not when the name is prefixed by The, as The Bennett Steel Co. For limited companies, or where the personal element is missing, it is better to address the Secretary, Manager, etc. (but not by name). Another caution : omit Messrs. if the name begins with a title, as Sir Alfred Ross & Sons.

messuage (legal), dwelling-house, with outbuildings and land; abbr. messe.

metallography, descriptive science of internal structure of metals.

metamorphosis, change of form or character.

meteorology, study of atmospheric conditions, especially in relation to weather forecasts.

métier (Fr.), trade, profession.

metre, 39·37 in.; abbr. m. Fr. *mètre;* Ger. *Meter.*

metropolis, *pl.* metropolises.

Meux. *See* Appendix II for pronunciation.

Meyer. *See* Appendix II for pronunciation.

Mexico. Unit of currency 1 peso = 100 centavos.

mezzanine, a low storey between two others, usually between ground and first.

mezzo (It.), half, medium; *pron.* medzo

mezzotint, print from an intaglio copper-plate engraved by hand.

mf, mezzo-forte (It.), rather loud.

mfd., manufactured, microfarad.

M.F.H., Master of Fox-hounds.

mfr., manufacturer.

Mg, magnesium (no point).

mg., milligram.

Mgr., Monsignor, Monseigneur.

Mho., unit of conductivity.

M.I.A.E., Member of the Institute of Automobile Engineers.

miasma, noxious exhalation; *pl.* miasmata.

Mich., Michigan.

Michaelmas, feast of St. Michael, 29th September.

Michelangelo Buonarroti, Italian painter, sculptor, and architect.

Michigan, abbr. Mich.

Mickfield, Suffolk.

Micklefield, Leeds.

Mickleton, Glos, Yorks

microcosm, the little world.

microfarad, abbr. mfd.

micro-organism, microscopic organism.

midday.

middle-aged.

Middle Ages, about A.D. 1000–1400.

middleman.

Middlestown, Yorks

Middleton, Derby, Leicestershire, Manchester, Norfolk,

T.T.—5

Northumberland, Shropshire, Staffs, Suffolk, Sussex, Yorks

Middletown, Armagh, Montgomeryshire.

midsummer.

Midsummer Day, 24th June.

mid-way.

midwinter.

M.I.E.E., Member of the Institution of Electrical Engineers.

mightst.

mignonette. Fr. *mignonnette.*

mile, miles, abbr. m. Fr. *mille, milles.*

milieu (Fr.), sphere, medium; *pl. milieux.*

Military Officers. *See* Appendix I for correct form of address.

mille (Fr.), a thousand. Same for plural; abbr. M. Also means a mile, with plural *milles.*

millennium, the promised thousand years of Christ's reign on earth.

milligram, ·015 grain; abbr. (*sing.* and *pl.*) mg.

millimetre, ·03937 in.; abbr. (*sing.* and *pl.*) mm.

Milltown, co. Kerry.

Milnes. *See* Appendix II for pronunciation.

M.I.Loco.E., Member of the Institution of Locomotive Engineers.

milreis, unit of currency of Brazil.

Milton, Berks, Cambridge, Derby, Dumfries, Hants, Northants, Oxford, Pembroke, Staffs, Wilts

M.I.Mar.E., Member of the Institute of Marine Engineers.

M.I.M.E., Member of the Institution of Mining Engineers (sometimes M.I.Min.E.).

M.I.Mech.E., Member of the Institution of Mechanical Engineers.

mimic, mimicking.

min., minim.

M.I.N.A., Member of the Institution of Naval Architects.

mincemeat.

mineralogical.

minim, a drop; abbr. min.

minimize.

minimum, *pl.* minima.

Minister Resident. *See* Appendix I for correct form of address.

M.Inst.C.E., Member of the Institution of Civil Engineers.

M.Inst.Gas E., Member of the Institution of Gas Engineers.

M.Inst.T., Member of the Institute of Transport.

minuet, slow dance in triple measure, or music in this style.

minute, minutes, abbr. **m., min.,** or the sign (').

minutia, small detail; usually in pl. **minutiae.**

minutiæ (Lat.), minute concerns.

M.I.P., Marine Insurance Policy.

M.I.P.E., Member of the Institute of Production Engineers.

mirabile dictu (Lat.), wonderful to tell.

mirabile visu (Lat.), wonderful to see.

M.I.R.E., Member of the Institution of Radio Engineers.

mis-. Use the hyphen when the word following this prefix begins with **s,** as otherwise there is a danger of mispronunciation.

miscellanea (*pl.*), collection of miscellaneous things.

miscellany, mixture; sometimes a collection of articles into one volume.

mischievous.

mise en scène (Fr.), scenery, surroundings of an event.

misfeasance, in law a transgression.

misfire. This is now the usual form, with *misfired* for past tense. If you use the two words *miss fire,* be careful to say *missed fire* for past tense.

misogamist, one who hates marriage.

misogynist, one who hates women.

Miss, a complete word; do not add a full stop.

mis-shaped, mis-shapen.

Mississippi, state and river in U.S.A.; abbr. Miss.

Missouri, abbr. Mo.

mistakable.

mistletoe.

mistral, cold NW. wind in South of France.

mitreing.

Mittagessen (Ger.), midday meal, lunch, or early dinner.

M.I.W.T., Member of the Institute of Wireless Technology.

M.L., Licentiate in Midwifery.

M.L.A., Member of the Legislative Assembly.

M.L.C., Member of the Legislative Council.

Mlle, Mademoiselle; *pl.* **Mlles** (no point).

M.M., Military Medal.

MM, 2000; Their Majesties. Fr. *Messieurs.*

mm., millimetre, millimetres.

M.M.A., Member of the Mechanical Association.

Mme (Fr.), Madame; *pl.* **Mmes** (no point).

Mn, manganese.

Mo., Missouri.

M.O., Medical Officer, Money Order.

mobile perpetuum (Lat.), something perpetually in motion.

mobilization.

moccasin, shoe worn by North-American Indians.

mocha, fine quality of coffee. Fr. *moka.*

mode (Fr.), method, fashion.

mode et forma (Lat.), in manner and form.

modeller.

moderato (It.), moderate; abbr. *mod.*

Moderator. Established Church of Scotland. *See* Appendix I for correct form of address.

modernize.

modicum, small quantity.

modiste (Fr.), milliner.

modus (Lat.), manner, mode.

M.O.H., Medical Officer of Health.

Mohammed, founder of Moslem religion.

moiré (Fr.), watered.

mois (Fr.), month.

molasses.

momentum, quantity of motion of moving body; *pl.* **momenta.** Popular meaning: impetus gained by movement.

Mon, Monmouthshire.

Mona Lisa.

mon ami (Fr.), my friend; *fem. mon amie.*

Monat (Ger.), month.

mon cher (Fr.), my dear; *fem. ma chère.*

monde (Fr.), world, men, society. *Tout le monde =* everybody.

Mon Dieu! (Fr.), a common ejaculation of surprise, etc.

monetary units of principal countries, *see* under names of countries.

money, abbr. moy. (legal).

moneys, moneyed. (Plural "monies" sometimes seen in old works.)

Monmouthshire, abbr. Mon (no point).

mono-, alone.

monochromatic, in one colour only.

monograph, a treatise on a single subject.

monopolize.

monosyllabic, consisting of words of one syllable.

Monro. *See* Appendix II for pronunciation.

Monseigneur, French title; abbr. *Mgr.;* *pl. Messeigneurs,* abbr. *Mgrs.*

Monsieur (Fr.), Mr., Sir; abbr. M. (never Mons); *pl.* Messieurs, abbr. MM.

Monsignor, title of officers of Papal Court, and others; abbr. Mgr. It. *Monsignore; pl. Monsignori.*

Monson. *See* Appendix II for pronunciation.

Montessori, system of education evolved in early twentieth century by Dr. Maria Montessori.

month, abbr. m., mo.

months. These take an initial capital, but in French they have either lower case or cap. The full forms for the months are desirable in correspondence. In invoice and other work they are shortened, and the recognized forms are Jan., Feb., Aug., Sept., Oct., Nov., Dec. The remainder, March, April, May, June, and July, should be typed in full, unless space is a consideration.

Mont-Saint-Michel, a fortified French rock off the coast of Normandy. Mount Saint Michael, or St. Michael's Mount, is in Cornwall.

Monzie. *See* Appendix II for pronunciation.

moonlight.

moonlit.

moorlands.

moping, giving way to listlessness.

moral. Use this for the moral of a story, and morale to mean the mental state or spirit of an individual or army. There is no need for italics.

moralize.

morass.

moratorium, legal permission to postpone payment of debts.

morceau (Fr.), fragment, snack, short musical composition; *pl. morceaux.*

moreover.

Moreton, Cheshire, Dorset, Essex, Shropshire. *See also* "Morton."

morganatic marriage, one contracted between man of high rank and woman of lower rank, the children of which have no claim to title or possessions of father.

Morgen (Ger.), morning.

morocco leather, no cap. needed. There are various

kinds of morocco leather: French (low grade), Levant (high grade), and Persian.

Morpheus, god of sleep.

Mors omnibus communis (Lat.), Death is common to all.

mortgage, abbr. mtge. (legal).

mortgagee, abbr. mtgee. (legal).

mortgagor, abbr. mtgor. (legal).

Morton, Derbyshire, Lincs

Moses'. For the sake of euphony no *s* is added for the possessive.

mosquito, *pl.* mosquitoes.

mot (Fr.), word.

mother-in-law, *pl.* mothers-in-law.

mother-of-pearl.

motif, central theme in musical composition; a lace ornament for a dress. Motive = the object that incites to action.

motion. This is the form in which a subject is presented to a Meeting. It does not become a Resolution until it has been carried.

motu proprio (Lat.), of his own accord.

mouchoir (Fr.), pocket-handkerchief.

mould.

mountain, abbr. Mt.

Mount Saint Michael, Cornwall, use *St. Michael's Mount.* Mont-Saint-Michel is off the coast of Normandy.

moutarde (Fr.), mustard.

mouthfuls.

mouthpiece.

mouton (Fr.), sheep, mutton.

moy. (legal), money.

M.P., pluralize by adding *s.* M.P.s. Reserve M.P.'s for singular possessive and M.P.s' for plural possessive.

mp (It.), *mezzo-piano,* rather soft.

M.P.S., Member of the Pharmaceutical Society; or of the Philological Society.

M.R., Master of the Rolls.

M.R.A.S., Member of the Royal Asiatic Society; or of the Royal Academy of Science.

M.R.C.C., Member of the Royal College of Chemistry.

M.R.C.P., Member of the Royal College of Physicians.

M.R.C.S., Member of the Royal College of Surgeons.

M.R.C.V.S., Member of the Royal College of Veterinary Surgeons.

M.R.G.S., Member of the Royal Geographical Society.

M.R.I., Member of the Royal Institution.

M.R.O., Member of the Register of Osteopaths.

M.R.San.I., Member of the Royal Sanitary Institute.

M.R.S.L., Member of the Royal Society of Literature.

M.R.S.T., Member of the Royal Society of Teachers.

M.R.U.S.I., Member of the Royal United Service Institution.

M.S., Master of Science, or Surgery; mid or medium shot (film scenario term).

MS., *manuscriptum* (Lat.), manuscript.

M.S.R., Member of the Society of Radiographers.

MSS., *manuscripta* (Lat.), manuscripts.

Mt., mount, mountain.

mtge. (legal), mortgage.

mtgee. (legal), mortgagee.

mtgor. (legal), mortgagor.

mucous (*adj.*), covered with mucus (*noun*), as, for example, mucous membrane. Note the difference between *adj.* and *noun*.

mufti, a Mohammedan priest. In mufti—the wearing of plain clothes instead of a uniform.

mulatto, offspring of European and Negro; *pl.* **mulattoes**.

mulligatawny soup.

multimillionaire, one who possesses several million pounds.

multiplication sign, use small x in typing.

multum in parvo (Lat.), much in little.

mur (Fr.), a wall.

mûr (Fr.), ripe, mature.

Mus.B., or **Bac.**, Bachelor of Music.

Mus.D., Doctor of Music. Use this form if the degree was taken at Cambridge or Manchester University, and D.Mus. if at Durham, Oxford, or London.

Mus.M., Master of Music, Cambridge.

Musulman, *pl.* **Musulmans**.

mutandum (Lat.), something to be altered.

mutatis mutandis (Lat.), with the necessary alterations.

mutual means reciprocal, that is, such a relationship as the friendship of Mary for John and John for Mary. To say "our mutual friend John" is not correct ("common" is the only word we have), but is frequently done, probably through the example set by Dickens and others.

mutuus consensus (Lat.), mutual consent.

M.V.O., Member of the Royal Victorian Order.

M.W.B., Metropolitan Water Board.

my being here. In these gerund constructions use my, not me. Example: " Do you object to my being here? "

mynheer, a Dutchman.

myopia, short-sightedness.

myrmidon, a hired ruffian ; policeman, etc.

mysticism, the practice of the mystics, but often used contemptuously.

N

N, nitrogen.

N., North, northern.

ñ, the Spanish *n* has the liquid sound of *ni* in pinion.

n/a, no acceptance.

N/A, no account (banking term).

Naboth's vineyard.

Nachmittag (Ger.), afternoon.

Nacht (Ger.), night.

nadir, time or place of deepest depression; opposite to zenith.

nainsook, muslin (originally Indian).

naïve, unaffected; **naïveté**, unaffectedness. These forms are likely to be replaced by *naive, naivety,* also *naively.* (From Fr. *naïf*; *fem. naïve.*)

N.A.L.G.O., National Association of Local Government Officers.

namby-pamby.

namely, use this in preference to *viz.*

namesake.

Nanking.

naphtha, note *Fels-naptha.*

Napier. *See* Appendix II for pronunciation.

narcissus, *pl.* **narcissi.**

N.A.R.M.A.T., National Association of Radio Manufacturers and Traders.

nasturtium, *pl.* **nasturtiums.**

Nat., Natal, National.

nationalization, the transfer of property to State ownership.

Natura abhorret vacuum (Lat.), Nature abhors a vacuum.

naturalize.

natus (Lat.), born; abbr. *n.*

naught, nothing. *Nought* should be confined to the name for the cipher, o.

Naval Officers. *See* Appendix I for correct form of address.

navet (Fr.), turnip.

Nazis. National Socialist Party of Germany, believers in form of government similar to Fascism.

N.B., New Brunswick; *nota bene*, mark well. Do not use this for Scotland (North Britain).

N.C.L., National Council of Labour.

N.C.O., Non-commissioned Officer.

N.C.U., National Cyclists' Union.

N.D., not dated.

NE., north-east.

né (Fr.), born; *fem. née.*

N/E, no effects (banking term).

Neapolitans, inhabitants of Naples.

nearby. This has recently become fairly popular as an adjective (e.g. " a nearby house "), though there is no dictionary sanction for it. When used adverbially, it should be in two words (e.g. " a house near by ").

Ne cede malis (Lat.). Do not yield to misfortune.

necessary, abbr. necy. (legal).

Necessitas non habet legem (Lat.), Necessity knows no law.

necessitous.

Nec temere, nec timide (Lat.), Neither with temerity nor timidity.

necy. (legal), necessary.

needlework.

ne'er, never (used in poetry).

ne'er-do-weel. As the expression is of northern origin, the Scottish *weel* is recommended.

Ne exeat (Lat.), Let him not depart.

ne exeat regno (Lat.), a writ restraining a person from leaving the kingdom.

négligé, free-and-easy attire, or a garment so worn (a French word that has become anglicized).

negligible, insignificant.

negotiate.

nein (Ger.), no.

neither, this is singular, and must be followed by singular verb. Use it when speaking of two things, not more. Be careful to follow with " nor," not " or."

nemine contradicente (Lat.), without opposition; abbr. *nem. con.*

nemine dissentiente (Lat.), without dissent; abbr. *nem. diss.*

nemo (Lat.), no one.

neophyte, a new convert (Gk. *neos* = new).

ne plus ultra (Lat.), nothing beyond; farthest point attainable.

nepotism, favouritism extended to one's relations.

nerve-racking, *see* note under " rack."

N'est-ce pas? (Fr.), Isn't it so?

net, not subject to discount.

Netherlands. Unit of currency 1 Dutch guilder = 100 cents.

neurasthenic, suffering, or a person suffering, from nervous depression.

neurosis, functional derangement due to nervous disorders. (From Gk. *neuron* = nerve); *pl.* neuroses.

neutralize.

never-ceasing.

nevermore.

nevertheless.

never-to-be-forgotten.

Newbiggin, Cumberland, Durham, Penrith.

Newbigging, Dundee, Lanarkshire.

new-comer.

newfangled, used rather derisively of new fashions or things.

New Jersey, abbr. N.J.

New Mill, Banffshire, Cornwall, Herts, Yorks

Newmills, Donegal, Fife, Tyrone.

New Mills, Montgomery, Stockport.

Newmilns, Ayrshire.

new paragraph, abbr. n.p.

newspapers. Type names of newspapers in quotes When printed, they appear in italics.

New Testament, abbr. N.T.

Newton, Cambs, Derbyshire, Lincs, Notts, Warwickshire, West Lothian.

Newtown, Berks, Cork, Glos, Hants, Montgomery, Tipperary.

New Year's Day.

nez retroussé (Fr.), turned-up nose.

N/F, no funds (banking term).

Ni, nickel.

niblick, a golf club.

Nicht wahr? (Ger.), Isn't it true?

nickel, abbr. Ni (no point).

nickel-plating.

nickname.

N.I.D., Naval Intelligence Division.

nidus, a nest, place where disease is bred; *pl.* nidi, niduses.

Nigel. *See* Appendix II for pronunciation.

night-dress.

nightfall.

nightmare.

nihil (Lat.), nothing; abbr. *nil* (no point).

nihilism, total rejection of current beliefs.

nil (Lat.), nothing, an abbreviation of *nihil*.

Nil desperandum (Lat.), Never despair.

Nil dicit (Lat.), He makes no reply.

nil ultra (Lat.), nothing beyond.

n'importe (Fr.), no matter.

nincompoop, a simpleton, blockhead.

nineties, apostrophe is seen usually (when referring to the 1890's), though many writers omit it. Be careful not to use the apostrophe in *twenties*, etc., referring to a person's age.

N.I.R.A., New Industrial Reconstruction Act (U.S.A.).

Nirvana, Buddhist idea of perfection, the extinction of individuality.

Nisi Dominus, frustra (Lat.), Unless God be with you, all your toil is vain.

nitrate, a salt that has nitric acid as its base.

nitrite, a salt of nitrous acid.

nitrogen, abbr. N (no point).

nitrogenize.

nitro-glycerine, an explosive liquid.

N.J., New Jersey.

N. lat., North latitude.

N.L.S.S., National Life Saving Society.

N/N, not to be noted (Bills of Exchange).

NNE., north-north-east.

NNW., north-north-west.

No., number; *pl.* **Nos.** (from It. *numero*).

N/O, no orders.

no account, abbr. N/A (banking term).

Noblesse oblige (Fr.), Rank imposes obligations.

no effects, abbr. N/E (banking term).

Noël (Fr.), Christmas.

no funds, abbr. N/F (banking term).

noggin, a small mug or wooden cup.

nogging, a partition of wooden posts with the spaces between filled up with bricks.

nolens volens (Lat.), whether he will or not.

nolle prosequi (Lat.), withdrawing a suit.

no-man's-land, unowned or debatable land.

nom de plume (Fr.), pen-name.

nom de théâtre (Fr.), stage name.

nomen genericum (Lat.), a generic name.

non-. Avoid compounds such as non-success, when there

are equivalents available. (For non-success use failure.)

nonagenarian, a person 90 years old.

non-commissioned officer, abbr. N.C.O.

non compos mentis (Lat.), lunatic (not master of his mind).

Nonconformist.

non constat (Lat.), it has not been shown, it is not clear.

non culpabilis (Lat.), not guilty; abbr. *non cul.*

non est (Lat.), it is not, it is wanting.

non est disputandem (Lat.), it is not to be disputed.

non est factum (Lat.), it is not done.

non est inventus (Lat.), it has not been found; abbr. *n.e.i.*

none the less.

non-existent.

non licet (Lat.), it is not allowed.

non obstante veredicto (Lat.), notwithstanding the verdict.

nonplus, nonplussed.

non possumus (Lat.), we cannot.

Non progredi est regredi (Lat.), Not to go forward is to go backward.

non prosequitue (Lat.), he does not prosecute.

non sequitur (Lat.), it does not follow.

Non sibi, sed patriae (Lat.), Not for oneself, but for one's country.

nonsuch, originally nonesuch, but now more often seen without the *e.*

noonday.

no one, two words.

nord (Fr.), north.

nord-est (Fr.), north-east.

nord-ouest (Fr.), north-west.

north. Use lower-case initial for north, south, east, and west, unless part of a name, as the Middle West, South Africa.

Northamptonshire, abbr. Northants (no point).

north-east, abbr. NE.

Northumberland, abbr. Northumb (no point).

Norway. Unit of currency 1 krone = 100 öre.

Nosce tempus (Lat.), Know thy time.

notabilia (Lat.), noteworthy things.

notanda (Lat.), things to be noted.

notatu dignum (Lat.), worthy of note.

notebook. This should be placed at the side of the

machine that is opposite to the carriage return lever, so that the view will not be obstructed by the arm as the carriage is returned at each line-end. The note-book should have a good inch margin, in which can be inserted special instructions, interpolations, etc. Each day's " take " should begin a new page, with the date written boldly.

note-paper, folding of; see note under " folding."

noticeable.

notitia (Lat.), a list; *pl. notitiae.*

notre (Fr.), *adj.* our. *Le nôtre, la nôtre* (possessive pronoun), ours. *Les nôtres,* our people, friends.

not sufficient, abbr. N/S (banking term).

Nottinghamshire, abbr. Notts (no point).

notwstg. (legal), notwithstanding.

nought, use this for the figure o, but *naught* in other connections.

nous, common sense (Greek, mind).

Nous verrons (Fr.), We shall see.

nouvelles (Fr.), news.

November, abbr. Nov.

novembre (Fr.), November. Upper- or lower-case initial may be used in French; abbr. 9ʳᵉ.

novus homo (Lat.), a self-made man.

nowadays.

nowhere.

n.p., new paragraph.

N.P., Notary Public.

N/S, not sufficient (banking term).

N.S., Nova Scotia; New Style (dating from 1752).

N.S.P.C.C., National Society for the Prevention of Cruelty to Children.

N.S.W., New South Wales.

N.T., New Testament.

nucleus, *pl.* nuclei.

Nuda veritas (Lat.), Truth needs no embellishment.

nudis verbis (Lat.), in plain words.

N.U.J., National Union of Journalists.

nulla bona (Lat.), no goods (upon which to levy).

nulla regula sine exceptione (Lat.), no rule without an exception.

nullifying.

nulli secundus (Lat.), inferior (or second) to none.

number, abbr. No; *pl.* Nos. Do not abbreviate unless followed by figures.

numbering pages. Pages of a MS. should be numbered in the middle, at the top. The second page of a letter should bear the name of addressee, number, and date. *See also* note under " pagination."

number of house. The practice of following this by a comma is fast dying out.

numerals, roman ; *see* note under " roman numerals."

Nummer (Ger.), number.

Nunc aut nunquam (Lat.), Now or never.

Nunc dimittis (Lat.), the canticle, " Lord, now lettest thou."

nunc est paratus (Lat.), never unprepared.

nunquam (Lat.), never.

nuptiae (Lat.), nuptials, wedding.

N.U.R., National Union of Railwaymen.

N.U.T., National Union of Teachers.

nutshell.

N.U.W.T., National Union of Women Teachers.

nux vomica, abbr. nux vom., a drug containing strychnine.

NW., compass point.

N.W., north-western postal district.

N.Y., New York state.

N.Z., New Zealand.

N.Z.A.F., New Zealand Air Force.

O

O, oxygen.

O', Irish name prefix. Use capital, with apostrophe, and follow on without space.

o', abbr. for of, used in poetry and in colloquial speech.

O and Oh! The practice is not fixed, but the general tendency is to use O for the vocative case, that is, when some person or thing is being addressed, and Oh in other constructions. Examples: "Oh! why was that?" "Oh no! I am sure it is false." "O Hamlet, what a falling-off was there!"

o/a, on account of.

oak-apple, hyphen for this and similar words.

oarsman.

oasis, *pl.* oases.

oatmeal.

obbligato (It.), part of a composition, or an accompaniment.

O.B.E., Order of the British Empire. The five classes of the order are:

MEN:
1. Knight Grand Cross, G.B.E.
2. Knight Commander, K.B.E.
3. Commander, C.B.E.
4. Officer, O.B.E.
5. Member, M.B.E.

WOMEN:
1. Dame Grand Cross, G.B.E.
2. Dame Commander, D.B.E.
3. Commander, C.B.E.
4. Officer, O.B.E.
5. Member, M.B.E.

obeisance.

Oberammergau, village in Bavaria famous for its Passion Play. Sometimes *Ober-Ammergau*.

obiit sine prole (Lat.), he, or she, died without issue.

obiter dicta (Lat.), things said by the way. (*dictum* = a saying.)

obituary, notice or account of death.

obligatory.

oblige, an outworn commercialism to be avoided.

oblivious *of*.

obloquy.

oboe, wind instrument; originally hautbois. The player is an oboist.

obscurantism, opposition to inquiry and reform.

obsequies, funeral rites. Not used in the singular.

obsequious, servile.

observanda (Lat.), things to be observed.

observon. (legal), observation.

obsession.

obsolescent, becoming obsolete, or out-of-date.

obstetrics, branch of medicine dealing with midwifery.

obstreperous.

obtd. (legal), obtained.

obverse, the side of a coin that bears the head or principal design.

O.C., Officer Commanding.

o'c., abbr. for o'clock. May be used in rough notes or drafts.

o/c, overcharge.

Occident, the West; western Europe. No capital for occidental.

occupon. (legal), occupation.

occurrence.

o'clock, type close up; abbr. (to be used sparingly) o'c.

Oct., October. Do not abbreviate in correspondence.

octavo note-paper measures 8 by 5 in. (properly called note-paper); abbr. 8vo

October, abbr. Oct..

octobre (Fr.), October. Upper- or lower-case initial may be used in French; abbr. 8bre.

octogenarian, a person 80 years old.

octopus, *pl.* octopuses.

O/D, on demand, overdraft.

odoriferous.

odor lucri (Lat.), the expectation of reward.

O.E., Old English.

œ, *see* note under " ligature."

œcumenical, representing the whole Christian world or universal Church.

O.E.D., the Oxford English Dictionary.

œil (Fr.), eye; *pl. yeux.*

œil-de-bœuf (Fr.), round or oval window; *pl. œils-de-bœuf.*

'er, over.

œsophagus, the gullet.

œuf (Fr.), egg.

œufs à l'indienne (Fr.), curried eggs.

œufs de Paques (Fr.), Easter eggs.

œuvre (Fr.), work, performance.

O.F., Old French.

offhandedness.

off-licence.

offscourings.

offshoot.

offside, football term.

oft-told, hyphen in this and similar words.

O.G.P.U., United State Political Administration (U.S.S.R.).

ogre, *fem.* ogress.

Oh, *see* note under " O."

ohm, unit of electrical resistance (from name of German physicist, G. S. Ohm).

O.H.M.S., On His Majesty's Service.

oho! interjection of surprise, etc.

O.I., *Officier de l'Instruction publique.*

oie (Fr.), goose.

oignon (Fr.), onion.

oil. Use the best typewriter oil. Apply one drop (by means of the needle-top usually supplied) ; too much will clog the machine. Consult mechanic as to the parts of *your* machine that should be oiled.

oilcloth.

oil-colour.

oil-painting.

oilskin.

O.K., all correct (slang term used mostly in commerce).

old. Note use of hyphens in : the four-year-olds, a ten-year-old boy, an old-world play, an old-clothes shop.

olden, archaic and literary. Old-time has replaced it.

old-fashioned.

Old Saxon, abbr. O.S.

old style, abbr. O.S.

old-womanish.

oleaginous, fatty, producing oil.

olfactory, concerned with smelling.

olive-oil.

olympiad, period of four years between the holding of the Olympic games.

O.M., Order of Merit.

Omar Khayyám, Persian poet.

omelet, more popular than the French *omelette.*

omen faustum (Lat.), favourable omen.

omissions in quoted sentences. Use three full stops

at beginning or in middle of sentence, and four at the end.

omitted.

omni-, all.

omnia (Lat.), all things.

Omnia ad Dei gloriam (Lat.), All things to the glory of God.

Omnia bona bonis (Lat.), All things are good to the good.

Omnia vincit amor (Lat.), Love conquers all things.

Omnia vincit labor (Lat.), Labour conquers all.

omnibus, *pl.* omnibuses. Bus is now a recognized word, and does not need to be preceded by an apostrophe.

Omnibus hoc vitium est (Lat.), This fault is (common) to all.

omnis Minervae homo (Lat.), " a Jack of all trades."

omniscience, infinite wisdom.

on account of, abbr. o/a.

one-and-twenty.

one-eyed.

oneness.

onerous, comprising a burden.

oneself.

one-sided.

only. Place this near to the word or phrase it qualifies, if in so doing you will not destroy the beauty of the sentence. Note that more precision is needed in writing than in speaking, when intonation can make the meaning clear. Consider " This child seems to act strangely only when in the company of others," and " This child only seems . . ." and " Only this child seems . . ."

onomatopoeic words, those formed from sounds associated with the object or action named.

onrush.

onset.

onside, football term.

onto, avoid this and use on or on to.

onus, responsibility. No plural.

onus probandi (Lat.), the burden of proof.

%, per cent.

% o, per thousand.

o.p., overproof, out of print.

op., opus (Lat.), work.

op. cit., *opere citato* (Lat.), in the work (or volume) quoted.

open-minded.

openness.

open-work.

opéra bouffe (Fr.), comic opera.

opere citato (Lat.), in the work (or volume) quoted; abbr. *op. cit.*

ophthalmic, pertaining to the eye.

opportunism, allowing circumstances of the moment to determine one's policy.

oppressor.

opprobrium, disgrace consequent upon some act or conduct.

optimates (Lat.), of the first rank, the chief men.

opus (Lat.), work; abbr. *op.*

opusculum (Lat.), a small work, an essay.

opus magnum (Lat.), a writer's or other artist's most important work. More usually *magnum opus.*

opus operatum (Lat.), a thing done.

O.R., Official Receiver; owner's risk.

or. (legal), other.

or. Use comma before this word in such phrases as " clerks, book-keepers, or typists."

-or. This is the Latin ending for many words representing agents or doers. The English termination -*er*, however, occurs in by far the larger number. The pronunciation helps little in deciding which spelling to use! When -*er* and -*or* coexist, -*or* has sometimes a more legal sense. Note also how in law the -*or* is changed to -*ee* to indicate the recipient of an action as opposed to the doer, e.g. lessor, lessee.

ora et labora (Lat.), worship and work.

orangeade.

ora pro nobis (Lat.), pray for us; abbr. O.P.N.

ordinal numbers, first, second, third, etc. The cardinal numbers are one, two, three, etc. Note that 1st, 2nd, etc., are not followed by full stop, as they are not strictly abbreviations.

Ordnance Survey, abbr. O.S.

ordre du jour (Fr.), agenda for a Meeting.

öre, coin used in Denmark, Norway, and Sweden.

ore rotundo (Lat.), with full utterance; imposing speech.

ore tenus (Lat.), with the mouth only.

organdie, a muslin. Fr. *organdi.*

organize.

orgy, *pl.* orgies.

orné (Fr.), decorated; *fem. ornée.*

orthochromatic, sensitive to yellow and green, as applied to photographic plate or film. Sometimes called iso-chromatic.

orthopaedic, related to the curing of deformities. (Gk. *orthos*, straight.)

O.S., Old Saxon, old style, Ordnance Survey, out-size.

o/s, out of stock, outstanding.

os (Lat.), a bone; *pl. ossa*.

O.S.B., Order of St. Benedict.

oscillate, to sway; oscillating current, an electric current which alternately reverses its direction in a circuit in a periodic manner.

O.S.F., Order of St. Francis.

O si sic omnia (Lat.), O that he had always done (or said) this!

Oslo, capital of Norway, formerly Christiania.

os rotundum (Lat.), eloquent delivery.

Ost (Ger.), east.

osteopathy, a system of drugless healing based on the theory that structural derangements are the chief cause of disease.

osteria (It.), an inn.

Osterreich, German for Austria.

ostler, a groom.

ostracized.

O.T., Old Testament.

O.T.C., Officers' Training Corps.

O tempora! O mores! (Lat.), O the times! O the manners! (How they have changed!)

other, abbr. or. (legal).

Otia dant vitia (Lat.), Leisure breeds vice.

Ottoman, a Turk; *pl.* Ottomans.

ottoman, a sofa; *pl.* ottomans.

O.U.A.C., Oxford University Athletic Club.

O.U.B.C., Oxford University Boat Club.

O.U.C.C., Oxford University Cricket Club.

O.U.D.S., Oxford University Dramatic Society.

ouest (Fr.), west.

O.U.G.C., Oxford University Golf Club.

ought, should. *See* notes under "naught" and "aught."

O.U.H.C., Oxford University Hockey Club.

oui-dire (Fr.), hearsay.

O.U.L.C., Oxford University Lacrosse Club.

O.U.L.T.C., Oxford University Lawn Tennis Club.

ounce, ounces, abbr. oz. The *z* is an abbreviation com-ing from the Italian forms of the fifteenth century, *onza, onze.*

O.U.S.C., Oxford University Swimming Club.

out-and-out.

outcome.

out-distance.

outdo.

outdoor, note out-of-door.

outgrowth.

out-herod Herod (to).

out of, abbr. ex.

out-of-date. Use hyphens only when adjective.

out of print, abbr. o.p.

out of stock, abbr. o/s.

out-patient.

outré (Fr.), exaggerated, outraging decorum.

outrival.

out-size, abbr. O.S.

outspread.

outstanding, abbr. o/s.

outward-bound.

ouvrier (Fr.), a workman; *fem. ouvrière.*

overboard.

overdo.

over-estimate.

overhead.

overlay (*verb*), to cover a surface with a coating; (*noun*) a coverlet.

overmantel.

overmuch.

overnight.

overproof, abbr. o.p.

overreach.

overrun (printers' term), to move words in printed matter from one line to the next.

overseas (*adj.*), more popular than oversea.

overseer.

Overstone, Northampton.

Overton, Hants, Lancaster, Shropshire, Warrington, Wilts

overwrought.

O.W., Office of Works.

Owen. *See* Appendix II for pronunciation.

Oxfordshire, abbr. Oxon (no point).

oxidation, the popular spelling, although *oxidization* is more accurate.

Oxon, Oxfordshire; also abbr. of Oxoniensis (of Oxford).

Oxonia (Lat.), Oxford.

oxygenator, apparatus for generating oxygen.

oyez! *pron.* ō-yez. The town crier's call for attention.

oz., ounce, or ounces. *See* note under " ounce."

P

p., page, particle, past, pole, *per* (by), *pro* (for).

p (It.), *piano*, softly.

P/A, Power of Attorney.

Pa., Pennsylvania.

p.a., per annum, yearly.

pace (Lat.), by leave of, with the consent of.

pacifism, usual, but *pacificism* more correct.

pacta conventa (Lat.), stipulations as agreed upon.

pactum (Lat.), an agreement, a pact.

pactum illicitum (Lat.), unlawful compact.

padlock.

padre, It., Port., and Sp. for father or priest. Military slang for chaplain.

paean, song of praise or triumph.

page. This is the matter printed on one side of a leaf; thus a leaf consists of two pages; abbr. p.; *pl.* pp.

Paget. *See* Appendix II for pronunciation.

pagination. Numbering of pages in the middle, at the top, is preferred by the printer. Do not number the first page of a chapter, but allow for it, and number throughout the MS., not each chapter separately. If a page is extracted, say, 55, mark the previous one 54/5. If an extra page is inserted, mark it 55A, and put at foot of 55, " 55A follows." In quoting pages, use the shortest form, e.g. 241–2, not 241–42.

paid, abbr. pd.

pain (Fr.), bread.

pair, abbr. pr.

palais (Fr.), palace.

palazzo (It.), a palace; *pl. palazzi.*

Palgrave. *See* Appendix II for pronunciation.

palliasse, a straw mattress. Fr. *paillasse* (from *paille* = straw), and sometimes so spelt in English.

Palmer. *See* Appendix II for pronunciation.

pan., panoramic (film scenario term); sometimes *pam.* to avoid confusion with *pan.* for panchromatic.

pan-, panto-, all.

panais (Fr.), parsnip.

panchromatic, fully colour-sensitive, as applied to photographic plates and films; abbr. pan.

pandemonium.

P. & O., Peninsular and Oriental Steam Navigation Company.

panegyrize, to write or speak in praise of.

panel, panelled.

panel envelopes, *see* note under " window envelopes."

pannikin, small drinking vessel.

panoramic, abbr. pan. *See* note under " pan."

pantechnicon.

paper, folding of, *see* note under " folding."

paper, right side of. The smoother surface is the right. If there is a watermark, the correct reading of this will indicate the right side.

paper sizes. The sizes of paper used by most typists are:—

Octavo, 8 × 5 in.
Half foolscap, 8 × 6½ in.
Quarto, 10 × 8 in.
Foolscap, 13 × 8 in.
Draft, 16 × 10½ in.
Brief, 16 × 13 in.

Papier (Ger.), paper.

papier (Fr.), paper.

papier-mâché, japanned pulp.

papyrus, *pl.* papyri.

par (of exchange), no point. When a £1 share is quoted at 20s., or £100 of stock may be bought for £100, it is said to be at par.

par., paragraph, parallel, parenthesis, parish.

par (Fr.), by, in, out of, through.

para., paragraph.

par accord (Fr.), by agreement.

parachute.

paradigm, example, pattern, especially of inflexion of noun, verb, etc.

paraffin.

paragraph, abbr. par., para., ¶.

paragraphing. Division into paragraphs should, if possible, be indicated in the notebook while the dictation is proceeding. Every fresh idea or logical change of thought needs a new paragraph, and well-written matter should be studied if the typist is weak in this important subject. It is well to avoid beginning a new page with the final line of a paragraph.

parakeet, small parrot.

parallel, abbr. par.

paralleled.

paralyse.

par amitié (Fr.), because of friendship.

paraphernalia, belongings, accessories, etc. The word is plural.

par avance (Fr.), in advance.

Parbleu! (Fr.), exclamation equivalent to our "By Jove!"

parcel, abbr. pcl. (legal).

parcelling.

parcel post, abbr. P.P.

parcht. (legal), parchment.

parentheses, the technical name for the curved signs commonly called brackets. The printer's bracket is a square sign (*see* note under "brackets, square"). Note the definite use of the parentheses (for references, interpolations, etc.), and also the increasing tendency to use dashes to enclose a parenthetical clause.

parenthesis, abbr. par.; *pl.* parentheses.

parenthetically, interposed.

par excellence (Fr.), by reason of special excellence.

par exemple (Fr.), for example.

par exprès (Fr.), by express.

par hasard (Fr.), by hazard.

pari passu (Lat.). in the same degree.

parish, abbr. par.

Parisian, of Paris, applied to people or articles.

Parisienne (Fr.), a woman of Paris.

park, abbr. pk.

parlars. (legal), particulars.

Parmesan, cheese made at Parma (Italy) and elsewhere.

parole, watchword (military) ; word of honour of prisoner that he will not escape.

parole (Fr.), word, promise.

paroxysm, a fit.

parquet, wooden flooring; also parquetry. Fr. *parquetterie*.

pars pro toto (Lat.), part for the whole.

part, abbr. pt.

parterre, part of garden laid with flower-beds, part of theatre behind orchestra.

particeps criminis (Lat.), a sharer in crime, whether as principal or accessary.

participator.

participle, abbr. p.

parti-coloured.

particularize.

particulars, abbr. parlars. (legal).

particulier (Fr.), a private individual.

partie (Fr.), part.

partim (Lat.), in part.

partisanship.

partout (Fr.), everywhere.

parts of machine. Secure from the typewriter company a booklet describing your machine, so that you can name the parts correctly when telephoning for a mechanic.

par voie télégraphique (Fr.), by telegraph; abbr. *p.v.t.*

pas de deux (Fr.), dance for two. (Pas = step.)

Pasha (civil). *See* Appendix I for correct form of address.

Pasha (military, Egyptian Army). *See* Appendix I for correct form of address.

P.A.S.I., Professional Associate Member of the Chartered Surveyors' Institution.

passé (Fr.), behind the times, faded, past the prime.

passe-partout, a master-key (literally, pass everywhere); also method of framing small pictures.

passers-by.

pas seul (Fr.), dance for one. (*Pas* = step; *seul* = alone.)

passim (Lat.), everywhere, here and there, throughout.

password.

past (*adj.*), abbr. p. Use *passed* for past tense of the verb.

Pasteurism, method of inoculation practised by French scientist, Pasteur.

pasteurize, to sterilize by heating. Initial capital no longer needed.

pâle (Fr.), paste.

pâté (Fr.), a pie.

pâté de fois gras (Fr.), pie, etc., of fatted goose liver.

pâte feuilletée (Fr.), puff paste.

pâte frisée (Fr.), short paste.

Pater (Lat.), Father; abbr. *P.*

paterfamilias (Lat.), the father of a family; *pl. patresfamilias.*

paternoster, the Lord's Prayer (literally Our Father).

pater patriae (Lat.), the father of his country.

pâtisserie (Fr.), pastry.

pâtissier (Fr.), pastry-cook; *fem. pâtissière.*

patois, the dialect of the common people of a district, not the written language.

Paton. *See* Appendix II for pronunciation.

patres conscripti (Lat.), the conscript fathers, the Roman Senate.

patronize.

patronymic, name derived from father or ancestor.

paucis verbis (Lat.), in few words.

pavé (Fr.), pavement.

pawnbroker.

pax Dei (Lat.), peace of God.

pax orbis terrarum (Lat.), the peace of the world.

pax regis (Lat.), peace of the King.

pax vobiscum (Lat.), peace be with you.

Paymaster-General, abbr. P.M.G.

payment, abbr. pt.

P.C., Parish Council, police constable, Privy Council, Privy Councillor.

p/c, petty cash, prices current.

p.c., post card.

pchsr. (legal), purchaser.

pcl. (legal), parcel.

P.D. or p.d., potential difference.

pd., paid.

P.D.A.D., Probate, Divorce, and Admiralty Division.

peaceable.

peacemaker.

pease-pudding.

peccadillo, trifling offence; *pl.* peccadilloes.

peccavi (Lat.), I have sinned.

pêche (Fr.), fishing, peach.

péché (Fr.), a sin.

peck, abbr. pk.

pecny. (legal), pecuniary.

pedalling.

pekinese (dog).

Peking.

pêle-mêle (Fr.), pell-mell, recklessly.

Pellew. *See* Appendix II for pronunciation.

P.E.N. Club. Founded 1921. The initials stand for Poets and Playwrights; Essayists and Editors; Novelists.

penalize.

penchant, a liking.

pendant. This is a *noun*, meaning a hanging ornament. Pendent is an *adjective*, meaning hanging. Pennant (*noun*) is in nautical use, meaning certain flags and pieces of rigging. Pennon (*noun*) is used in heraldry and in military connections for a pointed streamer and the like.

pendente lite (Lat.), pending or during the suit.

pendule (Fr.), *masc.* pendulum; *fem.* clock.

pendulum, *pl.* pendulums.

penes me (Lat.), in my possession or power.

penetralia (Lat.), secret recesses, the inmost recesses, sanctuary.

pengö, unit of currency of Hungary.

pen-name.

Pennan, Banff.

Pennant, Cardiganshire.

penniless.

Pennsylvania, abbr. Pa.

pennyroyal, a herb.

pennyweight, 24 grains; abbr. dwt. (*sing.* and *pl.*).

pensée (Fr.), thought.

pension (Fr.), boarding-house.

pensionnat (Fr.), boarding-school.

penta-, five.

Pentateuch, first five books of the Old Testament.

per, abbr. p.

per accidens (Lat.), by accident.

per ambages (Lat.), by roundabout expressions.

per angusta ad augusta (Lat.), through straightness to greatness.

per annum, abbr. p.a.

per ardua ad astra (Lat.), through difficulties to the stars.

per capita (Lat.), by the number of individuals (heads).

perceivable.

per cent Do not use a full stop after this. If the abbreviated form is required, it can be made by typing small *o*, shilling sign, and another *o* at slightly lower level. Do not mix signs and words; say 20% p.a., or twenty per cent per annum.

percentage.

percentile.

perceptible.

percolator, that which filters.

per consequens (Lat.), consequently.

per contra (Lat.), on the other hand; on the other side.

per curiam (Lat.), by the court.

per diem (Lat.), by the day.

perdu (Fr.), lost; *fem. perdue.*

père (Fr.), father.

perfce. (legal), performance.

per gradus (Lat.), by steps.

peri-, round.

periculum in mora (Lat.), there is danger in delay.

per interim (Lat.), in the meantime.

period, *see* note under " full stop."

per mensem (Lat.), by the month.

permissible.

per pro., or *p.p.*, is short for *per procurationem*, meaning by the agency of. The proxy's signature should therefore follow immediately after the *p.p.*

per se (Lat.), by himself, herself, itself, or themselves.

Persia (Iran). Unit of currency 1 rial = 100 denar.

persian morocco (no capital).

persil (Fr.), parsley.

persistence.

persl. (legal), personal.

persona grata (Lat.), a person in favour, a welcome guest.

persona ingrata (Lat.), a person who is not acceptable.

Personal. When typing *Personal* on an envelope, always place in the bottom left-hand corner, otherwise it will probably be obliterated by the Post Office stamp. Sometimes written on the back of the envelope, across the flap, so that it is impossible to open the envelope without seeing it.

personal, abbr. persl. (legal).

personality, distinctive personal character.

personalty, personal estate, except land and property thereon.

personnel, staff or body of persons.

per stirpes (Lat.), by families, or as a family.

per totam curiam (Lat.), unanimously.

per viam (Lat.), by way of.

pes (Lat.), a foot ; *pl. pedes.*

peseta, unit of currency of Spain.

peso, unit of currency in most S. American republics.

pessimi exempli (Lat.), of very bad example.

petalled.

Petersham, Surrey.

petersham, thick ribbed ribbon.

petit (Fr.), small ; *fem. petite.*

petite vitesse (Fr.), goods train ; abbr. *P.V.*

petitio principii (Lat.), a begging of the question.

Petrie. *See* Appendix II for pronunciation.

petrify, to change into stone, to stupefy with fear. Do not confuse with putrefy.

pettifogging, quibbling, wrangling (from pettifogger =
an inferior lawyer).

petty officer, abbr. P.O.

peu à peu (Fr.), little by little.

peut-être (Fr.), perhaps.

Pf., pfennig, small German copper coin; *pl. pfennige.*

Pfund (Ger.), pound, pounds.

phalanx, body of men, bone of toe or finger; *pl.*
phalanges.

phantasm, illusion, phantom. Note spelling of fantasy.

phantasmagoria, shifting scene of real or imaginary
figures. (The word is singular.)

Pharaoh.

pharisaical, self-righteous, hypocritical.

pharmaceutical, of the use or sale of drugs.

pharmacopoeia, book containing list of drugs, stock of
drugs.

pharynx, cavity communicating with nose, mouth, and
larynx.

Ph.B., *Philosophiae Baccalaureus* (Lat.), Bachelor of
Philosophy.

Ph.D., *Philosophiae Doctor* (Lat.), Doctor of Philosophy.

phenomenon, *pl.* phenomena.

philatelist, stamp collector.

Philip. This is the spelling of Christian name, but the
surname may be Phillip, Phillips, Philipps, etc.

philippic, a violent political speech (from the speech of
Demosthenes against Philip, King of Macedon).

philo-, love, loving.

philosophers' stone, substance said to change other
metals into gold.

philosophize.

phlebitis, inflammation of the veins.

phlegmatically, coldly, apathetically.

phosphorescence, luminosity.

phosphuretted.

photoelectric.

photographe (Fr.), photographer.

photographie (Fr.), photograph, photography.

photogravure, picture produced from photograph etched
into a metal plate or cylinder.

photolithography, a photographic method of reproducing
illustrations.

phrenology, study of the formation of head as index to
mental qualities.

phthisis, consumption.

physicist, student of physics or natural science.
physicking.
physiognomy (silent *g*).
physique, physical structure.
physique (Fr.), physics.
pianissimo (It.), very softly; abbr. *pp* (no point).
pianississimo (It.), as softly as possible; abbr. *ppp* (no point).
piano (It.), softly; abbr. *p* (no point).
piastre, Spanish silver coin, small Turkish coin.
piazza, public square, especially in Italian town.
pibroch, form of music played on bagpipe.
pica, standard of measurement for printers' type, one-sixth of an inch. On a typewriter, the size that gives ten characters to the inch.
Piccadilly.
piccalilli.
piccaninny, Negro baby.
piccolo, small flute.
picketing.
pick-me-up, stimulant.
pickpocket.
picnic, picnicking.
pictures. When quoting titles, enclose in quote marks.
pidgin-English, jargon used between Chinese and Europeans (from pidgin = business).
pièce (Fr.), piece, trick, head (of cattle), etc.
pièce de résistance (Fr.), most substantial dish of a meal. Often used figuratively.
piecemeal.
pied (Fr.), foot.
pied-à-terre (Fr.), temporary lodging; *pl. pieds-à-terre*.
pierre (Fr.), stone; (fig.) steel, rock.
pigeon-holed.
pigskin.
pigsties.
Pilgrims' Way.
pincers. There is no singular. Avoid using *pinchers*.
pint, abbr. pt.
pinxit (Lat.), he or she painted it; abbr. *pinx*.
pipefuls.
piquant, appetizing, stimulating.
piqué (Fr.), thick ribbed cotton material.
pit-a-pat.
più (It.), more.

pius (Lat.), holy; abbr. *p.*

pk., park, peck.

P/L, Profit and Loss.

pl., plural, place, plate.

P.L.A., Port of London Authority.

plagiarize, to use another person's writings as one's own.

plane sailing is the correct nautical term, but *plain* is commonly used and with some justification.

plaster of paris.

plateau, *pl.* plateaux.

platen, the printing roller of the typewriter.

platinum, abbr. Pt (no point).

plausible.

playgoer.

playhouse.

plays. Type in single spacing, on quarto paper, and underscore (or type in red) all parts not spoken. Names of characters at left-hand margin, in caps. Single parts are typed on octavo, with cover. Cues must be long enough to contain a helpful or distinctive word, and must be preceded by several full stops.

playwright.

plaza (Sp.), a public square, place, market.

pleb, person of the lower classes (Lat. *plebs* = the populace).

plebeian, common. This is one of the exceptions to the spelling rule "*i* precedes *e* except after *c.*"

plebiscite, direct vote of electors on important public question.

plebiscitum (Lat.), a decree of the populace.

plein air (Fr.), open air.

pleno jure (Lat.), with full power.

pleonasm is the using of more words than are necessary.

plie (Fr.), plaice.

Pliny. *See* Appendix II for pronunciation.

plumb, a leaden weight, perpendicular.

Plumptree. *See* Appendix II for pronunciation.

pluralizing figures. The plurals of foot, hour, ton, etc., should not be used until two is reached. Type 1½ mile, 1¼ minute. *See also* note under "apostrophe."

plurals. Words ending in *o*, preceded by consonant, usually take *es.* (Examples: cargoes, mosquitoes.)

plurals of abbreviations. Note that the following abbreviations do not change for the plural: c., ck., cm., cwt., dwt., gr., grm., in., ft., lb., mm., min., oz., pt., qt. (or Q.).

plus. This sign cannot be made satisfactorily on the typewriter, and it is best inserted afterwards in ink. It can be fitted on the typewriter (in place of a less-used sign) if desired.

plus tôt (Fr.), sooner.

plutôt (Fr.), rather.

P.M., Paymaster, post-mortem.

p.m., *post meridiem* (Lat.), afternoon. Use this abbreviation only when a figure precedes it.

P.M.G., Paymaster-General, Postmaster-General.

P.M.O., Principal Medical Officer.

p.n., promissory note.

pneumatic, acting by means of air.

P.O., Postal Order, Post Office, petty officer.

P.O.D., Pay on delivery, Post Office Department.

poetry. Type in single spacing, with double or treble between verses. Each line begins with capital. The verses as a whole should balance. Alternate rhyming lines should be indented, and all lines that rhyme generally commence at same degree of scale. Blank verse has no indentation. If quoting poetry, place quotes at beginning of first verse and end of last. Type name of author at end, preceded by a dash. (In typing MS. it will probably be found that each author has his own style, which should be ascertained.)

Point, abbr. Pt.

point-blank.

pois (Fr.), peas. *Petits pois* = green peas.

poisson (Fr.), fish.

poivre (Fr.), pepper.

Poland. Unit of currency 1 zloty = 100 groszy.

pole, abbr. p.

police-constable, abbr. P.C.

policyholder.

politesse (Fr.), politeness.

politic, expedient.

political, having relation to politics or government.

poly-, many.

polyanthus, *pl.* polyanthuses.

pommes (Fr.), apples.

pommes de terre (Fr.), potatoes.

pondere non numero (Lat.), by weight, not by count.

pons asinorum (Lat.), bridge of asses (5th proposition of 1st book of Euclid; hence anything difficult to beginners).

Ponsonby. *See* Appendix II for pronunciation.

Pontefract. *See* Appendix II for pronunciation.
pontifex (Lat.), a bishop; *pl. pontifices.*
P.O.O., Post Office Order.
poor-rate.
P.O.P., printing-out paper.
popularize.
populus (Lat.), people.
porc (Fr.), pork, pig.
Port, abbr. Pt.
porte-monnaie (Fr.), purse or pocket-book. Same in plural.
portière (Fr.), door curtain, etc.
portmanteau, *pl.* portmanteaux.
portray.
Portugal. Unit of currency 1 escudo.
P.O.S.B., Post Office Savings Bank.
poseur (Fr.), affected person; *fem. poseuse.*
posn. (legal), position.
possessive case, *see* note under " apostrophe."
posson. (legal), possession.
Possunt quia posse videntur (Lat.), They can, because they think they can.
post-, after.
post card.
post-date, to place on a document a later date than the actual one.
postea (Lat.), afterwards.
poste restante, department in post office where letters are kept till called for. See *Post Office Guide* for the regulations regarding this facility.
posthumous, occurring after death.
Postmaster-General, abbr. P.M.G.
postmistress.
post mortem (Lat.), after death; abbr. P.M.
Post nubilia, jubilia (Lat.), After sadness, gladness.
post obit (Lat.), a bond payable after death.
post obitum (Lat.), after death.
post office, abbr. P.O.
post paid, abbr. P.P.
postscript, not necessarily an afterthought; sometimes added to a letter to give emphasis to a particular point. Abbreviation P.S. (*postscriptum*), sometimes, and more logically, written PS. Plural PSS.
postulata (Lat.), things required.
potage (Fr.), soup.
potato, *pl.* potatoes.

pot-au-feu (Fr.), beef broth.

pot-pourri, a medley. (Actually dried petals kept for their perfume.) *Pron.* pō-poor-ē.

pouding (Fr.), pudding.

poudre (Fr.), powder, gunpowder.

poule (Fr.), hen.

poulet (Fr.), chicken.

Poulett. *See* Appendix II for pronunciation.

pound, abbr. lb. Sign for money = £ (no point). No *s* for plural in either case.

pour (Fr.), for.

pourparler (Fr.), conference, preliminary parley.

Powys. *See* Appendix II for pronunciation.

pp., pages.

P.P., parcel post, post paid.

p.p., per pro.

pp (It.), *pianissimo*, very softly, or *più piano*, softer.

p.p.i., policy proof of interest.

ppp (It.), *pianississimo*, as softly as possible.

PPS., a second postscript.

ppse. (legal), purpose.

P.P.U., Peace Pledge Union.

P.R., Proportional Representation.

pr., pair, pairs.

P.R.A., President of the Royal Academy.

practical, concerned with practice. Practicable = feasible, able to be carried out. Note the negatives unpractical and impracticable.

practice (noun).

practise (verb).

praecognita (Lat.), things previously known.

praemonitus, praemunitus (Lat.), forewarned, fore-armed.

Praha, national name for Prague.

pre-, before.

preces (Lat.), prayers.

pre-Christian.

precipitate, headlong.

precipitous, steep.

précis-writing, writing of summaries or extracts.

predilection, partiality.

pre-eminent. In this and other cases, where the main word begins with *e*, the prefix must be followed by hyphen.

pre-existence.

preferable *to.*

preferred.

prehistoric.

premes. (legal), premises.

premier (Fr.), first, best; *fem. première.*

premises, abbr. premes. (legal).

preoccupied.

prepay.

Pre-Raphaelite Brotherhood, abbr. P.R.B.

prerogative, an exclusive or peculiar privilege.

prescriptum (Lat.), a thing prescribed.

Press. Use capital when meaning newspapers, etc.

prestige, reputation, influence. (In French the word means glamour.)

presumably.

presuppose.

preventive. Use this form in preference to preventative.

pre-War, pre-war. Use as adjective, not adverb. Consider whether your reader will know to which war you are referring.

P.R.I.B.A., President of the Royal Institute of British Architects.

prima donna (Lat.), principal female singer.

prima facie (Lat.), as far as first appears.

primo (Lat.), in the first place.

primum cognitum (Lat.), the first thing known.

primum mobile (Lat.), the primary motive.

primus (Lat.), first.

Prince. *See* Appendix I for correct form of address.

princeps (Lat.), the first.

Princess. *See* Appendix I for correct form of address.

principal (*adj.*), first in rank or importance; (*noun*) sum of money, ruler, head of college, etc.

principle (*noun*), primary element, source, settled rule, etc.

Prinz (Ger.), prince; *pl.* Prinzen; *fem.* Prinzessin, *pl.* Prinzessinnen.

prise, to force open.

Private. When typing this on an envelope, always place it in the bottom left-hand corner. *See* note under "personal."

Privy Council, abbr. P.C.

Privy Councillor, abbr. P.C. *See* Appendix I for correct form of address

Privy Seal, abbr. P.S.

prix (Fr.), price, prize.

prix courant (Fr.), current price, price list.

pro, abbr. p.

pro-, before, forward, in front of, for, on behalf of, instead of.

Probatum est (Lat.), It has been tried and proved.

pro bono publico (Lat.), for the public good.

procès (Fr.), lawsuit.

procès-verbal (Fr.), official report; *pl. procès-verbaux.*

pro Deo et ecclesia (Lat.), for God and the Church.

prodon. (legal), production.

pro et con (Lat.), for and against.

Prof., Professor.

profanum vulgus (Lat.), the vulgar crowd.

Professor, abbr. Prof.

proffered.

prognosis, doctor's forecast of course of illness.

programme.

pro hac vice (Lat.), for this occasion.

projector.

proletariat, the labouring classes.

pro memoria (Lat.), for a memorial.

promissory note, abbr. p.n.

promotor fidei (Lat.), promoter of the faith.

prononcé (Fr.), prominent, decided; *fem. prononcée.*

pronounceable.

proof correcting, *see* note under "correction marks."

propagandist.

propagate.

pro patria (Lat.), for one's country.

propitiator.

proprietary, belonging to a private owner.

proprietor.

propriety, correctness of behaviour.

pro rata (Lat.), proportionately.

pro salute animae (Lat.), for the good of the soul.

pros and cons, arguments for and against.

proscenium, the space between curtain and orchestra (in ancient times the stage).

prosecon. (legal), prosecution.

proselytize, to convert from one party to another.

prospector.

pro tanto (Lat.), to that extent, for so much.

protégé, *fem.* protégée, person who is protected by another. (Fr. *protéger* = to protect.)

proteins.

pro tem. (Lat.), *pro tempore,* for the time being.

protester.

provable.

proven (not), a verdict (in Scots law) between guilty and not guilty, resulting in acquittal. Otherwise the word is archaic, and *proved* is used.

provisions (legal), abbr. provons.

proviso, a stipulation; abbr. provo. (legal); *pl.* provisos.

provo. (legal), proviso.

provons. (legal), provisions.

prox. (Lat.), *proximo*, next, not recommended for use in correspondence. Safer to mention name of month.

Proxime accessit (Lat.), He, or she, came very near (to winning a prize).

P.R.S., President of the Royal Society.

prudens futuri (Lat.), thoughtful of the future.

prunes (Fr.), plums.

prussian blue.

PS., *postscriptum* (Lat.), postscript. Often written P.S.

P.S., Privy Seal.

Ps., Psalm, Psalms.

p's and q's.

pseudo-, false.

pseudonym, an assumed name.

PSS., postscripts. (Lat. *postscripta*.)

psychiatrist, person treating mental disorders by psychological methods.

psycho-analyst.

psychology, the study of the mind.

Pt, platinum.

Pt., Point, Port.

pt., part, payment, pint, pints.

P.T.O., Please turn over.

ptomaine, a poison that comes from putrefaction.

publice (Lat.), publicly.

Pugh. *See* Appendix II for pronunciation.

pull, a proof.

pullover.

pumice-stone.

punctuation, *see* notes under individual marks.

pupa, *pl.* pupae.

purchasable.

purchaser, abbr. pchsr. (legal).

purée (Fr.), a thick soup, or anything reduced to pulp by cooking.

pur et simple (Fr.), unconditional, unqualified.

purlieus, surroundings.

purpose, abbr. ppse. (legal).

purst. (legal), pursuant.

pusillanimity, faint-heartedness.

putrefy.

Putsch (Ger.), attempted insurrection. Tendency **in** England to use lower-case instead of capital.

putt, golfing term.

P.V., *petite vitesse* (Fr.), goods train.

P.W.D., Public Works Department.

pygmy, a dwarf.

pyorrhoea.

pyrotechnics, display of, or art of making, fireworks. Also used figuratively.

Q

Q., quart, quarts.

q., query, quire, quires.

Q.E.D., *quod erat demonstrandum* (Lat.), which was to be proved or demonstrated.

Q.E.F., *quod erat faciendum* (Lat.), which was to be done.

Q.M., Quartermaster.

Q.M.G., Quartermaster-General.

Q.M.S., Quartermaster-Sergeant.

qr., quarter, quarters, quire, quires.

Q.S., quarter-sessions, Queen's Scholar.

qt. quart, quarts.

qua (Lat.), in the character of.

quad, quadrangle; quadrat, small metal block used by printers for spacing.

quadruplicate, to multiply by four; to make fourfold.

quaere (Lat.), enquire.

quaeritur (Lat.), it is asked; the question arises.

quaestio vexata (Lat.), an unsolved problem.

quam primum (Lat.), without delay.

quand même (Fr.), notwithstanding.

quantum, quantity, share.

quantum libet or *placet* (Lat.), as much as is desired (in prescriptions); abbr. *q.l., q.p.*

quantum meruit (Lat.), as much as he, or she, earned.

quantum sufficit (Lat.), a sufficient quantity (in prescriptions); abbr. *q.s.*

Quaritch. *See* Appendix II for pronunciation.

quarreller.

quarrelsome.

quart, quarts, abbr. Q. or qt.

quarter, quarters, abbr. qr.

quarter-days: Lady Day, 25th March; Midsummer, 24th June; Michaelmas, 29th September; Christmas, 25th December.

quarter-deck.

Quartermaster, abbr. Q.M.

Quartermaster-General, abbr. Q.M.G.

Quartermaster-Sergeant, abbr. Q.M.S.

quarter-plate (photography), $4\frac{1}{4} \times 3\frac{1}{4}$ in.

quarter-sessions.

quarterstaff, stout pole formerly used by peasants as weapon.

quartet, sometimes spelt *quartette.*

quartier (Ger.), quarter, piece, quarter of a town.

quartier général (Fr.), headquarters (military).

quarto, abbr. 4to (no point). Quarto letter-paper measures 10 × 8 in.

quash, to cancel.

quasi (Lat.), almost as if, in a manner.

quasi dicat (Lat.), as if one should say; abbr. *q.d.*

quasi dictum (Lat.), as if said; abbr. *q.d.*

quatrain, verse of four lines, usually with alternate rhymes.

Queen, The. *See* Appendix I for correct form of address.

Queenborough, Kent.

Queensborough, Louth.

Queensbury, Bradford.

Queen's College, Oxford, London, Belfast, Cork, Galway (apostrophe before *s*).

Queens' College, Cambridge.

Que faire? (Fr.), What is to be done?

quelque chose (Fr.), something.

Quel temps fait-il? (Fr.), What is the weather like?

Que m'importe? (Fr.), What does that matter to me?

quenelle (Fr.), a ball of forcemeat.

querulous.

query, abbr. qy.

question mark, to be used only when the question is a direct one. Not usually followed by any other stop, except the quotes.

questionnaire, a list of questions.

queue, line of persons waiting their turn, pigtail.

queue (Fr.), tail, queue.

quicker, quickest, when these are used as adverbs, they must be placed after the verb.

quicksilver.

quick-witted.

quid (Lat.), something, who, what, why.

quidam (Lat.), a certain person.

Quid faciendum? (Lat.), What is to be done?

quidnunc (Lat.), a gossip (*quid* = what, *nunc* = now).

quid pro quo (Lat.), compensation, something in return.

Quid rides? (Lat.), Why do you laugh?

quiet. This should be used as the verb, with *quieting* as present participle. *Quieten* is unnecessary.

Qui facit consentit (Lat.), Who keeps silence consents.

Qui facit per alium facit per se (Lat.), He who does an act by an agent is himself responsible.

Qui invidet minor est (Lat.), Who envies is inferior.

Qu'importe? (Fr.), What does it matter?

quincentenary, five-hundredth anniversary.

Quincey. *See* Appendix II for pronunciation.

Quinet. *See* Appendix II for pronunciation.

quinquennium, a five-year period ; *pl.* quinquennia.

quinsy, inflammation of the throat.

quintet, preferable to quintette.

quire, 24 sheets of writing paper ; abbr. q. or qr.

Qui s'excuse s'accuse (Fr.), To excuse oneself is to accuse oneself.

quisling. Vidkun Quisling. Norwegian major who took office under the Germans : hence the word has come to mean a traitor.

quisque (Lat.), everyone.

quite, used frequently in conversation, but should be employed sparingly in writing.

qui va là? (Fr.), who goes there ?

qui vive (on the), on the alert.

quod bene notandum (Lat.), which is to be carefully marked.

quod erat demonstrandum (Lat.), which was to be proved or demonstrated ; abbr. Q.E.D.

quod erat faciendum (Lat.), which was to be done ; abbr. Q.E.F.

quod est (Lat.), which is ; abbr. *q.e.*

quod vide (Lat.), which see ; abbr. *q.v.*

quo jure? (Lat.), by what right ? By what law ?

quondam (Lat.), formerly. In English the word means sometime, former, as " a quondam acquaintance of his."

quorum, a fixed number of members of committee, etc., who must be present to make proceedings valid ; *pl.* quorums.

quotation marks. Place these at the beginning of each paragraph, and at the end of final paragraph, but only at the beginning and end of poems. Indent quoted matter and set in single spacing. Use single quotes for the inner quotation and double for the main quoted passage. Quotes are usually placed outside the full stop and comma (even when this is illogical) for the sake of appearance. Quote the names of books, newspapers, plays, poems, ships, pictures, etc., but not the books of the Bible. Quotes are used by the typist to indicate inches and seconds, and as ditto marks.

quotations. Type in single spacing, so that they will stand out from the body of the work.

quotes, *see* under " quotation marks."

Quo vadis? (Lat.), Whither goest thou?

quo warranto? (Lat.), by what warrant or authority?

q.v., *quod vide* (Lat.), which see.

R., railway, right, road, river.

Ṛ, rupee (no point).

R.A., Rear-Admiral, Royal Academician, Royal Artillery.

R.A.A.F., Royal Australian Air Force.

R.A.C., Royal Automobile Club.

race-course.

rack, to stretch or torture. Wrack = seaweed. Wreck = ruin, especially of a ship; this has a collateral form *wrack*, but it survives only in the phrase "wrack and ruin," and even here tends to be spelt rack.

racket, the more popular spelling for all meanings.

raconteur, one skilled in the telling of anecdotes.

radiator.

radiographer, one who carries out X-ray photography and who treats under medical prescription.

radiologist, medical man who diagnoses disease by means of X-ray photographs.

radius, *pl.* radii.

R.A.F., Royal Air Force.

ragout, a rich meat stew. Fr. *ragoût.*

raie (Fr.), skate (fish).

raifort (Fr.), horseradish.

railway, abbr. R. or rail.

railway letters. These are letters conveyed by next available train, either to be called for, or to be posted on arrival. For particulars of this service see *Post Office Guide.*

rainfall.

rain-water.

raison d'être (Fr.), reason for existence.

Raleigh. *See* Appendix II for pronunciation.

rallentando (It.), gradually slower; abbr. *rall* (no point).

Ralph. *See* Appendix II for pronunciation.

R.A.M., Royal Academy of Music.

R.A.M.C., Royal Army Medical Corps.

ramekin, a dish of cheese, breadcrumbs, egg, etc., or the small mould in which the mixture is baked.

R.A.O.C., Royal Army Ordnance Corps.

rapprochement (Fr.), re-establishment of friendly relations, especially between States.

rara avis (Lat.), a rare bird, kind of person or thing rarely seen.

rarebit, *see* note under " welsh rabbit."

rarefy, to lessen the density of (air, etc.) ; to refine (a person's nature).

rarity.

R.A.S.C., Royal Army Service Corps.

rata (Lat.), individual share.

ratafia, biscuit, cherry, liqueur.

rateable.

rate-payer.

Rathaus (Ger.), town hall.

rationalize.

rattlesnake.

Rauchen verboten (Ger.), Smoking forbidden.

ravel.

ravelled.

raze, to destroy.

R.B., Rifle Brigade.

R.B.A., Royal Society of British Artists.

R.C., Red Cross, Roman Catholic.

R.C.A.F., Royal Canadian Air Force.

R.C.M., Royal College of Music.

R.C.O., Royal College of Organists.

R.C.P., Royal College of Physicians.

R.C.S., Royal College of Surgeons.

R.C.V.S., Royal College of Veterinary Surgeons.

R/D, Refer to drawer (banking term).

R.D., Royal Dragoons, Rural Dean ; Royal Naval Reserve Decoration.

Rd., road. As this abbreviation saves only one stroke in typing, it is not recommended.

R.D.C., Rural District Council.

R.D.I., Designer for Industry of the Royal Society of Arts.

R.E., Royal Engineers, Royal Exchange.

re (Lat.), with regard to. Do not use *re* in the body of a letter or article.

react.

readdress.

Reading. *See* Appendix II for pronunciation.

readjustment.

readmission.

ready-made.

reafforestation.

reagent, reactive substance.

realty, real estate property in land (law).

ream, 20 quires, consisting of 480 or 500 sheets; abbr. rm.

re-arrange. Hyphen necessary here to assist the correct reading of the word.

Reay. *See* Appendix II for pronunciation.

receptivity.

recession, withdrawal; *recessional hymn* = that sung while clergy and choir retire after service.

recg. (legal), reciting.

réchauffé, warmed-up dish.

recherche (Fr.), investigation; studied elegance.

recherché (Fr.), choice, far-fetched, sought-after; *fem. recherchée.*

recipe. This means a formula, especially for cooking. *Receipt* in this sense is obsolete, but is used in commerce to mean a written acknowledgment.

reciting, abbr. rect. (legal).

recognizable.

reconnaissance.

re-count, to count again. *Recount* means to relate. Note the distinction made by the hyphen.

re-cover, to cover again. Note the important part played by hyphen in distinguishing this word from *recover* = to regain possession of, get well, etc.

recrudescence, breaking out again.

recurred.

red, headings in. If you have not a bi-chrome ribbon, you can produce headings in red by inserting a piece of red carbon paper between the ribbon and the paper.

rédacteur (Fr.), editor; *fem. rédactrice.*

Redakteur (Ger.), editor.

Reddish, Cheshire.

Redditch, Worcestershire.

redecorate.

redemon. (legal), redemption.

Redhill, Bristol.

Red Hill, Surrey.

Redhills, Cavan.

red-hot.

redress, to remedy.

re-dress, to dress again.

reductio ad absurdum (Lat.), reducing an argument to an absurdity.

reductio ad impossibile (Lat.), an impossible conclusion.

re-dye.

Rees. *See* Appendix II for pronunciation.

re-establish. Hyphen needed in this and other instances where the two successive *e*'s would cause difficulty in reading.

referable.

referee.

referendum, name applied to a clause introduced into the Swiss Constitution in 1874 providing that certain laws should not become effective until ratified by the people generally. The word is often used more loosely; *pl.* referendums, referenda.

referring.

refer to drawer, abbr. R/D (banking term).

reflection, the more popular spelling. Fr. *réflexion.*

re-form. Note the meaning of this as distinct from *reform.* There are other instances where the hyphen makes a vital difference.

regd., registered.

Reg.-Gen., Registrar-General.

régime, a system of administration. This French word shows a tendency to lose its accent as well as its italicizing.

regiment, abbr. regt.

regina (Lat.), queen; abbr. *R.* or *Reg.*

Register Office, where marriages are conducted.

registered, abbr. regd.

registrable.

Registry Office, supplies domestic servants.

regium donum (Lat.), a royal grant.

Regnault. *See* Appendix II for pronunciation.

regnum (Lat.), a kingdom, or a badge of royalty.

Reg. Prof., Regius Professor.

regrettable.

regt., regiment.

regula (Lat.), a book of rules.

regulon. (legal), regulation.

rehabilitating. reinstating.

Reichsmark, German mark; abbr. Rm. (same for plural).

Reichspfennig, hundredth part of German Reichsmark.

reimbursement, refunding.

reinforcement.

relation, better than the somewhat popular *relative* as meaning a connection by blood or marriage.

relativity, a physical theory propounded by Professor Einstein and widely accepted by scientists.

re-letting.

religieuse (Fr.), a nun.

religieux (Fr.), *noun:* a friar. Same for plural. *Adj.* religious.

reliquiae (Lat.), relics.

remainder, abbr. remr. (legal).

remaindering a book, selling off copies at reduced price when demand has ceased.

re-mark, to mark afresh. Note the need for hyphen in this sense.

remerciement, remercîment (Fr.), thanks.

reminiscences.

removable.

remr. (legal), remainder.

rendezvous, meeting-place; same for plural. Fr. *rendez-vous.*

renommé (Fr.), renowned; *fem. renommée.*

renovator.

reorganize.

rep, a ribbed dress fabric.

reparable (accent on first syllable). This is used of abstract things (such as injury, etc.), and *repairable* of material things. The *nouns* are *reparations* and *repairs* respectively.

repartee, smart answer.

repellent.

repertoire, stock of items that a performer is ready to give. Used also to describe a company of players. In this sense the word is more often *repertory*, which also means a place for finding something, or a stock of information.

repertorium (Lat.), a summary, a catalogue.

repetatur (Lat.), let it be repeated.

replaceable.

replica, strictly a copy made by the artist himself, but often used loosely of an exact copy; *pl.* replicas.

repoussé, metal worked in relief.

reprehensible.

representative, abbr. rep.

repressible.

reprisal, retaliation.

reproducible.

République française (Fr.), French Republic.

reqd. (legal), required.

reqt. (legal), request.

reqtd. (legal), requested.

requiem, mass for the dead; *pl.* requiems.

requiescat in pace (Lat.), may he (or she) rest in peace; abbr. R.I.P.

required, abbr. reqd. (legal).

requons. or requns. (legal), requisitions.

reredos, ornamental screen at back of altar; *pl.* reredoses.

res (Lat.), a thing or things.

res communes (Lat.), things common to all.

reservist.

residuum, *pl.* residua.

resistant.

res judicata (Lat.), a thing already decided.

res nihili (Lat.), a nonentity.

resolution, *see* note under "motion."

resolvable.

resonator.

respecter.

respectively. This word has a definite work to do, but is often used when it is not helpful; abbr. resply. (legal).

respirator.

resplendent.

resply. (legal), respectively.

respondent, abbr. respt. (legal).

responsible.

respt. (legal), respondent.

respublica (Lat.), public property, the commonwealth.

res publicae (Lat.), things that belong to the State.

restaurateur (Fr.), restaurant proprietor.

Restauration (Ger.), refreshments.

résumé, a summary.

Resurgam (Lat.), I shall rise again.

resurgent, that which rises again.

resuscitate, to revive.

retd., returned.

R. et I. (Lat.), *Rex et Imperator,* King and Emperor.

retina, *pl.* retinas, retinae.

Retourné pour meilleure adresse (Fr.), Returned for better direction.

retraceable.

retrogression, deterioration.

retroussé (Fr.), turned up; *fem.* *retroussée.*

returned. abbr. retd.

Reuter, British and international news agency, founded by Baron J. de Reuter in 1849. *See* Appendix II for pronunciation.

Rev., Reverend; *pl.* **Revs.**

reveille, morning call (military) ; *pron.* rĕ-văl-ĭ.

Revelations, popular name for " The Revelation of St. John the Divine."

Revenons à nos moutons (Fr.), Let us return to our subject.

Reverend, usual abbr. Rev. Note that Christian name or initial must be used ; if it is not known, say Rev. Mr. Preachwell.

reversible.

reversion (legal), abbr. revon.

revise, a proof that embodies the corrections made in an earlier proof.

revivifying.

revocon. (legal), revocaticn.

revolutionize.

revon. (legal), reversion.

rex (Lat.), king ; abbr. *R.*

Rex regnat, sed non gubernat (Lat.), The king reigns, but does not govern.

rez-de-chaussée (Fr.), ground floor.

R.F.A., Royal Field Artillery.

R.G.A., Royal Garrison Artillery.

R.G.S., Royal Geographical Society.

R.H.A., Royal Horse Artillery.

rhapsodize.

R.H.G., Royal Horse Guards.

rhinoceros, *pl.* rhinoceroses.

rhododendron.

R.H.S., Royal Historical Society, Royal Horticultural Society, Royal Humane Society.

rhyme. Although rime would be the better word to use (Old Fr. *rime*), and would avoid confusion with rhythm, it is not often seen (except, of course, in its other meaning, i.e. to signify hoar-frost). *See* note under " rime."

Rhys. *See* Appendix II for pronunciation.

rhythm, metrical movement determined by the relation of long and short syllables in verse, etc. May be applied also to physical movement. It is essential for expert typewriting, and involves regularity of timing and evenness of depression.

R.I., Royal Institute of Painters in Water-Colours ; Royal Institution,

rial, unit of currency in Persia.

R.I.B.A., Royal Institute of British Architects.

ribbon switch. The ribbon switch is used to change

from one colour to another when using a two-colour ribbon, or to throw the ribbon out of action when preparing to cut a stencil.

rickshaw, abbreviation of *jinricksha,* light two-wheeled vehicle drawn by man, in Eastern countries.

rideable.

rider, clause added to a document.

right, abbr. R. In theatrical instructions almost always means the player's right.

Right Reverend, Bishop's title; abbr. The Right Rev.

rights of way, plural form of right of way.

rigorous.

rigour.

rime, hoar-frost. Writers dealing with literature and verse use this in the meaning of rhyme.

Ringwood, Hants

Ringwould, Kent.

R.I.P., *requiescat in pace* (Lat.), May he (or she) rest in peace.

Ripley, Derby, Surrey, Yorks

ris de veau (Fr.), sweetbread.

Riseley, Bedford, Berks

Risley, Derby, Lancs

risqué (Fr.), risky, offending against propriety; *fem. risquée.*

rissole (Eng. and Fr.), mince-meat fritter.

rissolé (Fr.), browned.

ritardando (It.), slower; abbr. *rit.* or *ritard.*

riverside.

riveted.

riz (Fr.), rice.

R.L.S., Returned Letter Section (formerly D.L.O., Dead Letter Office).

R.M., Resident Magistrate, Royal Mail, Royal Marines.

Rm., Reichsmark, German mark. Abbreviation same for plural.

rm., ream.

R.M.A., Radio Manufacturers' Association, Royal Marine Artillery, Royal Military Academy, Royal Military Asylum.

R.M.C., Royal Military College.

R.Met.S., Royal Meteorological Society.

R.M.S., Royal Mail Service, Royal Mail Steamer, Royal Microscopical Society.

R.M.S.P., Royal Mail Steam Packet Company.

R.N., Royal Navy.

R.N.A.V., Royal Naval Artillery Volunteers.

R.N.R., Royal Naval Reserve.

R.N.V.R., Royal Naval Volunteer Reserve.

R.O., Receiving Office, Relieving Officer, Royal Observatory.

Road. Do not abbreviate in ordinary circumstances, as only one stroke is saved.

road-hog, motorist or cyclist who disregards the safety of others.

roadway.

robe de cour (Fr.), court dress.

Roch, Pembrokeshire.

Roche, Cornwall.

rococo, over-decorative style of furniture and architecture, as practised in France in early eighteenth century.

Roget. *See* Appendix II for pronunciation.

rognons (Fr.), kidneys.

role, actor's part. Now anglicized. The French word is *rôle*.

roman numerals. Use ordinary capitals, no full stop. They are used for books of the Bible, inscriptions, chapter headings, names of monarchs, etc. (Say Henry V or Henry the Fifth, not Henry the Vth.) Note:

$$X = 10$$
$$L = 50$$
$$C = 100$$
$$D = 500$$
$$M = 1000$$

Lesser numbers prefixed to greater are deducted therefrom, e.g. IX, nine. A line drawn over a Roman number increases its value a thousandfold, e.g. $\overline{M} = 1,000,000$. Use small roman numerals for sub-sections, introductory pages of books, etc.

roman type, large. Machines can be fitted with this style of type, which gives nine characters to the inch, instead of ten (pica) and twelve (élite). Note: practice is very uncertain in regard to the cap. or lower-case initial for roman, but the tendency seems to be to drop the cap. in this and other old-established forms, such as indian ink, persian carpet, morocco leather, etc.

Romney. *See* Appendix II for pronunciation.

rondeau, a form of poem; *pl.* rondeaux.

rondel, a verse form.

rondo, piece of music in which return is made to the leading theme.

Röntgen rays, a form of light that penetrates substances impervious to ordinary rays.

Roquefort, a French cheese resembling Stilton.

rosary, or rosery. Either form may be used for rose-garden, but it is best to use rose-garden, and to reserve rosary for the Roman Catholic prayer, and string of beads.

rose (Fr.), *adj.* pink.

rose-water.

rostrum, oringinally the beak of Roman war-galley, and in this sense the plural is rostra. In the popular sense of pulpit the plural is generally rostrums.

rota, list of persons who are to perform duties in rotation; *pl.* rotas.

rotary, preferable to the longer rotatory (from Lat. *rota* = wheel).

rotary duplicators. These are operated by hand or electrically. The stencil is stretched round a cylinder and the ink applied automatically.

rôti (Fr.), roast meat.

rouble, Russian silver coin; abbr. R.

roué (Fr.), a dissipated person.

rouge et noir (Fr.), red and black, a card game played for money.

rough-and-ready. Hyphens required when the phrase is an adjective.

rough-cast.

rough-dry.

rough-hewn.

roughshod.

rouleau (Fr.), roll, twist, etc. Used in dressmaking to mean a roll of material employed decoratively; *pl. rouleaux*. Also English word (with plural *x* or *s*) meaning a packet of gold coins.

roundabout.

roundhead, member of Parliamentary party in seventeenth-century Civil War (from the style of hair-cutting).

round-robin, petition with signatures written in a circle so as to conceal their order.

round-shouldered.

rout-seat, light seat hired out for evening party, which was ordinally called a rout. Rout now used for disturbance, or for dispersal of troops; also a verb meaning to dig up or fetch out.

Rowe. *See* Appendix II for pronunciation.

rowlock, contrivance on a boat that supports the oar; *pron.* rŭl-uk.

Royal Air Force, abbr. R.A.F.

Royal Welch Fusiliers.

Roydon, Norfolk.

Royston, Herts, Yorks

Royton, Lancs

R.P., Reply paid.

r.p.m., revolutions per minute.

R.R.C., Royal Red Cross.

R.S., Royal Society.

R.S.G.B., Radio Society of Great Britain.

R.S.M., Regimental Sergeant-Major, Royal School of Marines.

R.S.O., railway sub-office.

R.S.P.B., Royal Society for the Protection of Birds.

R.S.P.C.A., Royal Society for Prevention of Cruelty to Animals.

R.S.V.P., *Répondez, s'il vous plait* (Fr.), Please reply.

R.T.C., Royal Tank Corps.

Rt. Hon., Right Honourable.

Rt. Rev., Right Reverend (title of a Bishop).

Rubáiyát, The, by Omar Khayyám, Persian poet. The word is the plural of rubâi, meaning a quatrain.

Rubicon, to cross the, to take an irrevocable step. (The Rubicon was the stream limiting Caesar's province and crossed by him before the war with Pompey.)

rubicund, high-coloured.

ruche (*noun* and *verb*), frilling, frill.

rucksack, *pron.* rŏŏksăk.

R.U.E., right upper entrance (stage directions), i.e. right of performer, not audience.

Rufford, Lancs

Rufforth, Yorks

rule, name used by printers for a dotted, straight, or wavy line.

ruled lines. You can type on ruled lines by releasing the line-space mechanism, and moving the platen by the twirler.

rule the roost, to domineer, as a fighting cock, over others. Some people use the expression " to rule the roast," as in superintending the cooking of the joint, but the first phrase is probably the more usual.

ruling, *see* note under " lines."

Rumania, now the popular spelling. Unit of currency 1 leu = 100 bani.

running head, the head-line at the top of a book, continued from page to page.

run on, term used in proof correcting, to signify that no break or new paragraph is to be made; abbr. r.o.

rupee, Indian unit of currency. Abbr. ℞; *pl.* ℞s (no point); tens of rupees ℞x.

rushlight.

Rushmere, Suffolk.

Rushmoor, Surrey.

Rushock, Worcestershire.

Rushwick, Worcester.

R.U.S.I., Royal United Service Institution.

rus in urbe (Lat.), the country in town.

Russia. Unit of currency 1 chervonetz = 10 old Russian gold roubles.

russia leather, reddish-brown leather used in binding.

Ruthven. *See* Appendix II for pronunciation.

R.V., Revised Version, Rifle Volunteers.

R.W., Right Worshipful, Right Worthy.

R.W.S., Royal Society of Painters in Water Colours.

℞x, tens of rupees (no point).

S

S, sulphur.

S., Saint, Signor, Society, south, Sunday.

s., second, seconds, shilling, shillings, signed, son, substantive, succeeded.

s (Fr.), *sur*, on, e.g. Trouville-sur-Mer.

$, American dollar mark. If this sign is not on the typewriter, it can be made by typing capital S and solidus. It should be typed close to and precede the figures.

:/S/: the repeat mark in music.

S.A., Salvation Army, South Africa.

S.A.A.F., South African Air Force.

sabotage, wanton destruction of property.

saccharin (*noun*), a substance of great sweetness obtained from coal-tar.

saccharine (*adj.*).

sackcloth.

sacré (Fr.), sacred; *fem.* *sacrée*.

sacrilegious, pertaining to sacrilege, profanity, an act of impiety; robbery committed in sacred building, etc.

sacrosanct, inviolable, secure against outrage.

S.A.E., stamped addressed envelope.

saga, Scandinavian myth, a legend; *pl.* sagas.

sagou (Fr.), sago.

sahib (Anglo-Indian), European in India; *fem.* *memsahib*.

saignant (Fr.), undertone; raw (wound, etc.); *fem.* *saignante*.

sailcloth.

sailer, a vessel. Sailor = a man who earns his livelihood on the sea.

Saint, abbr. S. or St. In indexing always place names beginning with St. under Saint. In French the abbreviation is *S.* or *St.* with fem. *Ste.* In German **Sankt**, abbr. *S.*, *pl.* *SS.*

St. Andrew's Day, 30th November.

St. Barnabas's Day, 11th June.

St. Bartholomew Day, 24th August.

St. David's Day, 1st March.

St. George's Day, 23rd April.

St. Ive, Liskeard (Cornwall).

St. Ives, Cornwall, Hants, Hunts

St. John. *See* Appendix II for pronunciation.

St. Leger. *See* Appendix II for pronunciation.

St. Martin's summer. This begins about 11th November.

St. Mellion, Cornwall.

St. Mellons, Cardiff.

St. Neot, Cornwall.

St. Neots, Hunts

St. Patrick's Day, 17th March.

St. Peter's Day, 29th June.

Saints' Days:

St. David, 1st March.

St. Patrick, 17th March.

St. George, 23rd April.

St. Barnabas, 11th June.

St. Peter, 29th June.

St. Swithun, 15th July.

St. Bartholomew, 24th August.

St. Andrew, 30th November.

St. Swithun's Day, 15th July.

St. Vitus's dance.

salaam, Oriental salutation.

salade (Fr.), salad; sometimes means lettuce only.

sal-ammoniac, ammonium chloride.

sale (Fr.), dirty, foul.

salé (Fr.), salted. *Sel* = salt.

saleable.

salicylic acid.

salle (Fr.), hall.

salle à manger (Fr.), dining-room.

salle d'attente (Fr.), waiting-room.

sally-lunn, a light tea-cake.

salmis (Fr.), a hash of game, etc.

Salmon. *See* Appendix II for pronunciation.

salon (Fr.), reception room, exhibition.

Salop, abbr. for Shropshire.

salt-cellar.

saltpetre.

salutary, beneficial.

salutation of letter. *See* note under "complimentary close."

Salve! (Lat.), Hail!

sal volatile, aromatic solution of ammonium carbonate.

salvo sensu (Lat.), the sense being preserved.

same. Avoid using *same* in place of it, him, her, them, they. *Same* would not be used in speaking, and this can be the guide.

sanatorium, *pl.* sanatoria.

sanatory, curative.

sanctorum (Lat.), a special retreat.

sanctum, a retreat, private study, etc.; *pl.* sanctums.

sanctum sanctorum (Lat.), the holy of holies.

sanctum simplicitas (Lat.), child-like simplicity.

Sandon, Essex, Herts, Stafford.

Sandown, Isle of Wight.

sand-paper.

sandstone.

Sandwich, Kent.

Sandwick, Orkney, Shetland.

Sandwith, Cumberland.

Sandys. *See* Appendix II for pronunciation.

sang-froid, coolness, composure.

sanitary, conducive to wholesomeness.

Sankt (Ger.), saint; abbr. *S.*

sans (abbr. of sans serif), type without serifs.

sans (Fr.), without. Sometimes used as an English word and given English pronunciation.

sans cérémonie (Fr.), without ceremony.

sans doute (Fr.), without doubt.

sans faute (Fr.), without fail.

Sanskrit, ancient language of India.

sans pareil (Fr.), without equal.

sans peur et sans reproche (Fr.), fearless and blameless.

sans souci (Fr.), without care.

Santa (It., Span.), female saint; abbr. *Sta.*

Santa Claus, a variation of St. Nicholas, which has come to us from the Dutch, through U.S.

saque, a loose coat.

sarcophagus, stone coffin; *pl.* sarcophagi.

sari, the long piece of cotton or silk which forms the garment of Hindu women.

sartor resartus (Lat.), the tailor patched or mended.

Sarum, ecclesiastical name for Salisbury.

satanic.

sateen.

satirize, to assail with satires.

satisfon. (legal), satisfaction.

Satis verborum (Lat.), No more need be said.

sauce piquante (Fr.), a sharp-tasting sauce.

saucisse (Fr.), sausage.

saucisson (Fr.), large sausage.

Sauerkraut (Ger.), cabbage, chopped and fermented.

saumon (Fr.), salmon.

sauté (Fr.), tossed in butter.

Sauterne, a French white wine.

sauve qui peut (Fr.), (let him find safety who can), precipitate flight.

S.A.V., stock at valuation.

savant, a learned person; *pl.* savants; *fem.* savante, *pl.* savantes.

Savile. *See* Appendix II for pronunciation.

savoir-faire (Fr.), tact, gumption.

Sb, antimony.

'sblood, an oath, corruption of " God's in's blood."

S.C., Staff Corps, South Carolina, Supreme Court.

Sc., Scottish.

sc., science, scruple.

s.c., small capitals (used in proof-correcting).

scalable.

scallop, a bivalve mollusc; shell in which cooked fish, etc., is served. As a verb it means to ornament the edge of a dress, etc., with scalloping.

scan, to examine the metre, in poetry. The other meaning " to run the eyes over " is in popular use, though originally the word meant " to examine intently."

scandalize.

S.C.A.P.A., Society for Checking the Abuses of Public Advertising.

scapegoat.

scarecrow.

scarlatina.

Sc.D., *Scientiae Doctor* (Lat.), Doctor of Science (Cambridge or Dublin University). D.Sc. if degree is taken at London, Oxford, or other University.

scena (It., Lat.), scene in a play. It. *pl.* scene; Lat. scenae.

scenario, outline of a play or film; *pron.* she-nar'io; *pl.* scenarii.

scène (Fr.), scene, stage.

schema (Lat.), an outline.

scherzo, light playful passage of music; *pron.* skärtsō; *pl.* scherzos.

Schiff (Ger.), boat.

Schloss (Ger.), castle; *pl. Schlösser.*

Schnapps (Dutch), gin.

scholium (Lat.), a marginal note.

schoolmistress.

schoolroom.

schottische, a dance.

science, abbr. sc.

scientific nomenclature. In quoting the Latin names of animals or plants, use an initial capital for the first part but not the second.

scimitar, a curved Oriental sword.

S.C.J., Supreme Court of Judicature.

-score. Compounds such as fourscore, etc., are written as one word.

Scot, native of Scotland; also Scotsman; Scotchman sometimes incorrectly used.

scot-free.

Scotland, use Scot. as abbreviation, provided it will not be misunderstood—never N.B.

Scottish (*adj.*). This is good usage both in Scotland and England.

scribes and Pharisees.

Scrimgeour. *See* Appendix II for pronunciation.

scrimmage. In Rugby football scrummage (abbr. scrum).

Scripsit (Lat.), He or she wrote it.

scriptio continuo (Lat.), continuous writing.

scriptorium (Lat.), a writing-room.

scruple, 20 grains; abbr. sc.

scrutineer.

scrutinize.

Sculpsit (Lat.), He or she engraved or carved it.

sculptures. When quoting titles enclose in quote marks.

Sculthorpe, Norfolk.

Scunthorpe, Lincs

S.C.W.S., Scottish Co-operative Wholesale Society.

s.d., sine die (Lat.), indefinitely.

S/E, Stock Exchange.

SE., compass point.

S.E., south-eastern postal district.

seafaring.

Seaford, Sussex.

Seaforde, co. Down.

sealing machines. Efficient machines, for sealing large numbers of envelopes, are on the market.

sealing-wax.

seamstress.

seaport.

seascape.

seasick, suffering from sea-sickness.

seasons. Capital not usually recommended, but may be used for special emphasis (spring, summer, etc.).

sec., second, seconds, secretary, section.

secession, withdrawing from fellowship or association.

second, abbr. s. or sec.

second-hand.

secretary, abbr. sec.

secretory (*adj.*), secreting.

section mark. A fair representation of this ( ) can be made by typing two large or two small *s*'s, one over and slightly below the other. (*Pl.* §§.) The longhand abbreviation for section is s., sec., or sect.

secularizing.

secundum legem (Lat.), according to law.

secundum ordinem (Lat.), in order.

secundum regulam (Lat.), according to rule.

secundum veritatem (Lat.), according to truth.

secy. (legal), security.

sederunt (Lat.), a meeting.

séduisant (Fr.), seductive, bewitching; *fem. séduisante.*

see-saw.

Seidlitz powder.

seigneur (Fr.), a person of rank.

seise. This spelling is more usual in legal phraseology, and *seize* in ordinary senses.

seismograph, instrument for recording earthquakes.

seize. This is one of the exceptions to the rule "*i* precedes *e* except after *c.*" Note siege.

séjour (Fr.), sojourn.

sel., *selig* (Ger.), deceased, late.

selector.

self-. Nearly all words with this prefix take the hyphen, e.g. self-conquest, self-supporting, self-created.

selfsame.

selvedge.

semble (Lat.), it seems, perhaps.

semi-. In all but well-established words semi- should be followed by a hyphen.

semicircle.

semicolon, a useful stop. Indicates a longer pause than the comma; links two parts of a double sentence when the conjunction is omitted. In typing, the semicolon is followed by two spaces.

semper (Lat.), always.

semper fidelis (Lat.), always faithful.

Sen., senior.

senatus consultum (Lat.), a decree of the senate.

Senhor (Port.), Mr.; *fem. Senhora.*

seniores priores (Lat.), elders first.

Señor (Span.), Mr.; *abbr.* Sr.; *Señores*, Messrs.; *abbr.*
Sres.; *fem.* **Señora**, Mrs.; *abbr.* Sra.; *Señorita*, Miss;
abbr. Srta. (Abbreviations not considered good practice.)

sensible (Fr.), sensitive.

sensu bono (Lat.), in a good sense.

sensu malo (Lat.), in a bad sense.

sentimentalize.

separator.

September, abbr. Sept.

Septembre (Fr.), September. Upper or lower-case may
be used for initial of months in French; abbr. *Sept.*, 7bre.

septimana (Lat.), a week.

septuagenarian, a person 70 years old.

sepultus (Lat.), buried.

sequens (Lat.), the following; abbr. *seq.*

sequentes or *sequentia* (Lat.), the following; abbr. *seqq.*

sequitur (Lat.), it follows.

seraph, *pl.* seraphs. Hebrew *pl.* **seraphim**.

Sergeant, for military and police rank. *Serjeant* in legal
titles.

seriatim, one after another.

serif, the short fine line at the end of the stroke of a
printed letter.

serum, *pl.* sera.

service. This word is used as a verb in garages, where
the workers speak of servicing a car, that is, making
minor adjustments.

serviceable.

sesquipedalia verba (Lat.), high-flown language, very
long words.

set-back, a hindrance; *pl.* set-backs.

setting-off, the transfer of ink from one sheet to the
next, either in duplicating (typewriting) or printing
processes.

settlt. (legal), settlement.

seventies. *See* note under "thirties."

sew, to fasten material. *Past-participle* sewn or sewed.
Sow applies to scattering seeds, and gives *sown* and
sowed.

sexagenarian, a person 60 years old.

s.g., specific gravity.

shallot, a kind of onion.

shan't, colloquial form of shall not.

Shakespeare, Shakespearian, and Shakespearean are more
popular than Shakspere, etc.

shanty, sailors' song. This is now the accepted spelling, though chanty (*cf.* chant) is obviously the correct one. Shanty also means a cabin or mean dwelling.

shareholder.

Shawford, Hants

Shawforth, Lancs

sheaf, *pl.* sheaves.

sheath (*noun*).

sheathe (*verb*).

Sheean, co. Mayo.

Sheen, Derbyshire.

sheep-dog.

Sheffield, Yorks

Shefford, Beds

Shelfield, Staffs

Shelford, Cambridge, Notts

shell-fish.

shelving.

Sherborne, Dorset, Glos

Sherbourne, Warwickshire.

Sherburn, Durham, Yorks

sherif, Mohammedan title.

sheriff.

Sheringham, Norfolk.

Sherington, Bucks

shew. This spelling is used only in Bible and Prayer Book, and in law; otherwise *show*.

shieling, Highland hut.

shilling, abbr. s.

shilling sign, familiar name for the solidus, the stroke sign that forms part of so many signs and abbreviations. Sometimes used in handwritten MSS. to represent *the*, and in technical works for *per* (e.g., lb./sq. in.).

Shillingstone, Dorset.

shillingsworth.

Shillington, Herts

shilly-shallying, hesitating, wasting time in deciding.

ships' names. These should have quotes, or, if printed, should appear in italic type.

shoeing.

shopfront.

shopkeeper.

shoplifting.

shorthand-typist.

short-sighted.

shoulder-heads, short headings inserted at intervals in printed matter, to break it up.

shoulder-note, note appearing at the top of page, at outer edge.

shouldst.

shovelfuls.

shovelled.

show. Do not use *shew* unless quoting from the Bible, etc. *See* note under " shew."

showcase.

showroom.

Shropshire, abbr. Salop (no point).

[*sic*] (Lat.). This is placed after a quoted phrase as signifying " Yes, he actually said that." It should be used only when there would otherwise be a doubt in the reader's mind.

Sic in originali (Lat.), So it stands in the original.

sic passim (Lat.), thus everywhere.

Sic transit gloria mundi (Lat.), Thus passes away the glory of the world.

side-note, a marginal note.

side-walk, American word for pavement.

siècle (Fr.), century.

siesta, midday rest.

sightseeing.

sigillum (Lat.), a seal.

signalized.

signatory, one who signs an agreement.

signe. (legal), signature.

signed, abbr. s.

Signor (It.), Mr.; *pl. Signori; fem. Signora,* Mrs., *pl. Signore. Signorina,* Miss, *pl. Signorine.*

signpost.

silhouette.

silkworm.

s'il vous plaît (Fr.), if you please.

Simila similibus curantur (Lat.), Like things are cured by like.

simile, the comparison of one thing with another; *pl.* similes.

Similis simili gaudet (Lat.), Birds of a feather flock together.

similiter (Lat.), in like manner.

Si monumentum requiris, circumspice (Lat.), If you seek (his) monument, look about you. (Epitaph to Sir Christopher Wren in St. Paul's cathedral.)

simplex munditiis (Lat.), simple yet elegant.

simpliciter (Lat.), absolutely, without limitation.

simulacrum (Lat.), an image, a deceptive substitute.

simultaneous *with*.

sine anno (Lat.), without the date.

sine die (Lat.), without naming a day.

sine invidia (Lat.), without envy.

sine loco et anno (Lat.), without place and date (applied to books that have no imprints).

sine praejudicio (Lat.), without prejudice.

sine prole (Lat.), without issue.

singeing, burning the tips of hair.

single quotes, used for a quotation within a quotation.

singr. (legal), singular.

Sinhalese, natives of Ceylon. This form is preferred to Singhalese, Cingalese, etc.

Sinn Fein. *See* Appendix II for pronunciation.

siphon.

siren, sea nymph, warning whistle.

sister-in-law, *pl.* sisters-in-law.

Si vis pacem para bellum (Lat.), If you wish for peace, make ready for war.

'sixties, the years 1860 to 1869. Apostrophe is seen usually, though many writers omit it. Be careful not to use it in speaking of a person's age.

sizable.

S.J., Society of Jesus (Jesuit Order).

ski, usually pronounced she; *pl.* skis. Ski-ing. *Ski'd* is better than *skied* for past tense.

skilful.

skill-less. Use the hyphen in this and similar words.

Skrine. *See* Appendix II for pronunciation.

sky-high.

skyline.

sky-scraper.

skywriting, the writing by an aeroplane of smoke messages in the sky.

S.L., serjeant-at-law.

slapdash.

sled, a drag in agriculture. Sledge or sleigh, a carriage for use on snow. (Sleigh is the U.S. and Canadian form.)

slipping of typewriter. *See* note under " typewriter, creeping of."

slipshod.

slough (ow), a bog; (ŭf) to cast off a skin.

S.M., Senior Magistrate, Sergeant-, Staff-, or Surgeon-Major.

smallpox.

smelling-salts.

smell-less.

smoky.

smooth, *verb* and *adj.* Note " She smooths the cloth," not " smoothes."

S.N., Shipping note.

snivelled.

snowfall.

S.O., sub-office.

So-and-so.

so-called. Use hyphen when an adjective.

société (Fr.), society.

Société anonyme (Fr.), joint-stock company, limited liability company.

soi-disant, self-styled, ostensible, professed, supposed. (Use one of these alternatives in preference to the foreign term.)

soirée, social evening party. Fr. *soir* = evening.

solatium (Lat.), compensation.

solecism, blunder in speaking, writing or behaviour.

solemnize.

sol-fa.

Solicitor-General, abbr. Sol.-Gen. or S.-G.

solicitude.

solidus, the " shilling sign " (/). It has many uses, in abbreviations, etc. *See* note under " shilling sign."

soliloquize.

soliloquy.

soling (boots).

solo, *pl.* solos.

solus, alone (used in stage directions).

solvable.

somebody else's. Use this as possessive form.

some day. This should never be written as one word.

someone.

Somers. *See* Appendix II for pronunciation.

Somersetshire, abbr. Som (no point).

Somerville. *See* Appendix II for pronunciation.

sometime (*adj.*), as in " the sometime Secretary." Otherwise use some time.

somnolent, sleepy.

son, abbr. s.

son-in-law, *pl.* sons-in-law.

soprano, *pl.* **sopranos**. It. *pl. soprani.*

sorbet, flavoured water-ice.

S O S, last signal for help. Adopted since 1912 because easy to transmit and distinguish in Morse. Does not mean " Save our souls."

so-so, passable.

sotto (It.), under.

sotto voce (It.), in an undertone; *pron.* vōchĕ.

soubrette, a lady who acts or sings in light comedy parts (originally a pert serving-maid).

soufflé (Fr.), light milky dish, generally containing whisked white of egg.

soulless.

Soult. *See* Appendix II for pronunciation.

soupçon, a very small quantity.

souper (Fr.), supper.

souris (Fr.), *masc.* smile; *fem.* mouse.

south, *see* note under " north."

South Africa, abbr. S.A.

South America, abbr. S.Amer.

South Carolina, abbr. S.C.

south-east, abbr. SE. for compass point; S.E. in ordinary usage.

Southwark. *See* Appendix II for pronunciation.

Southwell. *See* Appendix II for pronunciation.

south-west, abbr. SW. for compass point; S.W. in ordinary usage.

sou'wester, waterproof hat.

sow, *see* note under " sew."

Sowerby. *See* Appendix II for pronunciation.

S.P., Supra Protest.

spa. (legal), subpoena.

spacing after punctuation marks. The commonly accepted spacing follows the same order as the stops, viz. 3 spaces after full stop, exclamation mark, question mark; 2 spaces after semicolon or colon; 1 space after comma.

spacing, line. Single spacing is usual in business letters, unless they are very short. Double spacing is the rule for all literary matter; treble spacing for drafts of legal documents.

spadeful, *pl.* **spadefuls.**

Spain. Unit of currency 1 peseta = 100 centimos.

S.P.C.K., Society for Promoting Christian Knowledge.

speciality. Use this spelling for the ordinary meaning.

The form *specialty* is used in law to mean an instrument under seal.

specialization.

specialty, an instrument under seal (legal term).

specie, coin as distinct from paper money.

species, same *sing.* and *pl.*

specification. This is typed on foolscap, in double spacing, with extra spaces between paragraphs. The headings are typed in capitals in the wide margins.

specific gravity, abbr. sp. gr., also s.g.

spectrum, *pl.* usually spectra.

speculator.

speedometer.

speleological, having to do with the scientific study of caves.

spes (Lat.), hope.

spes mea Christus (Lat.), Christ my hope.

Spes tutissima caelis (Lat.), The safest hope is in heaven.

S.P.G., Society for the Propagation of the Gospel.

sp. gr., specific gravity, also abbr. s.g.

sphinx, *pl.* sphinxes.

spick-and-span, hyphenate when an *adj.*

spinach, *pron.* spinij.

spiritous, like spirit, refined.

spiritual, of spirit as opposed to matter.

spirituel, a negro song.

spirituelle, of refined mind or character.

spirituous, containing much alcohol.

split infinitive, the insertion of an adverb, etc., between *to* and the verb (e.g. to really enjoy). Be careful not to distort the sentence in order to avoid this construction, when " the remedy may be worse than the disease " !

spollation, plunder, pillage.

Spoonerism, accidental transposition of initial letters of words, e.g. " half-warmed fish " for " half-formed wish." (From Dr. W. A. Spooner.)

spoonful, *pl.* spoonfuls.

square, abbr. sq.

squarish.

squeegee, rubber-edged implement.

S.R., Southern Railway.

S.R. & O., Statutory Rules and Orders.

S/S or s.s., steamship.

S.S., Secretary of State, steamship, Straits Settlements, Sunday School.

S.S.C., Solicitor of the Supreme Court of Scotland.

SSE., south-south-east.

S.S.M., Squadron Sergeant-Major.

S.S.U., Sunday School Union.

SSW., south-south-west.

St., Saint, Street. *See* note under " Saint " with regard to indexing.

Sta (It., Span., Port.), *santa* (female saint).

stabilize.

staccato, distinct.

staff, *pl.* staffs, except in music and archaic senses, when it is *staves.*

Staffordshire, abbr. Staffs (no point).

Staff Sergeant.

stage-craft.

staggering. The grouping of business people as regards hours or holidays to avoid congestion. In the building trade, the term means the placing of uprights at intervals in zigzag formation ; in engineering, it might relate to placing of rivets or the spokes of a wheel.

stagy.

staid, solemn.

stalactite, deposit hanging from roof of cave.

stalagmite, deposit on floor of cave.

stalemate (chess).

stamp, abbr. stp. (legal).

stanch, to check a flow, especially of blood. *Staunch* is the adjective meaning loyal.

standardize.

standpoint.

standstill (*noun*).

stanza, *pl.* stanzas.

stapling machine. A useful little stapling press can be obtained for securing papers that are required to be fastened permanently. This is operated by hand, and there are larger machines that work automatically.

starfish.

starting-point.

statement, abbr. statt. (legal).

statim (Lat.), immediately.

stationary, fixed.

stationery, note-paper, etc.

statistician.

statistics. This is plural.

statt. (legal), statement.

status, rank.

status quo (Lat.), as things were or are.

status quo ante (Lat.), in the same state as before.

status quo ante bellum (Lat.), as it was before the war.

statutory, enacted by statute.

staunch (*adj.*), loyal.

stayed, stopped.

Ste, sainte (Fr.), female saint.

steadfast.

steamboat.

steam-engine.

steamship, abbr. s.s., S.S., or S/S.

steeplechase.

stencil, a waxed or composition sheet that is cut through by the type striking direct on to it. Used on rotary or flat duplicating machines. Type must be in good condition and clean, and capitals and fractions must be struck more heavily than the other characters. Paper must be used on the right side, which is smoother and more absorbent.

stencilled.

stepbrother, stepson, etc., need no hyphen.

stepping-stone.

sterilization.

sterling, abbr. stg.

stet, a word used in proof correction to signify that something crossed out is to remain as previously printed. Stet is written in the margin, and the reinstated word has dots placed beneath it.

Stet processus (Lat.), Let the process stand (title of an order suspending further action).

Stevenston, Ayrshire.

Steventon, Berks, Hants

Stevington, Bedford.

stg., sterling.

stigmatize.

stile, device to assist in getting over fence.

stiletto, *pl.* stilettos.

stillness.

stimulus, *pl.* stimuli.

stirps (Lat.), lineage.

stock at valuation, S.A.V.

stockbroker.

Stock Exchange, abbr. S/E.

stockholder.

stockinette.

stocktaking.

stoep, verandah or platform alongside a house (S. Africa); *pron.* stoop.

stopgap.

storey, more used than story in the building trade, though floor is more common than either; *pl.* **storeys.**

storyette.

Stourton. *See* Appendix II for pronunciation.

stowaway.

Stowe. *See* Appendix II for pronunciation.

stp. (legal), stamp.

straight away, immediately (slang).

straightforward.

straightway, immediately (archaic).

strait-laced.

Strasse (Ger.), street.

stratum, a layer of earth; *pl.* **strata.**

stratum super stratum (Lat.), layer above layer.

Street. Number of house in street need not be followed by comma. St. is the abbreviation for street, but it is better to type in full in letter-writing.

strictum jus (Lat.), strict law.

strongminded.

Strood, Kent.

Stroud, Glos, Hants

strychnine.

stumbling-block.

stupefy.

style, manner, custom; ancient writing tool; gnomon of sundial; part of flower.

stymie (golfing term).

suaviter in modo (Lat.), gentle in manner.

sub-, under.

sub-committee.

sub conditione (Lat.), under the condition.

subdivisible.

subdominant, the fourth note in the scale.

sub-editor.

sub judice (Lat.), under consideration.

sub-lease.

sublet.

sub-lieutenant.

subpoena (Lat.), a summons to appear as a witness (literally: under a penalty); abbr. spa. (legal).

sub rosa (Lat.) (under the rose), privately or secretly.

subsection.

subseqtly. (legal), subsequently.

subsidize.

sub sigillo (Lat.) (under the seal), in the strictest confidence.

sub silentio (Lat.), in hushed-up manner.

subsoil.

sub specie (Lat.), under appearance of.

substantive, abbr. s.

substituted, abbr. substtd. (legal).

substratum, *pl.* substrata.

substtd. (legal). substituted.

subterranean, underground.

subtlety, the state of being subtle, i.e. cunning, ingenious, acute. Modern forms of subtile and subtilty.

sub voce or *verbo* (Lat.), under a specified word.

subway.

succedaneum (Lat.), a substitute.

succeeded, abbr. s.

succon. (legal), succession.

succulent.

such-and-such.

suchlike, not recommended.

sud (Fr.), south.

Süd (Ger.), south.

suède, undressed kid used for gloves, etc.

sufficient, abbr. sufft. (legal).

sufficit (Lat.), it is sufficient.

Suffragan Bishop. *See* Appendix I for correct form of address.

sufft. (legal), sufficient.

sui juris (Lat.), of full age and capacity.

suing.

Suisse (Fr.), Switzerland; native of Switzerland.

suitcase.

suite, set of persons, rooms, or furniture.

suite (Fr.), continuation, retinue.

sulphur, abbr. S (no point).

sulphuretted, treated with sulphur.

summarize.

summa summarum (Lat.), sum total.

summer-time.

summon (*verb*). Use this spelling for ordinary meanings, but summons may be used in the sense of serve with a legal summons.

summons (*noun*). Legal abbr. sums. or sus.

summum bonum (Lat.), the chief good.

summum jus (Lat.), the extreme of justice.

sumptibus publicis (Lat.), at public expense.

sums. or sus. (legal), summons.

sunbonnet.

sundial.

sunstroke.

sun-worshipper.

super-, beyond, transcending. This prefix is used with many words, and is now employed loosely to mean anything that is out of the ordinary, e.g. super-cinema. Except in made-up words such as the example given, no hyphen is necessary.

superhuman.

superintendent.

superior characters, figures or letters placed a little above the line of typing. Seen in algebraic and chemical formulae, and in indications of footnotes. Use the variable line-spacer and turn the platen slightly backward.

supernumerary, in excess of the normal number.

super-saturated.

supersede. Other words ending with this sound are spelt -*cede*, with three exceptions: proceed, exceed, and succeed.

supersedeas (Lat.), a writ to stay proceedings.

supervise.

supervisor.

supposititious, substituted for the real.

suppurate, to fester.

sur (Fr.), upon; abbr. *s*.

sûr (Fr.), safe.

sur le tapis (Fr.), under consideration. English equivalent on the tapis, or on the carpet.

surmise.

surprise.

surreptitiously, stealthily.

Sursum corda! (Lat.), Lift up your hearts!

sur-tax.

surveillance, supervision.

survor. (legal), survivor.

svelte (Fr.), elegant.

SW., for compass point; otherwise S.W.

S.W., Senior Warden, south-western postal district.

swansdown.

swatch, a strip of material cut off as sample (term used in drapery trade).

Swede, native of Sweden.

swede, Swedish turnip.

Sweden. Unit of currency 1 krona = 100 öre.

sweet-brier.

sweetmeat, confectionery.

sweet-pea.

sweet-scented.

sweet-william, a garden plant.

S.W.G., standard wire gauge.

Swindon, Glos, Wilts, Worcs

Swinton, Berwickshire, Manchester, Ripon (Yorks).

switch, ribbon. This should be used only if the machine has a bi-chrome ribbon and it is desired to use the other portion for a short time. For the bulk of the work the switch should be on "black," and the ribbon itself should be reversed when one portion becomes worn.

Switzerland. Unit of currency 1 franc = 100 rappen or centimes. The Fr. for Switzerland is *la Suisse*; Ger. *die Schweiz*; It. *Svizzera*.

Sydenham. *See* Appendix II for pronunciation.

syllabus, *pl.* syllabuses.

symbolize.

sympathize.

symposium, set of contributions from various writers giving their views on a particular subject; *pl.* symposia.

synchronize, occur at same time; cause clocks to show a uniform time. Two electric currents are said to synchronize when they are of like phase and frequency.

syndicalism, a movement to destroy the capitalist system and transfer industrial control to representatives of the trades.

synonymous, having the same meaning.

synopsis, *pl.* synopses.

synthesis, composition; the opposite to analysis.

synthetic.

synthetize.

syringeing.

syrup.

systematize.

T

t., ton, tons.

tableau, picturesque presentation; *pl.* tableaux.

table d'hôte, an ordinary; a fixed-price dinner; *pl.* tables d'hôte. (Literal meaning = host's table.)

tablespoonfuls.

"tabloid," patented word; use legally restricted to products of Burroughs, Wellcome & Co.

taboo (*noun, adj.* and *verb.*) *Past tense* tabooed.

tabula (Lat.), a document.

tabular matter. Plan the work with care, if necessary on a rough piece of paper. Aim at securing balance. Set the tabulator stops for the column positions. Use double spacing generally between items. Check totals of columns. Do not rule with machine and pen on the same sheet. *See* notes under "column selector" and "lines, ruling."

tabulator. Make use of this for paragraph indentation, and for any tabular work.

tactics, *sing.* or *pl.*

tael, unit of currency of China.

taffeta, a silk fabric.

Tag (Ger.), day.

tail-piece, the name given to an ornamentation that sometimes appears at the end of a chapter or article. The typist can make a decorative tail-piece with a triangle of small *o*'s or other signs.

talisman, *pl.* talismans.

tallness.

tamable.

tambourine.

tam-o'-shanter.

Tannhäuser, opera by Wagner. *See* Appendix II for pronunciation.

tantalize.

tant mieux (Fr.), so much the better.

tant pis (Fr.), so much the worse.

tapis. *See* note under "*sur le tapis.*"

tariff.

tarpaulin.

tasselled.

tattoo, beat of drum, drumming with the fingers, indelible marks on skin.

Tauchnitz, publisher in Leipzig of well-known series of British and American authors. *See* Appendix II for pronunciation.

tautology, saying a thing twice over, in different words.

taxpayer.

taxying, term used in flying, when a plane runs along the ground under its own power.

tazza (It.), bowl; *pron.* tăt-să.

T.C.D., Trinity College, Dublin.

T.D., Territorial Decoration.

teacupfuls.

teapot.

teaspoonfuls.

Te Deum, hymn beginning *Te Deum laudamus* (We praise Thee, O God).

Tee (Ger.), tea.

teens, years of one's age from 13 to 19.

teetotaller.

teetotum.

tele-, afar.

telegrams. Type entirely in capitals and leave plenty of space between words. Make the meaning free from ambiguity, if necessary inserting full stops (charged at word rate). Telegrams are often sent by phone. They should be confirmed by letter.

teleprinter, an electrical typewriter which will transmit a message by means of a telephone or telegraph wire.

televise.

tempo (It.), time.

Tempora mutantur (Lat.), The times are changed.

temporary.

tempore (Lat.), in the time of.

Tempori parendum (Lat.), One must yield to the times.

temporize.

Tempus fugit (Lat.), Time flies.

Tempus omnia revelat (Lat.), Time reveals all things.

tenement, abbr. tenemt. (legal).

tenor, course, purport, drift.

Te nosce (Lat.), Know thyself.

terminus, *pl.* **termini.**

terminus ad quem (Lat.), the finish, the goal.

terminus a quo (Lat.), the starting-point.

terra-cotta, a kind of pottery. (It., baked earth.)

terra filius (Lat.), a son of the soil.

terra firma, solid earth, a safe footing.

terra incognito (Lat.), an unexplored country.

terrasse (Fr.), terrace; pavement in front of a café.

terrorize.

tertium quid (Lat.), a third something, especially between opposite things.

tessellated, formed of tesserae, blocks used in mosaic.

testament, abbr. testt. (legal).

testamur (Lat.), examination certificate.

testator, abbr. testor. (legal).

teste (Lat.), by the evidence of.

testor. (legal), testator.

testt. (legal), testament.

tête (Fr.), head.

tête-à-tête (Fr.), private conversation between two.

tête de veau (Fr.), calf's head.

text-book.

Teynham. *See* Appendix II for pronunciation.

tfer. (legal), transfer.

thabts. (legal), thereabouts.

Thalberg. *See* Appendix II for pronunciation.

Thanksgiving Day (U.S.A.), last Thursday in November.

that and which (difference between). Note the defining and restrictive function of *that* in the second sentence: (1) " The coats, *which* were illustrated in the catalogue, were cleared out on the first day of the sale." (2) " The coats *that* were illustrated in the catalogue were cleared out on the first day of the sale." The first sentence indicates that all the coats were illustrated and all were sold; the second sentence states that only those illustrated were sold.

thby. (legal), thereby.

thé (Fr.), tea.

théâtre (Fr.), theatre.

theca (Lat.), a case.

Theobald. *See* Appendix II for pronunciation.

theorize.

thereabouts, abbr. thabts. (legal).

thereby, abbr. thby. (legal).

therefor, sometimes used in formal sense, to mean for that, for it, etc. (e.g. " He will be reprimanded therefor "). Accent the second syllable; in *therefore* the first syllable is stressed.

therefrom, abbr. thfm. (legal).

therein, abbr. thrin. (legal).

thereof, abbr. thof. or throf. (legal).

thereon, abbr. thon. (legal).

thereto, abbr. thto. (legal).

therm, 100,000 British Thermal Units (B.Th.U.). A British Thermal Unit is the quantity of heat required to raise the temperature of 1 lb. of water 1° Fahr.

thermodynamics, relationship between heat and mechanical work.

thermometer.

thermos.

Thesaurus contains copious lists of related words, indispensable aid to the writer. Compiled by Peter Mark Roget, M.D., F.R.S., published in 1852, since enlarged.

thesis, written exposition, especially by one who is candidate for a degree; pl. theses.

thfm. (legal), therefrom.

thirties. When referring to a person's age (30 to 39 years), be careful not to use the apostrophe. In "the 'sixties," etc. (not referring to age), it is fairly general.

thof. or throf. (legal), thereof.

Thompson. See Appendix II for pronunciation.

Thoms. See Appendix II for pronunciation.

thon. (legal), thereon.

Thoreau. See Appendix II for pronunciation.

thoroughbred.

thoroughgoing.

though, abbr. tho'.

thraldom.

thrash, generally used for flogging, and thresh for beating out grain.

threefold.

threescore.

thresh, see note under "thrash."

threshold.

thrin. (legal), therein.

through, abbr. thro'.

thto. (legal), thereto.

tic douloureux, severe facial neuralgia.

tiffin (Anglo-Indian), lunch.

tilde, a wavy sign placed above the letter n (in Spanish) to show that it should be pronounced as if followed by y. Example: cañon.

till, now more usual than until.

timbale, a kind of pie made in a mould.

timbre-poste (Fr.), postage-stamp; pl. timbres-poste.

time of day. Avoid mixing figures and words; spell out phrases like half-past seven, a quarter to six. Use

a.m. and p.m. with figures, and do not say " this a.m."
for " this morning."

tingeing.

tin-plate, to coat with tin.

tinselled.

-tion. The termination with the sound of shun occurs
in over 2000 English words. It has various spellings
(e.g. musician, Persian, gentian), but by far the largest
group is that comprising the words ending in *-tion*.

tiptoeing.

tire, *see* note under " tyre."

'tis, abbreviation of it is. Note also it's.

titanic, of superhuman size or strength.

title-role, the part that gives a play its name.

t.l.o., total loss only.

T.L.R., Times Law Reports.

T.M.O., Telegraph Money Order.

T.O., turn over.

tobogganing.

Toc H, an association formed during the War of 1914–18 ;
the name is from the telegraphic abbreviation of Talbot
House, Poperinghe, a church institute named after
G. W. L. Talbot, a fallen officer.

to-day. The hyphen lingers in this and similar words,
but it serves no useful purpose.

to-do, a commotion.

toile (Fr.), cloth, curtain (theatrical).

toilette (Fr.), toilet, dress.

tomato, *pl.* tomatoes.

tome, volume, especially a heavy one. (Same word in
Fr.)

Tomline. *See* Appendix II for pronunciation.

to-morrow, *see* note under " to-day."

ton (Fr.), style, fashion, breeding.

Tonbridge. *See* Appendix II for pronunciation.

tonic sol-fa.

to-night, *see* note under " to-day."

tonsillitis.

toothbrush.

toothing, the indenting of certain lines in setting out
verse.

top-heavy.

topmast.

topmost.

topsy-turvy.

tormentor.

tornado, *pl.* tornadoes.

torpedo, *pl.* torpedoes.

tortoise, *pron.* tortus.

tortue claire (Fr.), clear turtle soup.

tortuous.

totalizator, the dictionary spelling, but *s* the more popular.

totidem verbis (Lat.), in so many words.

toties quoties (Lat.), as often as, on each occasion.

totis viribus (Lat.), with one's whole strength.

toto corde (Lat.), with the whole heart.

totum (Lat.), the whole.

touch typewriting. This involves locating the keys by sense of touch only, and using all the fingers. It is often taught by the aid of a cover that hides the keys. The results are a higher speed than can be attained otherwise, and less fatigue, as the operator's eyes remain on the copy instead of having to be shifted from copy to keys and back.

toupee, patch of false hair. *Toupet* is the French form.

tour (Fr.), *masc.* a tour, a circular; *fem.* a tower.

tour à tour (Fr.), in turn.

tour de force (Fr.), a feat of strength or skill.

tournados, small round fillets of beef, served as entrées.

tourniquet, instrument for stopping flow of blood (pron. toor-ne-ket).

tourte (Fr.), an open tart.

tout de même (Fr.), all the same.

tout de suite (Fr.), immediately.

tout d'un coup (Fr.), all at once.

tout ensemble (Fr.), the general effect. Ensemble (now an English word) is used with the same meaning.

toward. As an adjective this is archaic (e.g. " a storm is toward "). As a preposition, towards is more common.

towelling.

townsfolk.

Townshend. *See* Appendix II for pronunciation.

township.

toxicology, study of poisons.

tr., transpose.

t.r., tons register.

traceable.

trade-mark.

trade union, abbr. T.U.; *pl.* trade unions.

trade-unionist.

Trades Union Congress, abbr. T.U.C.

trafficker.

tragedian, actor of tragedy; *fem.* tragedienne.

trait, *pron.* trā; in U.S.A. trāt.

tranquil.

tranquillity.

trans-, across, beyond, through, into a different place.

transatlantic.

transcendent, surpassing.

transcontinental.

transfer, abbr. tfer. (legal).

transferable.

transferred.

transhipment.

translatable.

transmigration.

transmissible.

transmitter.

transpose, abbr. tr.

T.R.C., Teachers' Registration Council.

tree. (legal), trustee.

trek (South African), to travel by ox-wagon: trekker.

Tremayne. *See* Appendix II for pronunciation.

tremolo, musical term denoting intentionally tremulous effect.

tremor.

tremulous, quivering.

très bien (Fr.), very good.

trestle, supporting structure for table, etc.

Trevelyan. *See* Appendix II for pronunciation.

Treves. *See* Appendix II for pronunciation.

Trevor. *See* Appendix II for pronunciation.

T.R.H., Their Royal Highnesses.

tricoloured, of three colours.

trolley-bus.

troop, of soldiers.

troupe, of players.

trousseau, *pl.* trousseaux.

trumpeting.

trustee, abbr. tree. (legal).

try, should strictly be followed by infinitive (e.g. " Try to do it for me "). " Try and . . ." though less correct, is widely accepted.

tsetse fly.

T.S.F., French abbreviation for wireless—*télégraphie sans fil*, i.e. telegraphy without wire.

T.U., trade union.

tuberculosis.

T.U.C., Trades Union Congress.

Tues., Tuesday. Avoid abbreviations in correspondence.

tulle, fine silk net.

tumblerfuls.

tumultuous.

Tunbridge Wells.

tunnelled.

Tu quoque! (Lat.), Thou too!

tureen.

Turkey. Unit of currency 1 Turkish pound = 100 piastres.

turkey red.

turpentine.

Tuum est (Lat.), It is thine.

twenties. When used for the years (20–29) of a person's life, the apostrophe should not appear; when used for the years of a century it is fairly general.

'twere, contraction of it were.

'twixt, contraction of betwixt.

twofold.

'twould, contraction of it would.

tying, present participle of tie.

tympanum, ear-drum; *pl.* tympana. Timpani (*sing.* timpano) are the orchestral kettle-drums.

type machines. These machines are used for producing large numbers of copies. The type is set up. letter by letter, and prints either direct or through a ribbon.

typewriter, care of. Clean daily with duster and long-handled soft brush. Oil (sparingly) the carriage rails, using the best oil. It is well to consult a mechanic as to the parts of *your* machine that need oiling. When erasing (a rare operation for the touch typist) throw the carriage as far to one side as possible, so that the grit does not fall into the machine. Clean the type with stiff brush after any lengthy piece of typing. Cover machine so as to exclude all dust, and if possible put in cupboard at night.

typewriter, creeping of. It is not always practicable to fix the typewriter to the desk. If the machine "creeps," a cheap remedy may be applied in the form of small "feet" cut from a rubber sponge. These will cause the machine to cling to the table.

typewriter (music). It is possible to have certain musical signs fitted on to an ordinary typewriter. Experiments have also been made in America with a view to producing a special machine with keyboard largely devoted to musical signs.

typewriter, parts of, *see* note under " Parts of machine."

typewriter, the first. A typewriting machine was patented by Henry Mill in 1713, but it was not until 1872 that the first practical machine was put on the market. This was invented by C. Latham Scholes. It typed capitals only. The first shift-key typewriter (writing both caps. and small) appeared in 1878.

typewriter, weight of. The portable machines weigh from 8 to 14 lb., including cover. The full-size typewriter weighs 26 lb. or more.

typewriting charges. A scale of charges is recommended by the Incorporated Phonographic Society.

tyrannize.

tyre, band of metal or rubber round wheel. This spelling is popular, although tire is correct.

tyro, a novice.

Tyrwhitt. *See* Appendix II for pronunciation.

U

U.A., Underwriting Account.

u.A.w.g. (Ger.), *um Antwort wird gebeten,* please reply —or R.S.V.P.

uberrima fides (Lat.), superabounding faith.

ubi (Lat.), where.

Ubi libertas, ibi patria (Lat.), Where liberty is, there is my country.

ubique (Lat.), everywhere.

ubiquitous, being everywhere at the same time.

ubi supra (Lat.), where above-mentioned.

U.C., University College.

u.c., upper case (viz. capital letters).

U.D.C., Urban District Council, Union of Democratic Control.

U.K., United Kingdom.

ult., not recommended for use in correspondence; better to mention the month. (Lat. *ultimo* = last.)

ultima (Lat.), final, most remote.

ultima ratio (Lat.), the final argument.

ultima ratio regum (Lat.), the last argument of kings; hence, the force of war.

ultima thule (Lat.), the farthest boundary.

ultimatum, *pl.* ultimatums.

ultimum vale (Lat.), the last farewell.

ultimus (Lat.), the last.

ultimus Romanorum (Lat.), last of the Romans.

ultra (Lat.), beyond.

ultra licitum (Lat.), beyond what is permitted.

ultramarine, situated beyond the sea; blue pigment.

ultra-short.

ultra-violet.

ultra vires (Lat.), beyond one's powers.

umlaut, sign (¨) used in German to show modification of a vowel.

un-, words beginning with this prefix do not usually take a hyphen.

unanimity.

unauthorized.

una voce (Lat.), with one voice; unanimously.

unbiased, the more usual spelling.

unchristian.

und (Ger.), and.

under-. Words beginning with *under-* need no hyphen unless there would be a difficulty in pronouncing or the combination would appear clumsy.

under-exposure.

undergrowth.

underrate.

underscore. *See* notes under " lines, ruling " and " italic type."

under-secretary.

understudy.

under-tenancy.

under way, in progress, moving.

un-English.

uni-, one.

unilateral.

unique. Do not qualify this by more, quite, etc., as it is an absolute adjective, and admits of no comparison.

units of currency of the principal countries, *see* notes under the names of the individual countries.

unlicensed.

unmistakable.

uno animo (Lat.), unanimously.

unparalleled.

unpractical. Do not confuse with impracticable. *See* note under " practical."

unprecedented, having no precedent or previous example.

unrivalled.

U.N.R.R.A., United Nations Relief and Rehabilitation Administration.

unsaleable.

unserviceable.

unskilful.

untamable.

until, less used than *till.*

untrammelled, not hampered.

U.P., United Provinces, India.

uphill.

upholsterer.

upon, less common than *on,* but the choice between these two words is often decided by euphony.

upper case, a printer's term for the capital letters. In typewriting, the letters and signs that are made by depressing the shift key. Abbr. u.c.

Uppingham, Rutland.

Uppington, Shropshire.

upstairs.

up-to-date. Hyphenate only when *noun* follows immediately.

Ure. *See* Appendix II for pronunciation.

Urquhart. *See* Appendix II for pronunciation.

U.S., United Service.

U.S.A. Unit of currency 1 dollar = 100 cents.

usable.

user (legal), use.

U.S.I., United Service Institution.

U.S.N., United States Navy.

U.S.S.R., Union of Soviet Socialist Republics (For unit of currency *see* " Russia.")

usus loquendi (Lat.), usage in speaking.

ut dictum (Lat.), as said or directed.

utilitarianism, doctrine of the greatest happiness for the greatest number.

utilize.

ut infra (Lat.), as below.

Utopia, an ideal State.

ut supra (Lat.), as above.

Uvedale. *See* Appendix II for pronunciation.

U/W, underwriter.

Uwins. *See* Appendix II for pronunciation.

V

V, five (roman numerals).

v., verse, volt.

v., von (Ger.), of; *versus* (Lat.), against; *vice* (Lat.), in place of; *vide* (Lat.), see.

V.A., Vice-Admiral, Victoria and Albert (order of), for ladies.

Va., Virginia.

va., volt-ampere(s).

vaccinator.

vacillate, to fluctuate in opinion.

vacuum, *pl.* vacuums or vacua.

V.A.D., Voluntary Aid Detachment.

Vade in pace (Lat.), Go in peace.

vade-mecum, a small handbook to be carried about. (Lat. = go with me). Pronounce as four syllables.

vainglorious.

Vale! (Lat.), Farewell!

valet, man-servant.

valour, valorous.

valse (Fr.), waltz. Use the English form.

valuon. or valn. (legal), valuation.

van (Dutch), of; *van der*, of the. When these appear before names they usually have lower-case initials, but correspondent's signature should be noted and copied.

Vanbrough. *See* Appendix II for pronunciation.

vandyke collar, etc. (from name of Van Dyck, Flemish painter).

vanille (Fr.), vanilla.

vanitas vanitatum (Lat.), vanity of vanities.

vaporize.

vaporous.

variable spacer. Every typewriter contains mechanism which disengages the spacing apparatus and enables the cylinder to be turned to any point, as for algebraic characters or for typing on ruled lines.

variegated.

vasculum, botanist's collecting box; *pl.* vascula.

Vaughan. *See* Appendix II for pronunciation.

V.C., Vice-Chairman, Vice-Chancellor, Victoria Cross.

V.D.H., valvular disease of the heart.

vdrs. (legal), vendors.

veal-and-ham pie. Such word-groups must be hyphenated when forming an adjective.

veau (Fr.), calf, veal.

Veitch. *See* Appendix II for pronunciation.

veldt, tract of grass country in South Africa. (Dutch *veld.*)

vellum, smooth parchment.

Ven., Venerable.

vendetta, a blood feud.

Vendôme. *See* Appendix II for pronunciation.

vendors, abbr. vdrs. (legal).

venetian blind.

Veni, vidi, vici (Lat.), I came, I saw, I conquered.

ventilator.

ventis secundis (Lat.), with prosperous winds.

ventriloquism.

vera causa (Lat.), the true cause.

veracious, truthful.

veranda.

verba generalia (Lat.), general words.

verbatim, word for word.

verbatim et literatim (Lat.), word for word and letter for letter.

verboten (Ger.), forbidden.

verb. sap. (Lat.), *Verbum satis sapienti,* A word to the wise is sufficient.

verdigris, green substance formed on copper.

Veritas vincet (Lat.), Truth conquers.

vermicelli.

vermilion.

verse, abbr. v.; *pl.* vv. For hints on typing of verse, *see* note under "poetry."

vers libre, free verse, i.e. verses in which different metres are mixed, or the usual rules disregarded.

versus, against; abbr. *v.*

vertebra, *pl.* **vertebrae.**

vertebrate, animal having a spinal column; *pl.* **vertebrata.**

vertex, the highest point; *pl.* **vertexes or vertices.** *See* note under "apex."

Verulam. *See* Appendix II for pronunciation.

vessels' names to have quotes, or, if printed, to be in italics.

veto, *pl.* **vetoes.** (Lat. *veto =* I forbid.)

veuf (Fr.), widower.

veuve (Fr.), widow.

vexata quaestio (Lat.), a vexed question.

V.G., Vicar-General.

via (Lat.), by way of.

via crucis, via lucis (Lat.), the way of the cross, the way of light.

via media (Lat.), a mean between extremes.

via militaris (Lat.), military road.

Via trita, via tuta (Lat.), The beaten path is the safest.

Vice-. This is followed by a hyphen when prefixed to a name. It means "in the place of," and may be used in this sense (without initial cap) in the course of a sentence.

Viceroy of India. *See* Appendix I for correct form of address.

vice versa (Lat.).

vicissitudes.

victimize.

victualler, licensed inn-keeper (*pron.* vitler) ; **victualling** (*pron.* vitling).

vide (Lat.), literal meaning See! Should be used only when referring the reader to a book, chapter, verse, etc., and not in a general sense.

vide ante (Lat.), see before.

vide infra (Lat.), see below.

vide supra (Lat.), see above.

vie, vying.

vi et armis (Lat.), by main force.

vieux (Fr.), old.

viewpoint.

Vigilate et orate (Lat.), Watch and pray.

Vigor. *See* Appendix II for pronunciation.

vigour, vigorous.

vilify, to speak ill of.

villainous.

Villiers. *See* Appendix II for pronunciation.

Vincit omnia veritas (Lat.), Truth conquers all.

vin du pays (Fr.), wine of the neighbourhood.

vin ordinaire (Fr.), a cheap wine.

violoncello, abbr. 'cello.

Virginia, abbr. Va.

virginibus puerisque (Lat.), for girls and boys.

virtu, articles of, articles interesting because of their rarity, workmanship, etc. (Sometimes spelt *vertu.*)

virtuoso, one skilled in an art ; *pl.* **virtuosi** or **virtuosos.**

virtus et fide (Lat.), by virtue and faith.

Virtus incendit vires (Lat.), Virtue kindles one's vigour.

Virtus sola nobilitat (Lat.), Virtue alone ennobles.

virtute (Lat.), by virtue.

visa (Fr.), signature on a passport. Used as an English word, also the forms *viséd* and *viséing*, or *visaed, visae- ing*. Sometimes *visé* is used for the noun.

vis-à-vis (Fr.), face to face.

viscera, interior organs of the body (*pl.* form of Latin *viscus*).

Viscount or Baron. *See* Appendix I for correct form of address.

Viscountess. *See* Appendix I for correct form of address.

Viscount's daughter. *See* Appendix I for correct form of address.

Viscount's son. *See* Appendix I for correct form of address.

visé. See note under " visa."

vis inertiae (Lat.), passive resistance.

vis medicatrix naturae (Lat.), nature's power of heal- ing.

vis poetica (Lat.), poetic genius.

visualize.

vis viva (Lat.), living force.

Vita brevis, ars longa (Lat.), Life is short, art is long.

vitalize.

vitamins, vitamines.

vitiate, to corrupt, contaminate.

viticulture, grape-growing.

vitreous, pertaining to or consisting of glass.

vitriolic, having the qualities of vitriol (sulphuric acid). Figuratively: biting, very severe.

Viva! (It.), Long live!

Vivant rex et regina (Lat.), Long live the king and queen.

viva voce, orally. When used colloquially as noun may have plural *viva voces*.

Vivat respublica (Lat.), Long live the republic.

Vivat rex (Lat.), Long live the King.

Vive la République (Fr.), Long live the Republic!

Vive memor leti (Lat.), Live mindful of death.

Vive, vale (Lat.), Farewell and be happy.

vivisection.

viz. means namely, and stands for *videlicet* (Lat.), which comes from *videre licet* = " it is permitted to see." The *z* is not the letter in the alphabet, but the symbol used in medieval MSS. as a contraction for -*et*. There must always be a comma before viz. In most cases *namely* is preferred.

vocalize.

voce (It.), voice.

Voilà! (Fr.), Behold! There now!

Voilà tout (Fr.), That is all.

vol., volume.

volaille (Fr.), poultry.

vol-au-vent (Fr.), a pastry case filled with ragout of chicken, etc.

volcano, *pl.* volcanoes.

volente Deo (Lat.), God willing. More frequently *Deo volente.*

Volkslied (Ger.), folk-song; *pl. Volkslieder.*

volplane, *n.*, steep descent of a plane; *v.* to make such a descent.

volt-ampere(s), abbr. va.

volte-face (Fr.), a turning-round.

volume, abbr. vol.

von (Ger.), of. When appearing before a surname, it generally has lower-case initial.

voracious, greedy.

vortex, *pl.* vortexes or vortices. *See* note under " apex."

vouchsafed.

vox-humana (Lat.), reed-stop in an organ resembling human voice.

vox populi (Lat.), public opinion.

V.R., *Victoria Regina* (Lat.), Queen Victoria.

V.S., Veterinary Surgeon.

vulcanize.

vulgarize.

vv., verses.

vying, present participle of vie.

Vyvyan. *See* Appendix II for pronunciation.

W

W., west.

W.A., Western Australia.

Waddingham, Lincs

Waddington, Lancs, Lincoln.

Wadsworth. *See* Appendix II for pronunciation.

wages, this word is now plural.

Wagner. *See* Appendix II for pronunciation.

wagon, waggon.

wagon (Fr.), a railway carriage.

wagonette, waggonette.

wagon-lit (Fr.), sleeping car.

wainscoting.

Walford. *See* Appendix II for pronunciation.

walking-stick.

walk-over, an easy victory because of absence of competition.

Waller. *See* Appendix II for pronunciation.

wallflower.

wall-less.

wall-paper.

Walmesley. *See* Appendix II for pronunciation.

waltz, use this form in preference to the French *valse.*

Walzer (Ger.), waltz.

-ward. Words generally end in *-ward* for the *adj.* and *noun* (e.g. a westward position; a window to the westward), and *-wards* for the *adverb* (e.g. the boat moved westwards).

Waring. *See* Appendix II for pronunciation.

Warner. *See* Appendix II for pronunciation.

Warwickshire, abbr. War (no point).

Washfield, Devon.

Washford, Somerset.

wash-hand-stand, shorter and equally useful form: *wash-stand.*

washhouse.

wasn't, abbr. of was not.

Watchfield, Wilts

watchmaker.

watchword.

watercourse.

waterfall.

watering-place.

water-lily.

watermark, a design that appears in some makes of paper —helpful in ascertaining the right side.

waterproof.

watershed, a rise of land from which rivers flow.

water-tight.

waterworks.

Watten, Caithness.

Watton, Hertford, Norfolk, Yorks

Waugh. *See* Appendix II for pronunciation.

waxworks.

-ways, *see* note under "-wise."

W.B., way-bill.

W.C., west-central postal district.

W.D., War Department, Works Department.

W.E.A., Workers' Educational Association.

Weber. *See* Appendix II for pronunciation.

Weedon, Bucks, Northants

weekday.

week-end.

Weeton, Lancs, Leeds, Yorks

weight, abbr. wt.

weight of typewriter, *see* note under "typewriter, weight of."

weights. The abbreviations cwt., qr., lb., oz., and pt. do not take *s* for plural.

weird. This is one of the exceptions to the rule "*i* precedes *e* except after *c*."

Welborne, Norfolk.

Welbourn, Lincoln.

Welburn, York.

well-. When *well-* is linked to a participle and stands before a *noun,* the hyphen should be used, but not otherwise. Compare "a well-known man" with "His good deeds were well known."

well-being.

well-to-do.

well-wisher.

Welsh, modern spelling, except in the case of regiments, when *Welch* is used, except *Welsh Guards*.

welsh rabbit, more usual than rarebit.

Wemyss. *See* Appendix II for pronunciation.

west, *see* note under "north."

Westmorland.

w.f., wrong fount. This is an indication (used in proof-correcting) that the wrong style of type has been used.

The offending letter is circled, and *w.f.* written in the margin.

w.g., wire gauge.

wh., watt-hour.

whalebone.

wharf, *pl.* wharfs or wharves; abbr. whf.

Wharton. *See* Appendix II for pronunciation.

whas. (legal), whereas.

whate'er, poetical variant of whatever.

whatsr. (legal), whatsoever.

whby. (legal), whereby.

wheelbarrow.

wheelwright.

whereas, abbr. whas. (legal).

whereby, abbr. whby. (legal).

wherein, abbr. whrin. (legal).

wheresoever.

wherewithal.

whether, abbr. whr. (legal).

whether or no is allowable, the *no* representing not.

whf., wharf.

which and that (difference between), *see* note under " that and which."

while, preferable to whilst.

whirlpool.

whirlwind.

whisky, *pl.* whiskies.

whiskey, *pl.* whiskeys.

Whitbourne, Worcester.

Whitburn, Durham, West Lothian.

Whitchurch, Bristol, Bucks, Cardiff, Devon, Hants, Herefordshire, Reading, Shropshire, Warwickshire.

Whitechurch, Cork, Dorset.

white space, a printer's term to indicate space that is not occupied by printing. It has great artistic value. This should be appreciated by the typist in displaying her work.

whitewash.

whiting, a fish. Also prepared chalk; tendency to use *whitening* because the *verb* is now to whiten instead of to white.

Whit-Sunday [but Whitsun-day (15th May) in Scotland].

Whitsuntide.

Whittingehame, East Lothian.

Whittingham, Lancs, Northumberland.

Whittington, Lancs, Newcastle-on-Tyne, Shropshire, Staffs, Worcester.

whoever, used colloquially, both as subject and object. In literary use, whosoever is the subject and whomsoever the object.

whole-hearted.

whole plate (photography), $8\frac{1}{2} \times 6\frac{1}{2}$ in.

wholesomeness.

whomever (object), rarely used.

whomsoever, *see* note under " whoever."

whooping-cough.

whosoever, *see* note under " whoever."

whr. (legal), whether.

whrin. (legal), wherein.

wideawake. Use this form when meaning the broad felt hat and when an *adj.* preceding *noun*, but not in the sense of " She was wide awake."

widespread.

Wigton, Cumberland.

Wigtown, Wigtownshire.

wilful.

Will. Should be typed on foolscap, in double spacing. Usually there is no paragraph indentation. The attestation clause should be typed three spaces into the margin with room left beside it for testator's signature.

Willingdon, Sussex.

Willingham, Cambridge, Lincs.

Willington, Bedford, Chester, Derby, Durham, Kent.

Williton, Somerset.

will-o'-the-wisp.

willynilly.

Wiltshire, abbr. Wilts (no point).

window envelopes. These have a transparent panel through which the name and address may be seen. The typing of envelopes is thus saved, but the letter, invoice, etc., must be folded in a special way so as to expose the address.

winepress.

Winston, Durham.

Winstone, Glos.

Wis., Wisconsin.

-wise. In some words, *-ways* or *-wise* is used (e.g. endways, endwise, longways, longwise), but *-wise* is by far the commoner ending. It is usual, also, in words made from *nouns*, specially for the occasion.

Wishart. *See* Appendix II for pronunciation.

wishful.

wistaria, name of a plant (after the American scientist, Wistar).

withhold.

without, abbr. ex., witht. (legal).

witht. (legal), without.

witned. (legal), witnessed.

witneth. (legal), witnesseth.

wits' end (at).

witticism.

WNW., west-north-west (compass).

W.O., War Office.

Wodehouse. *See* Appendix II for pronunciation.

woebegone.

Wollaston, Northants

Wollaton, Nottingham.

Wollerton, Shropshire.

Wolsey. *See* Appendix II for pronunciation.

won't, colloquial form of will not.

woodcut.

woodenness.

Woodhouse, Leeds, Leicestershire, Sheffield.

Woodhouses, Lancs

woodland.

Woodleigh, Devon.

Woodley, Berks, Stockport.

woodpecker.

woodwork.

woolly.

Woolsack (House of Lords).

Woolston, Lancs

Woolton, Liverpool.

Worcestershire, abbr. Worcs (no point).

workaday.

worsted, a woollen yarn; first manufactured at Worstead in Norfolk.

wouldst.

W.P.B., colloquial contraction for waste-paper basket.

W.R.A., Wireless Retailers' Association.

wrack, seaweed. *See also* note under " rack."

wrapt, another form of *rapt*, which now usually means absorbed. *Wrapped* should be used for the past tense of wrap.

wreath (*noun*).

wreathe (*verb*).

wreck, *see* note under " rack."

wristband, *pron.* rizband.

write you, this is unidiomatic; use "write to you."

wrongdoing.

W.S., Writer to the Signet.

W/T, Wireless Telegraphy.

wt., weight.

wych-hazel, preferable to *witch-*.

Wyllie. *See* Appendix II for pronunciation.

Wyllie, Mon

Wylye, Wilts

X

X, ten (roman numerals).

X., Christ.

X^bre, Fr. abbreviation for *Décembre* (December).

XC, 90 (roman numerals).

x. cp., without coupon.

x.d. or ex div., without dividend.

xenomania, abnormal liking for things foreign.

x.i., without interest.

Xmas, Christmas (no point). An ugly abbreviation—to
be avoided.

Xn., Xtian., Christian.

X-ray.

xylonite, celluloid.

xylophone, instrument played with wooden hammers.

Y

Y., year.

yacht.

yard, abbr. yd.

yashmak, veil worn by Moslem women.

Y.B., year-book.

yd., yard, yards.

year-book, abbr. Y.B.

years. In quoting years, give the fewest figures that suffice, e.g. 1907–8, not 1907–08.

yen, unit of currency of Japan; *pl.* yen.

yes, *pl.* yeses.

yeux (Fr.), eyes; *pl.* of *œil.*

Y.H.A., Youth Hostels Association.

yieldg. (legal), yielding.

Y.L.I., Yorkshire Light Infantry.

Y.M.C.A., Young Men's Christian Association.

yodelling, special kind of singing practised by Swiss and Tyrolese mountaineers.

yoicks, an old fox-hunting cry.

Yorkshire, abbr. Yorks (no point).

you and I. This phrase is not invariably correct, as many people suppose. When the pronouns are in the objective, me should be used, e.g. " She sent the books for you and me."

yours (no apostrophe).

Yours faithfully, etc. *See* note under " complimentary close."

youthfulness.

yr., year, your, younger.

Yugoslavia (sometimes seen as Yugo-Slavia). *Adj.* Yugoslav. Unit of currency 1 dinar = 100 paras.

Y.W.C.A., Young Women's Christian Association.

Z

zenana, part of the house (in India) in which the women are secluded.

zenith, summit of ambition or happiness. Opposite to nadir.

Zeppelin, airship designed by Count Ferdinand von Zeppelin.

zigzagging.

zinc, abbr. Zn (no point).

zincography, printing from zinc.

zingaro (It.), a gipsy, *pl. zingari*; *fem. zingara, pl. zingare.*

zloty, unit of currency of Poland.

Zn, zinc.

zoology.

zouave, a French soldier. In English the word means a woman's short jacket similar to that of the soldier's uniform.

Zucker (Ger.), sugar.

Zug (Ger.), train.

Zwieback (Ger.), kind of rusk or biscuit.

SPECIAL SYMBOLS

$, dollar.

:/S/:, the repeat mark in music.

/, shilling.

§, section.

¶, paragraph.

%, per cent.

&, and.

@, at.

°, degree of a circle, latitude, longitude, temperature.

', a minute, 60th of a degree, a foot.

", a second, 360th of a degree, an inch.

See also "accents and diacritical marks" and "correction marks."

APPENDIX I

CORRECT FORM OF ADDRESS

Alderman.—*Address:* Alderman T. J. Brown, Alderman Sir Henry Brown, Alderman Mrs. (or Miss) E. Brown.

Ambassador.—*Address:* His Excellency (rank or title), H.B.M.'s Ambassador Extraordinary and Plenipotentiary to ——. *Begin:* My Lord . . . or according to rank. *End:* I have the honour to be, My Lord (*or* Sir), Your Excellency's obedient servant. The wife of an Ambassador has the courtesy title of " Her Excellency."

Archbishop.—*Address:* The Most Rev. His Grace the Lord Archbishop of ——. *Begin:* My Lord Archbishop, *or* Your Grace. *End:* I remain, My Lord Archbishop, Your Grace's obedient servant. *Socially:* My dear Lord, *or* My dear Lord Archbishop. *End:* I have the honour to remain, My dear Lord Archbishop, Your Grace's very faithfully, *or* Your Grace's very truly. The Archbishop of Armagh is addressed as " His Grace the Lord Primate of Ireland." The wife of an Archbishop has no title in right of her husband, but is simply " Mrs. A——."

Archdeacon.—*Address:* To the Venerable the Archdeacon of ——. *Begin:* Venerable Sir. *End:* I remain, Venerable Sir, Your most obedient servant. *Socially:* Dear Mr. Archdeacon, *or* Dear Archdeacon.

Baron.—*Address:* To the Right Honourable Lord ——. *Begin:* My Lord. *End:* I have the honour to be, My Lord, Your Lordship's obedient servant. *Socially:* Dear Lord ——. *End:* Very faithfully yours.

Baroness.—*Address:* To the Right Honourable Lady ——. *Begin:* Madam. *End:* I have the honour to be, Madam, Your Ladyship's obedient servant. *Socially:* Dear Lady ——. *End:* Very faithfully yours.

Baron's Daughter.—She has the title " Honourable " prefixed to her Christian name. If married, the only change is in her surname; if to a commoner, she is addressed as " The Honourable Mrs."; if to a Baronet or Knight, " The Honourable Lady."

Baron's Son.—*Address:* To the Honourable James ——. *Begin:* Sir. *End:* I remain, Sir, Your most obedient servant.

Baronet.—*Address:* To Sir John A——, Bart. *Begin:*

Sir. *End:* I remain, Sir, Your most obedient servant. *Socially:* Dear Sir Edward. *End:* Faithfully yours, *or* Sincerely yours.

Baronet's Wife.—*Address:* Lady —— (omit Christian name). *Begin:* Madam. *End:* I am, Madam, Your obedient servant.

Bishop.—*Address:* To the Right Reverend the Lord Bishop of ——. *Begin:* My Lord. *End:* I remain, My Lord, Your Lordship's obedient servant. *Socially:* My dear Lord, *or* My dear Lord Bishop, *or* Dear Bishop. *End:* Faithfully yours, *or* Truly yours. The wife of a Bishop has no title in right of her husband, but is simply " Mrs. ——." By virtue of his position, the Bishop of London is a member of the Privy Council, and is addressed: The Right Reverend and Right Honourable the Lord Bishop of London.

Bishop Retired.—*Address:* To the Right Reverend Bishop ——. *Begin:* Right Reverend Sir.

Bishop Suffragan.—*Address:* To the Right Reverend the Bishop Suffragan of ——. *Begin:* Right Reverend Sir.

Cardinal.—*Address:* His Eminence Cardinal ——. If he is also an Archbishop, His Eminence Cardinal ——, Archbishop of ——, *or* His Eminence Cardinal Archbishop of ——. *Begin:* My Lord Cardinal, *or* My Lord. *End:* I remain, My Lord, Your Eminence's obedient servant.

Clergyman (Rector, Vicar or Curate).—*Address:* To the Rev. John B——. *Begin:* Sir. *End:* I remain, Sir, Your obedient servant. *Socially:* Dear Mr. B——.

Colonial Bishops.—*See under* Bishop.

Countess.—*Address:* To the Right Honourable the Countess of ——. *Begin:* Madam. *End:* I have the honour to be, Madam, Your Ladyship's obedient servant. *Socially:* Dear Lady B——. *End:* Very faithfully yours, *or* Very sincerely yours.

County Court Judges.—*See under* Judges.

Dean.—*Address:* To the Very Rev. ——, Dean of ——. *Begin:* Very Reverend Sir. *End:* I remain, Reverend Sir, Your most obedient servant. *Socially:* Dear Dean. (Note: Use *Very Rev.* for Dean of a Cathedral and only *Rev.* for Dean of a College, or a Rural Dean.)

Duchess.—*Address:* To Her Grace the Duchess of ——. *Begin:* Your Grace (*or* Madam). *End:* I have the honour to be, Madam, Your Grace's obedient servant. *Socially:* My dear Duchess.

Duchess, Royal.—*Address:* To Her Royal Highness, The

Duchess of ——. *Begin:* Madam. *End:* I have the honour to be, Madam, Your Grace's obedient servant.

Duke.—*Address:* To His Grace the Duke of ——. *Begin:* My Lord Duke. *End:* I have the honour to be, My Lord Duke, Your Grace's obedient servant. *Socially:* My dear Duke.

Duke, Royal.—*Address:* To His Royal Highness the Duke of ——. *Begin:* Sir. *End:* I remain, Sir, Your Royal Highness's, &c.

Duke's Daughter.—Address personally as "Your Ladyship." *Begin:* Madam. *End:* I remain, Madam, Your Ladyship's most obedient servant. The title of "Lady" is prefixed to her Christian name. If married to any person not a peer, she retains her title and precedence, changing only her surname.

Duke's Eldest Son.—Takes his father's second title and is addressed as though he were really a Marquis or an Earl.

Duke's Younger Sons.—The title of "Lord" is prefixed to their Christian names. *Address:* Lord Robert ——. *Begin:* My Lord. The wife takes the title of "Lady." *Address:* Lady Robert ——.

Earl.—*Address:* To the Right Honourable the Earl of ——. *Begin:* My Lord. *End:* I have the honour to be, my Lord, Your Lordship's obedient servant.

Earl's Daughter.—*See under* Duke's Daughter.

Earl's Eldest Son.—Has his father's second title, and is addressed as if he were really a Viscount or a Baron.

Earl's Younger Son.—*See under* Baron's Son.

Earl's Wife.—*See under* Countess.

Envoy Extraordinary and Minister Plenipotentiary. —*Address:* To —— (according to rank), H.B.M.'s Envoy Extraordinary and Minister Plenipotentiary to ——.

Governors of British Overseas Possessions.—*Address:* To His Excellency Governor Sir William ——, *or* To His Excellency Sir William ——, Governor of Ceylon, *or* To His Excellency W. S——, Esq., Governor and Commander-in-Chief of British Guiana. *Begin:* Sir. *End:* I have the honour to be, Sir, Your Excellency's obedient servant. Consult *Whitaker's Almanack* as to precise title for the particular Dominion or Colony, e.g. Viceroy, Governor-General, Governor, Lieutenant-Governor, High Commissioner, Commissioner, Administrator, British Resident, Resident, or Captain-General.

Judges.—Lord Chief Justice. *Address:* To the Right Honourable Lord Chief Justice of England. *Begin:* My Lord. *End.* I have the honour to be, with great respect, Your Lordship's most obedient servant.

Puisne Judges.—*Address:* To the Honourable Mr. Justice ——.

County Court Judges of England and Wales.—*Address:* To His Honour Judge ——.

The King.—*Address:* To the King's Most Excellent Majesty. *Begin:* Sire, May it please Your Majesty. *End:* I remain, Your Majesty's faithful and dutiful servant.

Knight.—*Address:* To Sir Thomas Y——. *Begin:* Sir, *or* Dear Sir Thomas. *End:* I remain, Sir, Your most obedient servant.

Knight's Wife.—*See under* Baronet's Wife.

Lord Advocate.—*Address:* The Right Honourable Sir.

Lord Chancellor.—*Address:* To the Right Honourable ——, Lord High Chancellor of England. *Begin:* My Lord. *End:* I have the honour to be, my Lord, Your Lordship's obedient servant.

Lord High Commissioner to the General Assembly of the Church of Scotland.—*Address:* To His Grace the Lord High Commissioner.

Lord Justice General.—*Address:* To the Right Honourable Lord Justice General. *Begin:* My Lord.

Lord Mayor.—*Address:* To the Right Honourable the Lord Mayor. *Begin:* My Lord. *End:* Your Lordship's obedient servant. The wife has the title of "Lady Mayoress." Address personally as "Your Ladyship." *Begin:* Madam. *See also* Mayor.

Lords of Session (Judges in Scotland).—*Address:* To the Honourable Lord ——. *Begin:* My Lord. The wife has the title of "Lady." Address personally as "Your Ladyship." *Begin:* Madam.

Maids of Honour.—*Begin:* Madam. Have the title of "Honourable" prefixed to their Christian name, if they have not it already by courtesy.

Marchioness.—*Address:* To the Most Honourable the Marchioness of ——. *Begin:* My Lady, *or* Madam. *End:* I have the honour to be, My Lady (Madam), Your Ladyship's obedient servant.

Marquess.—*Address:* To the Most Honourable the Marquess of ——. *Begin:* My Lord Marquess, *or* My Lord. *End:* I have the honour to be, My Lord Marquess, Your (*or* Your Lordship's) obedient servant.

Marquess's Daughter.—*See under* Duke's Daughter.

Marquess's Eldest Son.—Takes his father's second title, and is addressed as if he were an Earl or a Viscount.

Marquess's Younger Son.—*See under* Duke's Younger Sons.

Mayor of a Borough.—*Address:* The Worshipful the Mayor of ——. *Begin:* Sir. *End:* I remain, Sir, your most obedient servant. *Socially:* My dear Mayor, *or* Dear Mr. Mayor.

Mayor of a City.—*Address:* The Right Worshipful the Mayor of ——. *Begin:* Sir. *End:* I remain, Sir, Your most obedient servant. *Socially:* My dear Mayor, *or* Dear Mr. Mayor.

Military Officers.—All officers in the Army above Lieutenant have their military rank prefixed to their name and title, e.g. General the Right Honourable Lord ——, P.C., G.C.B., *or* General Right Hon. Sir James ——, P.C., G.C.B., *or* Major-General Sir John ——, G.C.S.I.

Minister Resident.—*Address:* To ——, Esq. (or according to rank), H.B.M.'s Minister Resident to ——. *Begin:* Sir. *End:* According to rank or title.

Moderator of the Established Church of Scotland.—*Address:* To the Right Reverend the Moderator ——. *Begin:* Right Rev. Sir. *End:* I remain, Right Reverend Sir, Your most obedient servant.

Naval Officers.—Officers in the Navy above Sub-Lieutenant have their naval rank prefixed to their name and title, e.g. Admiral the Right Honourable Lord ——, P.C., G.C.B., *or* Admiral Right Hon. Sir George ——, P.C., G.C.B., *or* Rear-Admiral Sir Thomas ——, G.C.V.O.

Pasha (Civil).—*Address:* His Excellency (James Jones) Pasha. *Begin:* Excellency. *End:* I remain, Your Excellency's obedient servant.

Pasha (Military, Egyptian Army).—*Address:* His Excellency Ferik (Lieut.-General) —— Pasha, *or,* His Excellency Lewa (Maj.-General) —— Pasha. *Begin:* Excellency. *End:* I remain, Your Excellency's obedient servant.

Prince.—*Address:* His Royal Highness Prince ——. *Begin:* Sir. *End:* I remain, Sir, Your Royal Highness's obedient servant.

Princess.—*Address:* To Her Royal Highness Princess

——. *Begin:* Madam. *End:* I have the honour to be, Madam, Your Royal Highness's obedient servant.

Privy Councillor.—*Address:* The Right Honourable Thomas ——, *or* The Right Honourable Sir Thomas ——. *Begin:* Sir. *End:* I have the honour to be, Sir, Your obedient servant.

The Queen.—*Address:* To the Queen's Most Excellent Majesty. *Begin:* Madam, May it please Your Majesty. *End:* I remain, Madam, Your Majesty's obedient servant.

Suffragan Bishop.—*See under* Bishop Suffragan.

The Treasury.—*Address:* The Lords Commissioners of the Treasury, Whitehall, London, S.W.1. *Begin:* My Lords. *End:* I have the honour to be, Your Lordships' obedient servant.

Viceroy of India.—*See under* Governors of British Overseas Possessions.

Viscount.—*Address:* To the Right Honourable the Viscount —— (of ——). *Begin:* My Lord. *End:* I have the honour to be, my Lord, Your Lordship's obedient servant.

Viscountess.—*See under* Countess.

Viscount's Daughter.—*See under* Baron's Daughter.

Viscount's Son.—*See under* Baron's Son.

APPENDIX II

PRONUNCIATION OF PROPER NAMES

Abercrombie, *ab*-er-krum-be.
Agassiz, *ag*-a-se.
Alcester, *awl*-ster.
Arnaud, *ar*-no.
Assheton, *ash*-ton.
Augereau, *o*-zher-o.
Avebury, *ayve*-be-re.
Ayscough, *as*-kew, *as*-key,
ays-ko.
Aytoun, *a*-ton.

Bagehot, *bag*-ot or *baj*-ot.
Balcarres, bal-*kar*-ris.
Baring, *bare*-ing.
Barocci, ba-*rotch*-e.
Baumeister, *bow*-my-ster.
Bayard, *bay*-ard.
Beaconsfield,
beck-ons-field.
Beauchamp, *bee*-cham.
Beauclerc, *bo*-klerk.
Beaufort, *bo*-fort.
Beaulieu, *bew*-le.
Beaumarchais,
bo-*marsh*-ay.
Beaumont, *bo*-mont.
Bellew, bel-*yoo*.
Bellini, bel-*een*-e.
Bellot, *bel*-o.
Belvoir, *bee*-vor.
Benoit, be-*nwah*.
Berkeley, *bark*-le.
Berkshire, *bark*-sher.
Berlioz, *ber*-le-o.
Bertie, *bar*-te.
Bethune, *beet*-on.
Bewick, *bew*-ik.
Bledisloe, *bleds*-loo.

Bligh, bly.
Blount, blunt.
Blyth, bly, blīth.
Boleyn, *bull*-en.
Bolivar, bo-*le*-var.
Bompas, *bump*-us.
Boord, bord.
Borghese, bor-*gaze*-e.
Bourchier, *bou*-cher.
Bourke, burk.
Bourne, born or burn.
Breadalbane,
bre-*dawl*-ban.
Broke, brook.
Brougham, *broo*-am.
Buchanan, bu-*kan*-an.
Bunsen, *boon*-sen.
Burdett, bur-*dett*.
Burghley, *bur*-ley.

Cadogan, ka-*dug*-an.
Caius, keys.
Carnegie, *kar*-neg-e.
Cassilis, *kas*-sils.
Cecil, *sis*-il.
Chalmers, *chahm*-ers.
Charteris, *chart*-ers.
Chisholm, *chiz*-om.
Cholmeley,
Cholmondeley, or
Chomley, *chum*-le.
Cirencester, *sis*-i-ter.
Clerk, klark.
Clerke, klark.
Clowes, klouze.
Cockburn, *co*-burn.
Coke, kook.
Colquhoun, ko-*hoon*.
Combe, koom.

Comines, ko-*meen.*
Compton, *kum*-ton.
Constable, *kun*-sta-bl.
Corbould, *kor*-bold.
Couch, kooch.
Couper, *koo*-per.
Coutts, koots.
Coventry, *kuv*-en-tre.
Cowper, *cow*-per, *coo*-per.
Cozens, *kuz*-zens.
Creighton, *kray*-ton.
Crichton, *kri*-ton.
Curties, *kurt*-is.

Dalhousie, dal-*hoo*-ze.
Dalton, *dawl*-ton.
Dalziel, dee-*ell.*
Derby, *dar*-by.
Didot, *de*-do.
Dougal, *doo*-gal.
Duchesne, du-*karn.*
Duguid, *du*-gid.
Dysart, *dy*-sart.

Eardley, *eerd*-le.
Earle, ërl.
Eire, *ā*-rah (like Sarah).
Elgin, *elg*-in.
Ely, *ee*-le.
Erskine, *ers*-kin.
Euler, *oil*-er.
Ewart, *yu*-art.
Ewing, *yu*-ing.

Fabre, *fah*-br.
Falconer, *fawk*-ner.
Farquhar, *fark*-war.
Farquharson, *fark*-er-sun.
Featherston(e) haugh,
        pronounced in full.
Fenwick, *fen*-nik.
Fildes, fylds.
Forsyth, tor-*sythe.*
Fortescue, *fort*-es-kew.
Foulis, fowls.
Foulkes, fokes or fooks.
Fries, freez.

Galen, *gay*-len.
Gallagher, *gal*-la-her.
Gallwey, *gawl*-way.
Garioch, *gar*-rik, *gar*-i-ok.
Geddes, *ged*-es.
Gee, jee.
Genlis, *zhon*-leess.
Geoffrey, *jeff*-re.
Geoghegan, *gay*-gan.
Gerard, *jer*-rard.
Gloucester, *glos*-ter.
Gough, goff.
Gould, goold.
Gower, gore, gower.
Greenhalgh, *green*-halje,
        green-halg.
Greig, greg.
Grosvenor, *gro*-ven-or.

Hakluyt, *hak*-loyt.
Hardinge, *hard*-ing.
Hawarden, *har*-den
        (village).
Hawarden, *hay*-ward-en
        (peer).
Heathcote, *heth*-cot.
Hepburn, *heb*-burn.
Hertford, *har*-ford.
Hervey, *har*-ve.
Holmes, homes.
Home, hume, home.
Homfray, *hum*-fre.
Horace, hor-*as.*
Hotham, *huth*-am.
Houghton, *ho*-ton, *how*-ton.

Ian, *e*-ahn.
Inge, ing.
Ingelow, *ing*-lo.
Ingres, *an*-gr.
Inigo, *in*-e-go.
Innes, *in*-is.
Isidore, *is*-e-dor.
Iveagh, *ive*-ah or *iv*-y.

Jansen, *yan*-sen.

Kearney, *kar*-ne.
Keble, *kee*-bl.
Keith, keeth.
Kekewich, *kek*-wich.
Kerr, ker, kar.
Kirkby, *kir*-be.
Knollys, noles.
Kyrle, kurl.

Latham, *lay*-tham.
Laudon, *low*-don.
Layard, laird.
Leconfield, *lek*-on-field.
Leigh, lee (place-name
  sometimes, lie).
Leighton, *lay*-ton.
Le Queux, le-*kew*.
Lever, *lee*-ver.
Lindsay, *lin*-ze.
Loudon, Loudoun,
              low-don.

Macbean, mak-*bain*.
Mackay, ma-*ky*.
Maclachlan, mak-*loch*-lan.
Macleod, ma-*kloud*.
Mahon, mahn.
Mainwaring, *man*-ner-ing.
Marjoribanks,
              marsh-banks.
Maugham, mawm.
Melhuish, *mel*-lish.
Mempes, memps.
Mentone, men-tō-nĕ.
Menzies, *ming*-es, *meng*-es.
Meux, mews.
Meyer, *my*-er.
Milnes, mils.
Monro, mun-*ro*.
Monson, *mun*-son.
Monzie, mo-*nee*.

Napier, *nay*-peer.
Nigel, *ny*-jel.

Owen, *o*-en.

Paget, *paj*-et.
Palgrave, *pawl*-grave.
Palmer, *pahm*-er.
Paton, *pay*-ton.
Pellew, pe-*loo*.
Petrie, *pee*-tree.
Pliny, *plin*-e.
Plumptree, *plum*-tree.
Ponsonby, *pun*-sun-be.
Pontefract, *pum*-fret (per-
  sonal name), *pon*-te-
  fract (town).
Poulett, *paw*-let.
Powys, *po*-iss.
Pugh, pew.

Quaritch, *quor*-ritch.
Quincey, *kwin*-se.
Quinet, *kee*-nay.

Raleigh, rally, *rah*-ley.
Ralph, rafe, ralf.
Reading, *red*-ing.
Reay, ray.
Rees, reece.
Regnault, *ray*-nyo.
Reuter, *roy*-ter.
Rhys, reece. •
Roget, *ro*-zhay.
Romney, *rum*-ne.
Ruthven, rĭvn.

St. John (personal name),
  sin-jun.
St. Leger, sellinger (oc-
  casionally Saint Leger).
Salmon, *sal*-mon, *sam*-on.
Sandys, sands.
Savile, *sav*-il.
Scrimgeour, *skrim*-jor.
Sinn Fein, shin fain.
Skrine, skreen.
Somers, *sum*-ers.
Somerville, *sum*-er-vil.
Soult, soolt.
Southwark, *suth*-ark.

Southwell, *suth*-el (also as spelt).
Sowerby, *sour*-be.
Stourton, *stur*-ton.
Stowe, sto.
Sydenham, *sid*-en-am.

Tannhäuser, tan-*hoi*-zr.
Tauchnitz, *towk*-nitz.
Teynham, *ten*-ham.
Thalberg, *tal*-berg.
Theobald, *tib*-ald.
Thompson, *tom*-son.
Thoms, toms.
Thoreau, *tho*-ro.
Tomline, *tom*-lin.
Tonbridge, *tun*-bridj.
Townshend, *towns*-end.
Tremayne, tre-*main*.
Trevelyan, tre-*vel*-yan.
Treves, treeves.
Trevor, *trev*-or.
Tyrwhitt, tïrit.

Ure, yewr.
Urquhart, *urk*-ut.

Uvedale, *yewv*-dale.
Uwins, *ew*-inz.

Vanbrough, *van*-broo.
Vaughan, vawn.
Veitch, veech.
Vendôme, *von*-dome.
Verulam, *ver*-ru-lam.
Vigor, *vy*-gor.
Villiers, *vil*-ers.
Vyvyan, *viv*-yan.

Wadsworth, *wods*-wurth.
Wagner, *vahg*-ner.
Walford, *wall*-ford.
Waller, *wol*-er.
Walmesley, *wawms*-le.
Waring, *ware*-ing.
Warner, *worn*-er.
Waugh, waw.
Weber, *vay*-ber.
Wemyss, weemz.
Wharton, *whor*-ton.
Wodehouse, *wood*-house.
Wolsey, *wool*-ze.
Wyllie, *wy*-le.

APPENDIX III

THE ARCHITECTURE AND LAY-OUT OF LETTERS

CONSIDERATION of the finished appearance of typed letters is well worth while. The quality of the actual typing itself may be good, but may be nullified if no attention has been paid to the arrangement and presentation.

Every typewritten letter should embody these architectural qualities: balance, proportion, and unity. The degree of good taste and judgment of the individual typist will influence her interpretation of all these factors, but generally the desired results can be attained by observing the following simple rules.

Balance.—Consider the length of the letter to be typed. If it is short, reduce the measure of the typed lines by setting the margins accordingly. If the letter is likely to fill the sheet, set the margins to give a wider measure of type line. If the letter must undoubtedly go over on to a second or third sheet, set the margins so as to give a moderately wide measure of type line. Watch your work when nearing the end of the letter, and avoid taking a second sheet for only one line.

Whether the letter be short, medium, or long, margins at left, right, and at bottom should be adequate: ample enough to convey a sense of "holding" the massed grouping of typed matter on the sheet. Skimped, meagre margins give a cramped effect, and actually make reading less easy. Aim at making the right-hand margin as level as possible: (*a*) by setting the right-hand margin stop and heeding the warning bell; and (*b*) by proper division of words at line-ends.

In ordinary business correspondence the name and address of the addressee is placed at the head of the letter. Each line of this should be in line with—

should "square" with—the left-hand margin; and, whether the body of the letter be single-spaced or double-spaced, this matter should form a compact, neat group, *single*-spaced.

In nearly all official correspondence, and in many legal offices, it is the practice to group the name and address of the addressee at the foot of the letter.

The date, in ordinary business correspondence, should appear on the right-hand side to "square" with the *average* limit of the body matter—the *average* right-hand margin. The most usual and most easily read form is:

13th December, 2060.

but some people prefer a more fanciful arrangement.

Proportion.—This is closely associated with the factor of balance, dealt with in the preceding paragraphs. Good proportion is attained by properly relating the size and shape of the grouped typed matter to the size and shape of the sheet, and to the margins.

Unity.—The impression of unity is achieved when massing, margins, balance, and proportion are harmonized, and when a sense of order and planned arrangement is conveyed by the finished work.

On the following pages are reproduced actual typed letters, examples of good and bad lay-out.

TELEPHONE MULCORN 0434 (2 LINES)   TELEGRAMS CERTIFICATE ESTBLND. LONDON

JORDAN & SONS, LIMITED
PUBLISHERS

ALSO AT
13, BROAD STREET PLACE,
E.C.2

Our Ref. JGB/MC

Your Ref.

116 CHANCERY LANE
LONDON: W.C.2

1st August, 2060.

B. A. Fairman, Esq., B.Com.,
21 Grove Crescent,
Palmers Green, N.EC.

Dear Mr. Fairman,

I have your letter of yesterday, enclosing synopsis of your proposed work on "World Trade in the Future."

If you can arrange to call here at 2.30 p.m. on Wednesday, the 6th inst., I shall be pleased to discuss the matter with you.

Yours very truly,

EDITOR

A good example of proper adjustment of line measure, grouping, and white space when the letter is a short one.

JORDAN & SONS, LIMITED

PUBLISHERS

116 CHANCERY LANE
LONDON: W.C.2

Our Ref: R/ST

Your Ref:

Friday,
Twenty-first
June,
2090

Mrs. J. A. McIntyre,
21A, St. Thomas's Road,
NEWCASTLE-ON-TYNE.

Dear Madam,

Thank you for your letter of yesterday's date
asking our advice about a textbook on typewriting.

We suggest you cannot do better than use our
"Typewriting Self-taught," which has proved very popular
and is specially suitable for the intelligent adult
working at home without supervision. It should cover
all you need in order to be able to type your own articles and verses.

You can order the work through a local bookseller, or, if you prefer, we will post it direct on
receipt of remittance for 1s. 2d. to include postage.

Yours faithfully,
JORDAN & SONS, LIMITED,

Director

An attractive, well-balanced letter of medium length. Note the
measure of the type lines, and the evenness of the right-hand
margin. A fanciful arrangement of the date is shown.

The advantages to be gained by converting a business into a Private Limited Company may be summarised as follows:—

The liability of the Members is limited to the amount unpaid (if any) on the Shares held by them.

The respective interests of the persons engaged in the business can be easily provided for.

The conversion enables the proprietor of the business (or any other shareholder) to determine precisely and intelligibly the interests of beneficiaries under his Will, thus facilitating the distribution of his estate by his executors.

The appointment, retirement, or removal of Directors is effected in a simple manner.

Facilities are afforded for obtaining additional Capital and borrowing money, and for amalgamating or establishing reciprocal interests with other bodies.

Employees may, with adequate safeguards, be afforded an opportunity of acquiring interests in the business corresponding to their respective positions and responsibilities, or Shares may be allotted for services rendered or in pursuance of a profit-sharing policy. The maximum number of Members is fifty (exclusive of employees and of ex-employees who on leaving the employment of the Company have retained Shares acquired by them during that employment), and thus the number of persons who may be associated in the enterprise is far greater than could be included as Partners in a workable Partnership.

Neither the continuance of the business nor the position of the remaining Members is affected by the death of one of their number, as no obligation rests upon the survivors to realise the interest of the deceased in the Company. Similarly the retirement of a Member by the disposal of his Shares does not concern the other Members.

The liability of the Executors acting for deceased Shareholders of a Company is clearly defined.

The disposal of the whole or part of the business to any other company, firm, or person is facilitated.

In all these respects Limited Companies and also Members thereof individually are in a more advantageous position than general Partnerships (unregistered) or Partnerships registered under The Limited Partnerships Act, 1907, and the Members thereof.

A Private Company enjoys, as compared with a Public Company, many privileges. Thus - (1) A Private Company may consist of two persons. (This is an important consideration where the business is managed by two or three members of a family who desire to be exclusively interested in the Company, for a Public Company must have at least seven Members. (2) A Private Company is relieved from the obligation imposed on every Public Company to lodge with the Registrar of Companies every year a copy of its last balance sheet. (The copy of the balance sheet required to be lodged by a Public Company has to be included in the Annual Return. By its relief from the obligation to render with each Annual Return a copy of its balance sheet a Private Company has a distinct advantage over a Public Company, for its affairs are not unduly disclosed to competitors and others). (3) A Private Company is not required to hold a Statutory

Dull and overcrowded. Too wide a measure, with inadequate margins. A formidable reading proposition.

18th April, 2000.

Albert Diffuso, Esq.,

"Loose Ends",

Obscure Road,

Scatterton.

Dear Sir,

We beg to acknowledge your letter.

We do not stock the make of lawn mower you
mention.

We have one with five blades, 10 inches cut,
fitted with adjustable screws.

The handles are variable, and main parts run on
ball bearings.

There is a grass box.

Trusting this meets your requirements,

Yours faithfully,

THE UNCERTAIN APPLIANCE CO.

An example of disorder. Note the lack of "shape," the impression
of aimless wandering, the lopsidedness, and the wide spacing between
the lines. Wholly unattractive.

Our ref: G Dept.   7th September, 2060

Albert Diffuso, Esq.,
"Loose Ends,"
Obscure Road,
SCATTERTON.

Dear Sir,

　　　　Thanks for your letter of the 6th inst. regarding a
lawn mower.

　　　　It so happens that we do not stock the particular
make you mention, but we stock one with five blades, 10 inches
cut, fitted with adjustable screws, variable handles, main
parts mounted on ball bearings.　　There is a grass box.　　The
price is 45/-.

　　　　Descriptive leaflet is enclosed.

　　　　So strong is our confidence in this make of lawn
mower that we are prepared to deliver it on approval, for a
practical trial on your own lawn.

　　　　　　　　　　　　　　　Yours faithfully,
　　　　　　　　　　　　　　　THE VULCAN MACHINE CO., LTD.

　　　　　　　　　　　　　　　　Secretary.

Enc:　Leaflet No. 22.

An improvement. Note the effect of squared grouping of the address
and the more pleasing margins.

7th September, 2060.

Our ref: G Dept.

Albert Diffuso, Esq.,
"Loose Ends,"
Obscure Road,
SCATTERTON.

Dear Sir,

Thanks for your letter of the 6th inst.
regarding a lawn mower.

It so happens that we do not stock the particular make you mention, but we stock one with five
blades, 10 inches cut, fitted with adjustable screws,
variable handles, main parts mounted on ball bearings.
There is a grass box.   The price is 45/-.

Descriptive leaflet is enclosed.

So strong is our confidence in this type of
lawn mower that we are prepared to deliver it on approval, for a practical trial on your own lawn.

Yours faithfully,
THE VULCAN MACHINE CO., LTD.

Secretary.

Enc: Leaflet No. 22.

Better still. Here there is a sense of order, neat grouping, and
admirable use of white space.